Henry H.H. Remak

West European Studies
Indiana University
Bloomington, Indiana
47405

D1605559

JEAN MONNET:
THE PATH TO EUROPEAN UNITY

Also by Douglas Brinkley

AFTER THE CREATION: Dean Acheson and American Foreign
    Policy, 1953-1971

DEAN ACHESON AND THE MAKING OF U.S. FOREIGN
    POLICY (*editor*)

DRIVEN PATRIOT: The Life and Times of James Forrestal
    (*co-author*)

Also by Clifford Hackett

CAUTIOUS REVOLUTION: The European Community Arrives

Jean Monnet:
The Path to European Unity

Edited by
Douglas Brinkley and Clifford Hackett

Introduction by George W. Ball

St. Martin's Press   New York

First published in the United States of America in 1991

ISBN 0–312–04773–8

Library of Congress-in-Publication Data
Jean Monnet : the path to European unity / edited by Douglas Brinkley
and Clifford Hackett.
      p.   cm.
   Includes bibliographical references and index.
   ISBN 0–312–04773–8
     1. Monnet, Jean, 1888–   . 2. Statesmen—Europe—Biography.
   3. European federation. I. Brinkley, Douglas. II. Hackett,
   Clifford P.
   D413.M56J43   1991
   940.5'092—dc20
   [B]   90–39706
                                                              CIP

Contents

Preface

When the Jean Monnet Council began its work in early 1988, it was the Monnet centennial. There was naturally much talk about how the new American organization should mark Monnet's anniversary in the year in which France would place his ashes in the Pantheon, the greatest honor which the grandest nation-state has devised to honor one of its citzens. Out of such concerns came this book.

This volume resulted from the intersection of several generations of admirers of Jean Monnet. The April 1988 Council session, with a wide range of people interested in Monnet, decided that a book of essays representing both European and American writers was the most appropriate tribute from the country this remarkable Frenchman liked so much and where he had so many friends.

The editors, who know Monnet only from his historical reputation, represent two generations of his admirers: those who remember the early post-war years and Monnet's work, and those too young for such recollections but who now recognize his enormous accomplishments. Another generation, those who worked directly with Monnet and knew those accomplishments and his characteristics firsthand, are also well represented in this unusual collection.

Selecting the essays was not an easy task. So much had been written about Monnet that even reprinting the best would take far more than one large volume. Furthermore, much of that writing was in other languages so that translations, with all of their hazards, might be required. Finally, there were still aspects of Monnet's life not fully explored for which new writing was needed. We decided, therefore, on a mixed volume of American and European authors, and of both new and published pieces, including some translations which we commissioned.

A brief word about the authors is appropriate for while each is an expert on some (or several) aspects of Monnet and his work, not every one of them is well-known in this country.

The introduction by George W. Ball, who is well known for his work in the State Department and as a commentator on foreign affairs, sets Monnet briefly and carefully between the worlds of Europe and America, moving easily between the two. Ball worked with Monnet from the early days of World War II, later advised him in the Commissairiat du Plan in Paris after the war, gradually developed a deep friendship with him over the decades and had an American Thanksgiving dinner with him in Houjarray, the Monnet home outside Paris, just months before Monnet died there in 1979 at the age of ninety-one.

The European authors include François Duchene and Richard Mayne, two Englishmen who worked closely with Monnet from the 1950s when he was engaged in constructing the foundations of the European Community whose institutions today remain his finest monument. Their essays are both remarkable etchings of Monnet, yet quite different from each other; Duchene's shrewdly analyzes the Monnet method, a topic he has studied for several years; Mayne writes a brief biography of the 'Gray Eminence', full of personal touches and clear insights.

Three Frenchmen, each close to Monnet for many years, are represented by newly-translated accounts of Monnet's influence in both European events and in their own quite distinctive lives. The first is François Fontaine, who worked with Monnet for over thirty years, and who wrote the fine piece 'Forward With Jean Monnet' partly, he notes, to encourage other close friends to share their recollections and partly because Monnet himself was so sparing in his *Memoirs* in giving space to the personal side of his long life. Fontaine tries in his essay to point out some features of that life with rare insight and great admiration.

A second French compatriot of Monnet represented here is Robert Marjolin from whose own memoirs, *Le travail d'une vie*, two sections are excerpted here: the first on Monnet and de Gaulle, the other on the European Community. Both show Marjolin's sharp insights and the second also unveils the limits of Marjolin's admiration of Monnet's work in constructing a supranational Europe.

The final essay by a Frenchman, and the last in the book, is a moving tribute by Jacques Van Helmont, 'Jean Monnet As He Was'. This small essay, possible only by one who knew Monnet intimately and observed him incessantly, is sparse. It contains few adjectives, little praise, and is largely a recitation of some mundane aspects of Monnet the man: how he breathed, and worried about his health; how he travelled; how he worried decisions and events almost to death until he dominated them; how he lived with change, and why he found the United States and its citizens so compatible.

The American authors begin with Robert Nathan's firsthand account of Monnet during World War II when they worked together to plan the great increases in American military production from their relatively modest perches in the expanding Washington power game in the early 1940s.

Irwin Wall and John Gillingham, two American historians, tell fascinating stories of Monnet as head of France's first Plan from 1946–52 and as head of the High Authority of the European Coal and Steel Community, respectively. Together these accounts bridge the movement of Monnet from private citizen and banker, pressed into wartime service as experienced expediter, to government planner and master builder of the new institutions of postwar Europe.

The result, as with all writing, must speak for itself. We can only commend the authors for their contributions and their generosity in making them available to the Jean Monnet Council for this volume.

D.B. and C.H.

Acknowledgements

The editors are grateful to the publishers George Weiden-feld and Nicolson, London, for the use of the excerpts from their edition of Robert Marjolin's *Memoirs*; to Professor Henri Rieben, and the Fondation Jean Monnet Pour l'Europe and the Centre de recherches européennes in Lausanne which he directs, for permission to translate and use the essays by François Fontaine and Jacques Van Helmont, which originally appeared in French in the Cahiers Rouge series of those remarkable institutions; and to *The American Scholar* where the essay by Richard Mayne first appeared in August 1984.

They are also grateful to the support given in the preparation of the manuscript by Hofstra University's Secretarial Services and the Center for American-Netherlands Studies.

Finally, they wish to acknowledge the support and understanding of the Jean Monnet Council (incorporated as the American Council for Jean Monnet Studies), the sponsor of this volume which is one of the Council's major efforts to make Monnet and his accomplishments better known in the United States.

The Contributors

George W. Ball is one of America's foremost experts on US-European affairs. He served as Under Secretary of State in the Kennedy and Johnson administrations (1961–6). An international lawyer, Ball worked closely with Jean Monnet on plans for the new European Coal and Steel Community. He later represented it and several other Common Market agencies in the US.

Douglas Brinkley is Assistant Professor of History and Teaching Fellow, New College, Hofstra University, where he is also co-director of the Center For American-Netherlands Studies. He earned his doctorate from Georgetown University and has since authored several articles on US diplomatic history in addition to *After the Creation; Dean Acheson and American Foreign Policy 1953–1971* (New Haven, Conn., 1991).

François Duchene is an English collaborator of Monnet who worked directly with him in 1952–5 at the Coal and Steel Community and in 1958–63 at the Action Committee. Duchene is completing a major analysis of the working methods of Monnet's varied accomplishments.

François Fontaine is one of France's preeminent spokesmen on European integration affairs. Besides working with Jean Monnet for more than thirty years and collaborating on the *Memoirs*, Fontaine has had two other careers: as a best-selling novelist of ancient Rome and as an information official of the European Community for many years.

John Gillingham is Professor of History at the University of Missouri-St Louis where he has also served as Director of the Truman Era Research Program. He has recently completed his third book, *Coal, Steel and the Rebirth of Europe, 1945–1955: The Germans and French from Reunification to Economic Community* (Cambridge, 1991). He is researching a biography of Jean Monnet.

Clifford Hackett is Executive Director of the American Council For Jean Monnet Studies. Following ten years in the foreign service, he spent more than thirteen years working on Capitol Hill where he became interested in the European

Community. He recently finished a book on its history and institutions, *Cautious Revolution: The European Community Arrives* (Westport, Conn., 1990).

Robert Marjolin was an internationally known economist who played a leading role in the post-World War II restructuring of Europe. Although not entirely sympathetic with certain aspects of Monnet's supranationalism, they worked closely together for many years. He completed his *Memoirs 1911–1986* shortly before his death.

Richard Mayne is an English writer who worked with Monnet in 1956–8 and again in 1963–6 in the Action Committee for a United States of Europe. He has written several well-received books on post-war Europe and translated Monnet's *Memoirs* into English. He is also a broadcaster and book and film critic.

Robert R. Nathan is one of Washington's leading international economic consultants. One of Monnet's few early acquaintances still living, Robert Nathan is a well-known American economist and political leader who still directs his own consulting firm assisting governments and business on complex economic analyses.

Jacques Van Helmont is an astute French analyst of European Community affairs. When he started to work on the post-war Plan for France in 1946, he began a close relationship with Monnet and his work which included the entire life span of the Action Committee until it was disbanded in 1975 upon Monnet's retirement.

Irwin M. Wall is Professor of History at the University of California, Riverside. He is the author of *French Communism and the Era of Stalin: The Quest for Unity and Integration, 1945–1962* (Westport, Conn., 1983) and numerous articles on contemporary French history. His latest book, *L'Influence americaine sur la politique francaise, 1945–1954* (Paris, 1989) is currently being revised for English language publication.

Introduction
George W. Ball

Over the long reaches of history, ambitious men and women have sought to achieve the unity of Europe – usually by military might. But no serious peaceful progress was made until after the Second World War when Jean Monnet set in motion the long march toward unity by proposing a European Coal and Steel Community.

Coal and steel had special significance in the early 1950s, since those commodities had provided the basic raw materials for fighting two world wars. Monnet, who passionately abhorred war as both cruel and irrational, perceptively foresaw that the pooling of coal and steel might not only soften national rivalries but also help tie West Germany tightly to the West. What was needed was to reconcile dominant but disparate motivations: the French interest in gaining and maintaining equality with Germany and the German interest in achieving political rehabilitation.

We have by now become so suffocatingly aware of the Cold War that we find it hard to realize that the dark specter overhanging Europe in the early postwar years was not what Mr Reagan referred to as the 'evil empire' but rather the threat of a resurgent Germany.

In that atmosphere Monnet clearly predicted that, when the bombs finally stopped falling in Europe, the French government would be moved by conditioned reflex to try, as its predecessors had unsuccessfully tried in the past, to block Germany's aggressive tendencies by massive force and to inhibit its economic recovery. At the same time America, seeking to rehabilitate Germany as the engine of European economic recovery, was assisting that truncated new state to rebuild.

Monnet sought a fresh solution that would reconcile both these pressures. Under the Schuman Plan which he proposed, Germany would be permitted, even encouraged, to rebuild, but within the framework of a united Europe rather than merely as a nation state. Of course, a united Europe would not be easy to achieve; Monnet had seen too many well-intended but futile efforts to achieve effective cooperation among governments, and he knew that without some transfer of sovereignty from the national governments the result would be mere organized impotence.

Yet, given the realities of day-to-day national politics, how could he ever achieve the necessary transfer of substantial power from governments to European institutions? Monnet knew that he could never persuade governments to give up sovereignty over a wide spectrum of their affairs; but, he thought, they might well be persuaded to yield major attributes of their sovereignty in a limited economic sector. His strategy was roughly equivalent to a tank warfare tactic General de Gaulle had futilely advocated in the late thirties: concentrate all available power at a specific point, then spread out behind the lines. Once a breakthrough had been accomplished with regard to coal and steel, Monnet believed that the jurisdiction of the new institutions could then be expanded.

There was well-conceived method in this apparent madness. All of us working with Monnet well understood that it was quite unreasonable to carve a single economic sector out of the jurisdiction of national governments and subject it to the control of international institutions. Yet, with his usual perspicacity, Monnet recognized that the very irrationality of the scheme would compel progress and might then start a chain reaction. The awkwardness and complexity resulting from the singling-out of coal and steel would compel member governments to pool other production as well.

That assumption was, of course, validated by events, but only after two transient diversions: abortive efforts to bring about a European army and to pool the development of nuclear power through Euratom. Still those detours did not prevent the six nations of the Coal and Steel Community in 1957 from signing the Treaty of Rome, which called into being a European Economic Community empowered to create and supervise a common market.

Like the Coal and Steel Community, the EEC was designed for the future with full-fledged institutions – an executive, a court and an assembly. Yet because over the years the executive body, the Commission, seemed to have contracted the traditional symptoms of creeping hypertrophy – a huge bureaucracy and a swollen budget – many Americans came to take the Community for granted, and to assume that it would remain a half-completed edifice.

What its critics failed to foresee, however, was the traumatic impact of intensifying economic competition, primarily from Japan and the little dragons of Asia. That recent development slowly brought home to Europe's industrialists, financiers and businessmen the reluctant recognition that, as economic and commercial units, the nation states of Europe were anachronisms – no longer adequate for the current age of rapid travel, instant communications and computers that enable management to function effectively at long distance. In that new environment the European nations found their internal markets too limited to permit their industries to realize the full economies of scale indispensable to their effective competition in the expanding world market, while the rapid internationalization of financial markets and transactions sharply emphasized the need to save Europe from the high costs of its economic fragmentation.

These ideas again inspired a fresh initiative when, on becoming President of the European Commission in 1985, a former French Finance Minister, Jacques Delors, proposed the completion of a vast European internal market. Delors not only presented his scheme to the member governments but enlisted Lord Cockfield, the commissioner of the Internal Market and a former businessman, to give the plan concrete form. Cockfield prepared a White Paper listing nearly 300 measures needed to bring about a single integrated market where there could be free movement of goods, services, people and capital, and he provided a detailed timetable for the member governments of the Community to adopt the necessary common legislation by 31 December 1992.

The achievement of Cockfield's deadline was aided when those governments enacted a measure quaintly called the 'Single European Act'. That act increased the powers of the institutions of the European Community; in particular it facilitated the task of meeting the 1992 deadline by providing that most of the Cockfield measures could be enacted by a mere 'qualified majority' of the Council of Ministers rather than by unanimity.

Delors' scheme gained additional momentum when, in a case involving the import of a cassis drink, the European Court of Justice upheld and applied a provision of the Single European Act granting the Council of Ministers of the European Community power to 'decide that provisions in force in a member state must be recognized as being equivalent to those applied by another'. When coupled with the Single European Act, that decision could well mean for Europe what the interstate commerce clause has meant for America.

I shall not review here the complicated problems requiring resolution before complete economic integration can be even substantially achieved. No doubt there will be some slippage and by no means all of its provisions will be in place by 1992. It is problematical, for example, how soon Europe will be able to get rid of customs houses on national boundaries, since the free movement of peoples contemplated by Delors' concept involves not merely duty collections, which will be eliminated, but police and demographic controls, which present greater problems. So I cannot predict when the Milanese doctor will be able to set up practice in Lyons without being subject to qualifying examinations. Quite likely the most rapid progress will be made in the financial area since funds are, by their nature, fungible and their movement instantaneous and invisible.

Meanwhile, the scheme is getting a mixed press in America. Some of our larger enterprises see the opening of new opportunities and are rushing to exploit them; yet the same business mentality that denounced the Coal and Steel Community as merely a cartel is now loudly predicting that the new European single market will be – or in time will become – an economic citadel with its gates bolted against our own production. Of course, I do not doubt that the spirit of Colbert still hovers over some sectors of Europe's economic life – and particularly agriculture – but it will be countered, as it was thirty years ago, by even stronger anti-protectionist pressures. All one can be sure of is that the new single European economy will not be born without labor pains.

But if no one can tell with precision what specific items of the agenda will be realized by 1992, substantial progress is steadily and rapidly being made and, particularly among younger Europeans, the movement has acquired remarkable momentum. But, because events are moving so fast and unpredictably, I shall refrain from offering a detailed analysis of the prospects of the European Single Market, and instead address a more agreeable, though essentially nostalgic task: to reflect a little about Jean Monnet.

We recently marked the centenary year of Jean Monnet's birth and, at long last, he is being recognized in France as the father of European unity. Indeed, in November 1988 his ashes were transferred to the Pantheon, to rest among those of other French immortals.

I knew Jean Monnet well for the last three decades of his life, and, along with a handful of other Americans and a number of Europeans, worked closely with him for at least twenty years.

Since, in retrospect, Monnet's methods of operation may be quite as interesting as his philosophical thoughts about Europe, I shall limit myself to a few words regarding the rationale that inspired Monnet's initiatives and comment briefly on his idiosyncratic methods. The fact that he redrew the economic map of Europe so extensively without ever holding elective office makes him almost unique in history. Monnet had a clear view of the role he could effectively play. European ministers with large governmental responsibilities or American cabinet secretaries presiding over large departments are, he believed, so occupied with day-to-day problems that they have no time to think or plan for the future. Monnet saw himself as a man who did not think about problems in long time spans, and he took fruitful advantage of the old adage that the man of vision has no power while the man of power frequently has no vision. It was his role, as he saw it, to provide vision to the man of power, to furnish the conceptual basis for action to be taken by governments.

One secret of Jean's effectiveness, many of us suspected, was his lack of personal ambition; because he never challenged a political figure as a rival, he could easily gain his audience. Nor was Monnet in the slightest degree impressed by rank; he was quite prepared to spend days with junior civil servants, and he achieved his most formidable objectives not by going directly to the top, but by first working with those modest toilers in the governmental vineyards who actually prepared the first drafts of documents and provided their bosses with advice and information. He had an infallible instinct for the *loci* of power and he quickly discovered, from his wide circle of friends, who in any political situation was worth educating.

Monnet, furthermore, had the advantage of a richly diverse career in which he had been employed in his father's brandy business, traveling the world selling cognac. Then, during the First World War as a young man of twenty-six, he arranged through a family solicitor for an audience with Prime Minister Viviani. He proved so effective in persuading Viviani of the desperate need to coordinate the Anglo-French supply effort that Viviani sent him to London as a member of the French Liaison Committee, where he met Arthur Salter and other rising young Britons who were to form his close friends over many years.

Thereafter he engaged in a variety of activities all heavily colored by his interests in a more pacific world order. At the age of thirty he became Deputy Secretary-General of the League of Nations where, among other things, he led the negotiations regarding Silesia and the Saar, and the rehabilitation of Austria. Then, after a respite while he resuscitated the family brandy business, he joined the Paris branch of a New York investment banking firm, which floated loans for the Polish and Rumanian Governments, which ultimately took him to Wall Street, where he played a major role in large affairs, involved himself in a major struggle with Giannini and, in the course of his work, acquired a distinguished group of American friends, including John Foster Dulles and Jack McCloy. He then served for a year in Shanghai developing and negotiating a reconstruction plan that would attract Chinese and international capital.

Before the Second World War broke out he arranged to be sent to America by the French Air Ministry to negotiate the purchase of aircraft and, foreseeing America's ultimate involvement, he helped persuade President Roosevelt of the need for a vast expansion of American war production. When France was about to fall, he arranged, through his

British friends, to gain the agreement of Winston Churchill for an offer to the French of equal citizenship with the British, but unfortunately, by the time the document had been prepared and taken to Bordeaux, where the French Government was then in exile, Petain had taken over and France had surrendered.

Jean Monnet was known to his friends as an incorrigible optimist, yet his optimism did not stem from a Panglossian conviction that all was for the best in the best of all possible worlds but rather from a belief in the logic of events and the essential rationality of man – a dauntless faith in the ineluctable direction of deeply-moving forces. Thus, as I constantly discovered on working with him, he was never put off course by disappointments; instead he would say with a Gallic shrug, 'What has happened has happened, but it does not affect anything fundamental. We must find a way around it.' His resilience reflected an attitude he found expressed in a passage from a biography of Ibn Saud written by a French author which Monnet showed me very early in our work together. It contained the passage: 'A Western visitor asked Ibn Saud the secret of his success. Ibn Saud replied, "God appeared to me in the desert when I was a young man and said something which has guided my actions throughout my life. He told me: 'For me, everything is a means – even the obstacles'."'[1]

I vividly recalled that advice on one occasion, just after the preparatory conference on the Coal and Steel Community had begun on 20 June 1950. On Sunday, 25 June, I had gone to Houjarray, Monnet's thatch-roofed house near Paris, for a day of work, and during the afternoon three or four Europeans from other delegations also arrived. Then the telephone rang with the shocking news that the North Korean army had invaded South Korea.

Monnet reacted after only a moment's reflection. 'You Americans', he said to me, 'will never permit the Communists to succeed with such aggression. You cannot afford to let them begin the erosion of lines drawn during the postwar years. Yet an American intervention in Korea could clearly jeopardize the Schuman Plan. It may create panic in Europe, and it will almost certainly increase American insistence on a larger German role in the defense of the West. We both know what the rearming of Germany could mean.'

Although Monnet feared that the prospect of a rearmed Germany could lead Frenchmen to hesitate before entering the Coal and Steel Community with the Germans, he reacted as usual to the appearance of a new obstacle; what we should do, he insisted, was to follow God's advice to Ibn Saud and make it a means to our larger objective.

To forestall the rearmament of Germany as a nation state, Monnet decided to push forward far sooner than he had intended with a scheme to organize Europe's defense roughly along the lines of the Schuman Plan. So he enlisted the support of Prime Minister René Pleven, who had earlier assisted Monnet in the League of Nations Polish loan negotiations. Monnet's tactic was to persuade the French government to take a public position rejecting German rearmament on a national basis, but suggesting instead the formation of a European army including units from Germany with a European Defense Community. On 24 October 1950, Pleven presented such a plan to the French Assembly, which approved it, thus marking the beginning of what the late Raymond Aron was to describe as 'the greatest ideological and political debate France had known since the Dreyfus Affair'. In the end, of course, the European Defense Community foundered on the rock of French nationalism. But meanwhile, the European concept was kept alive by other measures.

Perhaps Monnet's greatest disappoinment was his failure to persuade the British to join from the beginning in his efforts to build Europe – first through the Schuman Plan and later the Economic Community. He knew the British well, and he greatly respected their skills in politics and institution building. Yet, though he spent long hours trying to persuade his British friends to 'be present at the creation', he was not dismayed – or even surprised – when they held off. The British, he said, had an infallible instinct for *fait accompli*; 'if we go forward and show concrete results, they will join at the right time'.

Of course, history proved him right. When the British began to fear that their cherished 'special relationship' with the United States might be imperiled by America's fascination with the new European institutions, they took steps to join; and, though Britain's first efforts were frustrated by De Gaulle's narrow nationalism, Great Britain finally took its place in Brussels. Meanwhile, lacking British help, Monnet went forward with what then seemed the unorthodox scheme of founding European union not on the historic Anglo-French entente but on a Franco-German base.

It was a shock to conservative Frenchmen that France should even be talking to the Germans about a common effort so soon after the war; to tie French fortunes to those of Germany in a European context was for many unthinkable. To offer Germany equality with other European nations, which Monnet thought essential, required the sublimation of French feelings of national inferiority, while it broke with the pretensions of French leaders to diplomatic superiority. The fact that Monnet succeeded in using Franco-German *rapprochement* as the basic component in the structure of the new Europe was greatly helped by the presence in Bonn of Chancellor Adenauer and of Jack McCloy, then High Commissioner. Both men had the wisdom to comprehend Monnet's vision.

Monnet was completely aware of the implications of what he was trying to start, saying, 'One change begets another. The chain reaction has only begun. We are starting a process of continuous reform which can shape tomorrow's world more lastingly than the principles of revolution so widespread outside the West.' Though Monnet had no illusions about the possibility of changing human nature, he was convinced that by altering the conditions under which people lived, they would adapt to the new reality. 'Europe', he said, 'will not be conjured up at a stroke, nor by an overall design, it will be attained by concrete achievements generating an active community of interest.' That was the point of the Schuman Plan and of the Economic Community which followed. Those schemes upset old balances of power and applied pressure at limited, but vital, points to change political prospects.

When I first began working with Monnet, he showed me a passage from a Swiss writer, Henri-Frédéric Amiel – to whom I had not given a thought since my undergraduate days – and commended it to me as the ultimate wisdom. Amiel had written, 'The experience of each person is a new beginning. Only institutions grow wiser: they store up the collective experience and, from this experience and wisdom, men subject to the same laws will gradually find, not their nature changed but that their behavior does.' And Amiel added, 'It is institutions that govern relationships between people. They are the real pillars of civilization.'[2]

Recently a brilliant European, half-British, half-Swiss, named François Duchene, has undertaken to analyze Monnet's concepts and methods in a study which is summarized in his essay in this volume. He notes not only that Monnet believed that institutions could shape popular conduct but also that equality before common rules was as urgently needed between nations as between individuals; only thus could one create a sense of joint responsibility for the application of those rules to all participants in a community.

With an astute sense of timing, Monnet was firmly convinced that novel ideas should be advanced at moments when the contradictions of the *status quo* forced political leaders to question their own assumptions. Thus, as he himself wrote in his memoirs, 'I have always believed that Europe will be established through crises and that the outcome will be the sum of the outcomes of those crises'.

Monnet was able to succeed, Duchene suggests, because his principal period of creativeness occurred within the quarter century between 1938 and 1963 – a war and post-war period, when most of continental Europe had been destroyed and institutions and networks of loyalty deeply shaken.

His working methods were extraordinary. Although he produced highly persuasive documents, I never saw him write anything himself. He simply talked while people wrote and for a long time I was one of his amanuenses – even a simple letter went through as many as twenty drafts. Unfortunately for my comfort, he thought most effectively when he walked, and whenever I would stay overnight at his house in Houjarray, he and I would have breakfast, together, then Jean would hand me a cane, open the door and say, 'Start talking'.

I would try to fill him in about developments in America or whatever else I thought might interest him. Then, as we climbed up over the pleasant hills, he would suddenly grab my arm and point out a bucolic scene saying, 'Isn't that beautiful! Can you imagine a more lovely view than this? This is a great country and we must see that its qualities are put to good use'. Then, he would turn and, just as abruptly, seize my arm and say, 'Start talking again'.

NOTES

1. Quoted in Jean Monnet, *Memoirs* (Garden City, New York, 1978), 399.
2. A similar version of the Amiel aphorism is quoted in Monnet's *Memoirs*, op. cit., 393.

1 Forward with Jean Monnet

François Fontaine

Translated by Margot Lyon

PREFACE

For more than thirty years I lived a great experience that went beyond my limits. I lived close to a man who at one and the same time shaped things in detail and on a world scale. I was a little heedless, not always aware of my luck. Later I realized that my life would have no other meaning than to have been the witness of an historic achievement. I helped, to the utmost of my powers, its author to write the story of this achievement and to draw its lessons from it. It would have been wise to stop there. Jean Monnet said all he wanted to say. But reticence stopped him short of fully revealing himself and for that reason his *Memoirs*, written in the first person, are too discreet about the richness of his nature and the deep sources of his creative genius. Certainly there is no lack of testimonies to him, but they add little to the picture of him that is already becoming fixed. There is still time to enrich that image, to widen the somewhat narrow circle of repetitive stories. I have tried to do this, with the single aim of provoking all those who knew him to go further into their recollections, and to correct or complete this sketch.

I

It is by looking at the way Jean Monnet lived that one could wonder about the nature of genius in action. His public and private behavior, and the way he spent his time, seemed to have nothing mysterious about them. No doubt the word 'genius' might seem inappropriate in his case. We are used to the romantic definition of genius, meaning someone who operates in dramatic circumstances, at the outer limits of the normal. Yet, looking at the results of his action, we are forced to admit that this man, plain in appearance and speech, not concerned to astonish or even to be publicly known, possessed the faculty to a very rare degree of influencing his fellow-men and transforming the state of society.

The way he repeated, or rather renewed, his great enterprises at different stages in his life showed that it was not just a question of strokes of luck. His aptitude for mobilizing the power of other people for the common good and for seizing circumstances, anywhere, to introduce progress or to restore peace, was a natural gift. In fact it is a gift that nature is niggardly in distributing, and is not to be confused with the other kind of lucidity and instinct for seizing the moment, that ambitious men use for their own profit.

But this gift would not have been enough to situate him well above his contemporaries. There are plenty of men in every period who like to lobby so as to influence the political scene. Jean Monnet possessed, in addition and exclusively, a high moral vision that is very rarely found among men behind the scenes, who mostly use their abilities to pull down rather than to build up, and to divide rather than to unite. It is this combination of distinctive features that constitutes creative genius in a given society and, in certain circumstances, enables that genius to act for the common interest. And it is in this sense that one can speak of the genius of Jean Monnet, who made his mark on the men of his time without wishing or seeming to raise himself above them.

Genius does not always sparkle, either at its source or in its expression. It can be sober, and not seem different from a set of ordinary capacities. In this case it derives from a certain combination of these capacities which, distributed by genetic chance, begin to diverge systematically compared with established norms. From then on, other unexpected results and a new series of structures are produced. If this phenomenon is well-controlled, if it stays within legitimate limits, if it is strong enough, directed fairly high, and introduced at a certain point to change the fundamental structures of society, it can make things move forward. Everything depends on the way it is applied, the level being a matter of morals, the time and place a matter of intuition and later of obstinacy. Jean Monnet did not lack obstinacy. It was not a character trait with him, nor stubbornness, but an unbelievable capacity to concentrate his attention on a single point. He fixed on an idea as long as he thought it right and necessary. It became an *idée fixe*, overshadowing all others or subordinating all others to itself. Was concentration ever an effort for him? What does it owe to his upbringing and to his willpower, or to practice that became habit?

We would need to have watched him as a thoughtful small boy, looking at the monotonous landscape of a region of France dedicated to a single crop; and later as a young man who had grown up among people obsessed by a single product. Inattentiveness was unknown in the family circle. Distillation of the grapes and the patient wait for the wine's maturing had filled the family's working lives for several generations. Even so, carelessness was possible. But it could ruin you. Seriousness was consubstantial with this society of puritans. Nobody remembered much laughter going on. There were better things to do. Perhaps some went off to do their laughing elsewhere. But they came back to the vines strung together in endless straight lines, and to the rows of barrels lined up in the dark cellars.

Everything was large-scale in Cognac, and nothing was excessive. You never saw all the wealth and you never exercised all the power. They were secrets that everybody knew very well, but that the community had an interest in protecting. The State must not get to know them, and people outside did not need to know them. The little boy quickly learned that there was no point in concerning yourself with what other people were doing. The Hennessy family dominated everything, but J. G. Monnet was independent, or rather he had grouped the independents together. Martell had a world reputation, so J.G. would have to make himself known in places the big firms had not yet tried to reach. They had the monopoly, but J.G. would have the imagination. The little boy was trained to take initiatives, taught the art of going out to persuade. He had been impregnated naturally with the basic virtues – respect for quality and practicing patience – because these constituted the moral code of Cognac's professional growers.

At the basis of genius there is a life of hard work, that gives birth to the phenomenal child. Such a child is not rare, but generally it dreams and breathes uneasily. Often the child hides away. Only his mother knows or senses why. Jean Monnet's mother knew that in Cognac the menfolk were basically unstable, and needed to be. But there were several ways of being so. Monnet's father was restless, and his family were often glad to see him go. The son was determined. There was no question of holding him back. Moreover, it was not easy for both of them to live together at home. The father was charming and capricious, but he went round in circles like the tendrils of the vine. The son would become his natural support if he could wait and bear the waiting, like all the younger generations of Cognac's little monarchies.

The war and its sequels put the inevitable confrontation back by ten years. But it was not so much a confrontation between two closely-linked men as one between two concepts of trading, in a decisive period. If the father had to be sacrificed, this had nothing to do with Oedipus. The inescapable human drama was not really at the center of the clash. At issue was the management of stocks. It was now necessary to sell the old brandies, in the same way as one might sell gold so as to reactivate business. It was Keynes, putting an end to the conservative Guizot era. It was also a sacrifice of quality to quantity.

If the father is identified with the family wealth, yes, there was ritual murder. But this selling-off could also be compared to the myth of the Biblical Fall: in Cognac the oldest stock is traditionally nicknamed the 'Paradise'. But the Monnet household did not go in for such tales. Everything had a down-to-earth objective, even explosions of rage. Passions were depersonalized. The House of Monnet took precedence over the family, as the family did over its individuals. And, dominating over all, was dignity.

Dignity in behavior was something Jean Monnet never lacked. It is impossible to know how far this quality was innate in him, but one can well imagine that he found it sound and convenient to shun petty thinking. He did not like to speak ill of other people, and did not let conversation degenerate. His intolerance on this point, and his hesitations about judging and condemning, showed he was vigilant. He was careful not to give way to impulses, or to the easy way out, either inwardly in his thinking or outwardly in his person. He was not at all what one would call consciously imposing, or an aristocrat either, in his bearing. But vulgarity was deeply repugnant to him. He did not make any great fuss over this, but he would simply say, 'That doesn't interest me' or, 'Let's not waste our time on that kind of talk.'

The moral code of the Charente peasants is a mixture of superstition and wisdom. An irrational fear of offending the powers of nature by excess goes very well with an atavistic feeling for discretion and for thrift. Not too much could still be too much. The basic principle is to stay a bit below other people's line of fire – whether it is a close neighbor or, even more, 'the stranger who is not from these parts'. This redundant phrase underlines very ancient suspicions about anything or anyone who comes to show off, or to spy, or to impose anything. You recognize the stranger by the fact that he talks loud, wears light-colored clothes, and is always in a hurry. Suspicions of this kind are universal peasant reflexes, but in Charente they are even stronger. It would be wrong to say that Jean Monnet did not inherit any of them. The region has produced other great entrepreneurs and long-distance travelers, artists who were pure products of this land of extreme moderation and extreme prudence; not the products of mutation. And the word 'extreme' is chosen deliberately. It means that the apparent nonchalance due to the climate is in fact carefully calculated: never draw attention to yourself, and don't waste your strength. The men who have given the world the best examples of Charente's virtues left the place early, driven by youthful impatience for action. Most of them have never gone back. But it has influenced them all their lives.

For centuries, Cognac has distilled a mixture of the people of Charente with some Scottish and some Irish, and a few Swedish elements as well. All these imported Puritans must have had a lot in common with the local Protestants, because the mixture they formed together was a homogeneous blend, even if it emphasized the local characteristics. The fact that the leading merchants were Anglo-Saxon in origin mattered less, as time went on, than where the clients could be found. For the most part, clients lived in the same latitude. The language was English. If the Charente growers bought their clothes in London it was perhaps to impress the clients, or perhaps for reasons of convenience and price, but certainly not – like the Parisians – for the snob value of English suits. Besides, London chic was so discreet that it was not even noticed in Cognac. In later years, one would not notice that Jean Monnet dressed well unless someone drew your attention to the fact. He gave more the impression of a man in country clothes. You admired his nailed boots, but you did not suspect his dark shoes were made to measure. You had to look at old photographs to notice the changes in style of the clothes he wore. For instance, when did he stop wearing a vest with a gusset in favor of the knitted cardigan that was considered so informal by his generation? He had spent many years in countries where elegance was combined with comfort. When and where did he buy a cap, and how old was his eternal grey felt hat? In this as in so many other ways, all he had to do was to go on being himself, to be an innovator when he was back in France at the end of the Second World War.

Let us not leave Cognac without examining all its influences. Let us not forget that at thirty-five, after World War I and the beginnings of the League of Nations, Jean Monnet went back to Cognac to settle there for a period of time whose length he could not foresee. He would have stayed there, he used to say, if it were necessary. That was the way he saw things, but it would not have lasted in those quiet surroundings, given his active temperament and his imaginative flair, when the local industry was conservative by its very nature. His abilities were for modernizing management, not production methods. Once the business side was straightened out he would have gone off again, undoubtedly. Nonetheless, being impregnated as a child, strongly reinforced all the old local virtues in this man of Cognac, now an international administrator. This booster shot fixed in him for evermore his inherited protection against the toxins of cosmopolitanism. He did not need to go back to Cognac ever again. From then on, nothing could prevail over his peasant nature.

He was not miserly in the way most people of Charente are. It is a region that has experienced periods of severe scarcity and therefore never stops saving its money against an uncertain future. He was thrifty, but in the style of the big

Cognac firms, spending what is necessary for health care, social status and the good name of the family business. The Monnet household opened up a little to important clients, who were invited to stay to lunch, and even to stay overnight for a lack of any suitable hotels. But the shutters were regularly closed before nightfall. 'People might see us' Jean Monnet's mother would say, anxiously. He laughed at that remark, but he did not like to exhibit himself either. Although he was not often alone, he did not really keep open house. The people he chose to have around him regularly were few in number but very close. He gave his confidence very selectively. Once he accepted people he used the same ones a great deal, mainly to keep him informed, to try out his ideas and to put them into shape.

There were thresholds to his intimacy, insurmountable barriers. There were inviolable moments, and in any case very long periods of waiting and of being observed by Monnet. This defensive attitude – frequent and entirely normal among public figures – was with him a way of placing other people, according to their use, value and loyalty. In his eyes nobody was of any interest or importance in himself, but only according to an objective that could either be close or long-term. He developed his initiatives in secret, making inquiries without seeming to. When the moment to act arrived, he decided who was indispensable, brusquely stirring up friendships that had lain dormant for a long time or unexpectedly renewing distant contacts, taking an expert away from his work. He plagued them without any consideration, alternating charm and moral aggression. To win them over was already a great gain to the undertaking that he could not carry through without them. Their resistance stimulated him, but if he failed with them, that was a bad sign. He pressued them in a way that was so unexpected and so insistent that he could only justify it by communicating his own convictions. He did not give orders. In the last resort he insisted on an urgent need, 'Believe me, do what I say. There is no other solution.'

He did not always manage to hide the fact that he was interested in a person's utility but nobody held this against him because his lack of personal gain or ambition was so evident. People agreed to serve him because it was clear that he was serving an idea. Little by little you would find yourself committed, and then trapped. You became the most important man around. Then you were astonished at being less important, and finally you were pained at not being important anymore. The pressure, the operation-charm and the tyranny were all aimed at someone else who was now more directly useful. Sometimes you were called back and found you were once more the central point, without any explanation. The only way really to fall from favor was not to accept being edged out with good grace. Such people ought not to have understood for themselves that they had not lacked merit, but that the center of the problem had moved for a while, unknown to them. The ones who were most impatient, or the proudest, went off to serve somewhere else – where, with or without their goodwill, they would be used again by Jean Monnet.

He had very few friends, but the habit of making his way forward with the same people generated a feeling that had no name, not even fidelity. Everything was unspoken. You had to avoid reading too much into signs of familiarity. For him they were a way of relaxing the atmosphere between two periods of concentration; or a reward to people who had done some good work. He would look interested in some anecdote about politics, his eyes would crease and he would laugh, 'Oh, that's a good one! Are you sure about that? I can hardly believe it'. But he would already be thinking about something else – or rather, he was going on thinking about the same thing. There was no mistake; these short-lived complicities were the sign of his indifference to whatever it was that you enjoyed so much. That is, to what you were.

With his closest and most constant companions he did not bother to charm or to see that there were amusing little work breaks. All he did to be pleasant and to relax them was to change from one serious subject to another. In fact, as a young man he had chosen partners made of the same stuff as himself, the sort that is strong, consistent and hardwearing: they were a few foreign lawyers, top civil servants, bankers and newspapermen who like himself, far away from him but for the same reasons as him, were respected actors on the international stage. These demands and this discernment are signs of immense pride, and also of a considered decision never to compromise with mediocrity. The young man from Charente was miserly in paying respect and economical in giving his admiration. Nor did he like to waste time with the intruders he frequently found in his way. But he must have cut himself off from the easy-going pleasures of camaraderie.

He was familiar with journalists, the way one is in the United States, at all levels – it is better to invite them yourself into your company than to have to put up with their indiscretion. He respected their job and had no prejudice against their methods. 'Their work is difficult and indispensable' he said, 'so one should be very clear right from the start. There should be confidence on both sides.' He hardly ever needed to regret that he had spoken too frankly with one of them. The newsman who is explicitly given secret information knows what he risks if he betrays it. Jean Monnet had every kind of security at his disposal. Newspaper owners used to come for an intimate chat with him once or twice a year. Nobody was present during their general exchange of views, which led to no particular piece of news. He was seen, too, staking all his credit in favor of the survival and independence of a leading French daily, although it was far from supporting his ideas. The balance of power being safeguarded this way, misunderstandings need not be feared. Giving press conferences were ordeals for him without any appeal, and so were held as rarely as possible. Formal interviews were dramas where every word was carefully traded; they were only reluctantly granted. Wide-ranging conversations, on the contrary, happened almost every day without any difficulty.

He himself started them off readily, like a recreation for the mind. They happened most often at mealtimes, with one or two of his associates who were used to the simple pattern of eating he preferred. They would talk of the political situation, of people, of his memories of China. At his table Jean Monnet echoed the pattern of family lunchtimes, with the stranger passing through who supplied them with news. His curiosity seemed inexhaustible. But as the conversation grew livelier, you could see him gradually withdrawing from it. His face would grow redder. He would push his plate away. At such moments his extraordinary concentration mechanism began to work, and his *idée fixe* would reassert itself. Whatever the subject being discussed around the table, he would raise his hand very slightly and you would hear his voice, low-pitched, 'Let's stop talking about all that; we can't do anything about it. Let's get back to our own affairs.' There would be a long silence. Then, 'We have no choice. If we do nothing, events will decide for us . . . Look at what's happening in Germany . . .' It was probably the time when, in Cognac, you started talking about the harvest to the guest who most certainly would not be familiar with the particular savor of end-of-the-meal exchanges.

He made a few exceptions to this reserved style of behavior. He made use of his spare time during journeys, or in his rare vacations when he got intensely bored. He would go on with his endless inquiry by getting the opinions of taxi drivers, hotel porters, gardeners. He was incapable of trivial exchanges – except on the weather, which he was always concerned about – so he carried on the conversation as if he were talking with an expert. And so he drew the best out of everyone he spoke with. Very often he got one of those astonishingly revealing reflections that simple folk express when their judgment is appealed to. They saw at once that Jean Monnet was a man you would not talk lightly with. He showed that their views were important to him, though generally nobody cared about them. So he must really want to know. And you gave him the most striking formula possible. 'Tell me . . . tell me . . .' he would insist if they hesitated. But if they went too far, he would stop listening. He would have stopped when you brought out your formula, and he would be turning it over in his mind. After a moment he would interrupt you, 'What you said just now is very important. Tell me it again . . .' He wanted to be sure that it was not just vague talk.

For that other category of people he talked to, the journalists, he always had time, as we have seen, particularly when a situation worried him or he was working out a project in his head. 'Come and have lunch with me', he would say to them on the telephone, 'I'd like to have your views.' This habit dated from the League of Nations when, with his friends Pierre Comert and Henri Bonnet, he learned that secrecy is not an end in itself as diplomats would like to think – and as people thought back in Cognac. You could soon easily become its prisoner. Perhaps he had followed the lessons of Léon Bourgeois or Henri de Jouvenel. He rounded off this teaching by his contact with the leading English-language reporters. Later, he used the press like a virtuoso. A whole book would not be enough to tell the story of his relationship with journalists, and to describe the role he made them play in the conception and development of his enterprises. Such a book would be a practical manual, but it would also be a treatise on the ethics of information. He would not have achieved great things without the great world press. With it, he had a pact of sincerity.

II

Leading Frenchmen enjoyed the paradox for a long time, that this doctor *honoris causa* of the leading American and European universities had never even finished his university preparatory studies. As a child he had certainly had severe difficulties with his schooling. In elementary school he found it impossible to sit still on the school bench, and had to be allowed to move around the classroom. At the age of ten they sent him as a weekly boarder to Pons; but he was soon back at home. These days, his behavior would have been seen as promising and the school would rightly have been thought in the wrong. At the time he was considered to be handicapped, except for business, and except in Cognac where the essential requirement was to learn English, early. So Monnet's parents did not dramatize: Gaston, the younger boy, was more intellectual, so Jean would be the practical one. They would send him to England to learn the language. But first of all, in any case, he would have to go through the apprenticeship to learn the techniques for producing cognac. The storehouse keeper, the *maitre de chais*, was the great initiator. And the workshop for making the barrels had its secrets too.

The young Monnet watched all this without trying to penetrate the secrets. Already he had learned to watch out not to burden himself with the technicalities that other people would make better use of than he. He had the same approach to wine distillation as he had later to atomic fission.

If he never stopped asking questions, he was not interested in scientific minutiae and deliberately limited the range of his curiosity. You could just as often hear him say, 'Don't explain to me...' as 'Explain to me', but the two remarks did not concern the same point. He knew that a few well thought-out questions could produce what he wanted to know about the most complex technical difficulties. One could get their scope by bringing them down to their simplest outline. He was not interested in the processes for making either a brandy cask or a ton of steel. He respected the specialist knowledge of the artisans or the engineers concerned. But he cared a great deal about their securing the supplies they needed, and about their sales outlets. He had learned that even if goods were generally well-made, transportation was limited and poor, which meant that the merchandise itself wound up by becoming less good. Removing obstacles to men's activity was his own tireless activity.

He accepted the mysteries of distillation like dogmas, and also the brandy's aging process in oak casks marvelously adapted to their purpose. But he did not understand art for art's sake, nor that procedures could be an end in themselves. He rejected the dogma in Cognac 'Paradise' where brandy a century old could go on acquiring unlimited quality. When he was young, people were still talking nostalgically of the time when the priceless casks were reluctantly loaded on to the Charente boats, where the river flowed peacefully beside the storeroom *chais*. He himself on the contrary admired Monsieur Boucher, who had invented the industrially-molded bottles that were filled with only moderately old brandy, and packed by the dozen into wooden crates for transportation by the train load. 'This Monsieur Boucher', he would say, 'saved Cognac from economic decline, but he's not respected because he didn't belong to the merchant élite. If there's a statue to him anywhere, it must be somewhere up in the north of France.' (But people say they have seen Boucher's sculpted bust, half-hidden in the shade in Cognac's public garden.)

Modernization had begun with the twentieth century, and men who clung to the old traditions were ruined. Dramatist Jacques Chardonne had written a play, 'Sentimental Destinies', about the families who had stayed single-mindedly and obstinately attached to the old ways and had dragged their firms along with their reveries of a former age. Jean Monnet's generation rejected that kind of play-acting. Did Monnet know Chardonne's magnificent saga of the cognac dynasties, where he would have rediscovered the biblical personalities that he had respected? He never read novels and had barely heard of Chardonne. 'Tell me what he said', he would ask, if one insisted. But he would soon interrupt. 'With us, things didn't happen that way. We didn't ask questions. We did what was to be done.'

His psychology was capable of extraordinary penetration, going straight to the heart of the problem, disregarding the meanderings of literature, and refusing attractive hypotheses. That romantic situations existed in Cognac, and even within his own simple family atmosphere, had no interest for him. He only recalled a few anecdotes showing a certain way of seeing life, that he liked to tell. He had taken some general ideas from them, but rejected speculations about them that seemed too ingenious. He got this from his mother's side. They said she had no imagination, but she must have spent treasures of imagination to keep in check the temper Jean inherited from his father. For there was something of the Don Quixote in the Monnet branch of the family. It was a rare phenomenon in Charente, but when it appeared, the womenfolk automatically restored the balance. His mother's family, the Demelles, were no Sancho Panzas but reserved people who disliked noise and restlessness. They wanted to live out their modest lives in dignity, which was not easy. The Monnet side was always ready to take risks.

Young Jean lived with this tension between his elders, picturesque rather than dramatic, and had learned lessons from it. But most of all he was the product of it, and if one does not easily distinguish both sides of these characteristics in him – the daring imagination and the prudent good sense – it is because they were mixed together very early, at the biological stage. Only late in life did he take some pleasure in sorting out his inheritance. He recalled with affection his father's modest origins and his first contact with Monsieur Salignac, whose firm Monnet senior subsequently owned. 'Hey you, boy, take your clogs off before you come in,' Salignac said to Godard the errand boy who brought him a letter. Then the mother interrupted her husband, 'But, you know, this story doesn't interest anybody. It happened that way and that's all'. Monnet thought this story explained a lot; it explains Monnet himself too. Often he would throw cold water on your imagination and cut down your build-up. 'Don't try to see too much in things. He said that because that's what he thought', he would say. In fact he himself would not have understood people so well if he had not been more curious about them than his mother. But no doubt like her, he did not care to hear unusual connections made, that one ought to be discreet about. What did the wooden shoes matter in the long history of the relations between Monnet and Salignac? They were too insignificant to mention.

However, he was always ready to tell this old story – and also the one about his grandfather wearing his Sunday clothes to go and pay his taxes. This was not seen as grandfather's eccentricity; it was a respectable rite. To these non-churchgoers, doing one's duty toward the State was a solemn procedure. On Sunday mornings, while the mother was at church, Monnet's father went to look after a farmers' mutual aid society. He told another story about clothes, which, unlike the wooden clogs, was very significant: Monsieur Barraut, a grower from Segonzac, was a Protestant preacher of the Reformed Church. After the service, still wearing his old-fashioned frock coat jacket, he went straight off to plow among his vines. 'He's a man who knows his Bible' people said admiringly. Monnet told stories with these insights, but without lingering on them. They gave the detail that summed up the life-style and values of those times. Any more would have been romanticizing, which was to be carefully avoided.

All the same, Monsieur Barraut was a yardstick who was used as an example more than once. He incarnated the vinegrower, the basic feature of the native soil, the small landowner who was indispensable to the big firms, although they imposed their conditions on him. Monsieur Barraut's horizon was not limited to his field. He felt concerned in the prosperity of the big firms, who fixed the prices but bought his entire crop. When young Jean went to see him after a trip abroad, without stopping his plowing Monsieur Barraut asked, 'So, how are things in Winnipeg?' On Saturday mornings the Monnet firm was open to him, as it was to all the other suppliers who came from the small farms of the Grande Champagne region. He was asked to stay to lunch. He was perhaps one of the small stockholders in the Vine-growers' Society, founded by Monsieur Salignac as a coopera-tive for the small independent producers. This system, quite widespread among minor industries, was daring for the still feudalized farming world. Ideas of mutual action did not come naturally to the peasants of Charente. But wasn't it the only way for the small owner to escape subjection to the big firms? Monnet senior knew from experience that it was not always easy to keep a steady hand on a group of stockholders united under the independence banner – the Salignac heirs had been ousted by only one vote in J. G. Monnet's favor. He needed to negotiate quite as much among his own associates as with the clients. His son was to remember this. Jean Monnet never imposed a decision on his own authority.

He grew up in the shadow of the Hennessy and Martell monopolies. Even if they did him no harm, since they organized everybody's prosperity, and even if he never lost a degree of esteem for them – he kept up friendly relations with the head of the Hennessy firm – there is no doubt his hostility toward dominant positions developed in his family circle. Consideration is not the same as respect. 'Stick closely to the meaning of words', he would say. The word 'respect' was too loaded in his eyes; he did not see the point of using it. 'Consideration' was quite enough for him, provided one did not get too far away from its literal sense. Similarly, he did not know how to conjugate the verb 'obey'. If a reporter asked him who had been his teachers, he would reply, 'It is a question that has never had any meaning for me'. But if it is true he did not submit to any other man or authority throughout his life, this was not a privilege bestowed on him. He had bought it by his effort and paid for it by giving up a great deal. It was all born from his early upbringing and from his early resolutions, and produced in turn his strong and incorruptible character, that only necessity could bend. The price had sometimes seemed high to him. When he was approached to take up politics, and tempted by the idea, he had quickly realized that he could not 'belong' to any party. The very phrase seemed inconceivable to him; there was no need for any other argument. At the time, he regretted this a little. It was in 1945. Thirty years later he was still glad he had steered clear.

People in Cognac voted republican, but the Monnet family was radical-socialist and Catholic. They were not active in politics nor in local government, but the father believed in the need for associations – for mutual help – and in cooperatives – the Vinegrowers' Society. Oddly, Monnet junior had no interest in the organization of the cognac trade; he did not see the advantage of combining the firms or uniting their efforts. Development of the family firm was his only concern. But his father's example was not to be lost. He recalled his methods to mind in circumstances where collective action had become a life-or-death problem. He admitted he had never felt the need before he saw, in 1914, the waste of war resources. This had given him the idea of organizing transportation methods on an allied basis.

At that time it was still a matter of private business operations, but the general interest was at stake, and requisitioning was about to transfer the entire supplies question into the domain of public responsibility. The father was very surprised that his son went off to the rescue of world trade and the allied war effort before he had even displayed his abilities in Cognac. Monnet senior liked proper respect for the hierarchies. 'We have leaders for those things . . . besides, you think you're busy with world affairs, but you will be glad to come back to the family firm.' The truth is that Jean Monnet did not see himself as involved in world affairs. He was doing service in a sector that was still civilian; he could not make himself useful in any better way, since he had been declared unfit for military service. He could have settled for merely trying to put some order into the private transportation of wheat through a few telephone calls. Instead he set up the biggest public market ever seen, and the first pooling of international resources.

Later he was to say that he had not planned this, nor was he driven by ambition. It was not false modesty. But the aim to do great things, that he had begun empirically, came to him when he found out that he had discovered, without knowing it, a sort of enmeshing activity that was endless. That everything was connected together, and that his linking method worked so well, was his first and only revelation; he was to draw innumerable consequences from this discovery, but he would only see its immense range later on. Though each of his undertakings followed the same overall approach, following the same methods, he had the impression of acting each time according to the inspiration of the moment – even when, in 1939, he referred back to notes written in 1916. He would have been astonished to hear one talk of his political philosophy, and of his method's general principles. It was when he looked back, almost at the end of the road, that he saw the unity in his life. From then on his one wish was to describe it, so that other men might perhaps go further. What is certain, in any case, is that when he was twenty he did not foresee the scope of his action and never said: I shall change the world.

Could anyone with second sight have predicted his great destiny? You might as well believe that someone could have forecast the dangers the world was going to face. For Jean Monnet the optimist was the man of great crises. He was never so lucid as when other men were not lucid anymore. He used to say that without the wars he would have gone on selling cognac. There was doubtless a tendency deep inside him to react to violence and to attacks on liberty, a tendency that mobilized itself within him when these disorders threatened fundamental balances. However, he was not what is called an orderly man. He could work in a degree of confusion, and he by no means feared the kind of activity that shifted the contours of a given situation. But he had such a physical horror of blind force that he could see it coming from far off, and did not wait till it reached the door before he set up the wall of collective action against it. He would have liked to write a book in two parts: 'Today force, tomorrow law'. Somebody suggested instead: 'The law of force and the force of law', but he thought this more striking formula was less true. He was right. It weakened the idea, because it mixed up two ideas in the same word. There should be one word for physical force and another for moral force.

In his view violence did not stop at the end of World War I. It took the form of injustice. The 'unequal peace' of Versailles had seemed to him heavy with threat, all the more unnatural because the instruments of common prosperity then existed. If only the organizations that had combined allied resources had not been disbanded but instead had been enlarged gradually to fit the dimensions of Europe. But the victors wanted to push the advantages they had won to their limits; they even did their utmost to defraud each other. With the vigor of youth and the momentum he had acquired, Jean Monnet continued a line of action whose nature victory had scarcely altered, and which was none the less urgent with the return of peace. But nobody wanted to be bothered with regulating mechanisms. And the 'organized peace' seemed useless or utopian, not to say heretical – economic planning was the system that reigned in the paradise of the Soviet Union. The little team that had built the League of Nations was dissolved in the uncontrolled liberalism of the interwar period. Whether he went back to Cognac where he was still needed, or stayed in Geneva where they could already do without him, was not the great turning point of his life and he did not dramatize it. In his recollection, there was nothing useful to do in this blinkered and weary period. It was also a shorter period than one thinks.

The period between the wars was not in fact an interval where a whole generation of survivors wasted itself in mediocrity. For men like Jean Monnet, scarcely fifteen years separated the last convulsions of the First World War and the preliminary tremors of the Second. He went back to Cognac in 1923 after helping to settle the aftermath of one conflict, and he was in Washington in 1938. In the short interval he had had time to travel a lot, to make and to lose money; and probably to get bored, because he was not the adventurer he might have seemed. His one great enterprise, in line with his liking for difficulty, was to get married. With his partner he made his marriage into a magnificently balanced construction.

He never lost interest in cognac. Although he had transferred all his powers in the firm to other members of his family, and although he never mixed private and public affairs, he kept himself informed on how the firm was doing. His cousins were seen quietly going into his office. They were the most patient of all his visitors, called after all the rest, so that nobody could think – but who cared? – that they were privileged. They left after a long confession, with advice, perhaps reprimands, because they had to answer for the honor of the family, and its name. To have the Monnet name on the best tables all over the world meant great care must be taken to ensure the product was worthy even if, and especially if, Monnet himself was no longer in charge. Until he sold his last holding in the firm, in 1960, he kept this moral and material link with this ancestral reality. There is no way of measuring its profound influence. Neither the pretense at lack of interest, nor genuine distinterestedness, could prove that the son of J. G. Monnet had lost all concern for his heritage.

His relationship to money was mysterious. But the same being true for most Frenchmen, it ought to be easy to find the key. In fact, no key was better hidden in all of our society, and in this way Jean Monnet was no different from other Cognac people – who had taken over many Anglo-Saxon attitudes, except naively flaunting their money. Nobody ever knew if he were rich, and even he himself did not know, no doubt because he had decided one day, to keep his mind free, not to know any longer. For a native of Charente the size of his possessions can become a primordial concern, a worry, a factor hindering decisiveness. Jean Monnet had understood, in middle age, that no personal considerations should weigh in his choices any longer. He needed to be able to change position, and workplace, to face crises wherever they were happening, and to be ready to resign or expatriate himself to keep his independence. So he lost the taste for ownership and the habit of counting. Occasionally however, at slack times, atavism overcame him and he would shut himself up with an accountant, whom he would make count the sums over a hundred times. Then he would forget the total. Though for a while he was director of a great world bank, it was because other people's money is a serious matter, toward which you do not have the same attitude as a small vinegrower would. Also, a mass of money becomes an abstraction, which needs thinking about, with a sense of the general interest. But the experience was too unfamiliar, and he soon grew tired of it. The 1929 crash wiped out what he had been able to earn and quickly ended his personal venture into finance.

This venture had been the same as that of so many men of his generation that we would be wrong to attach too much importance to it. It was possible to make a quick fortune, so it was fashionable to try. How the boss of Transamerica, the partner in Blair and Co., lived through it all we do not know. We can imagine, but what would be the point? Jean Monnet never spent more than a few seconds recalling this somewhat unreal period. He found the thread of his recollections again with his marriage, and with China where he accumulated most of his experience. Of the Great American Depression he remembered the energy and the imagination of the man who put an end to it. He liked Roosevelt who in his eyes personified the grandeur of public office. When Roosevelt died, he wept.

To end this section on money, let us sum it up in the picture of the cognac merchant, who is elegant and likes quality in everything, is accustomed to the best Victorian hotels and is generous with the hall porter who sees to the incidental problems. In the brandy trade you did not skimp on the travel expenses. In his home there was a style of comfort that was called 'British', with the countryside not far off – if possible, beside the door. Guests at the meal table were mostly people passing through. Social activities were rare, and he did not move in fashionable circles. Life was close to domesticity, and centered round the family, if not on the familiar. It all involved expense, but all things considered, it was a quiet life-style. The man one has seen involved in great affairs and whom history will remember was this kind of man, who had re-established the well-tempered comfort of his origins. Toward the end he realized that his resources were small and that he had put his private fortune at the service of his public activity. Then, you saw him negotiating the sale of his *Memoirs* like an old winegrower selling the last of his vintage barrels.

His *Memoirs* owe very little to his memory, which registered actual events badly. He only retained their essence. His recollections were entirely distilled into his experiences, so that the rare precise circumstances he remembered were of particular moments that illustrated his thinking. Why has this physical characteristic or that word, that anecdote survived the general neglect? We can suppose they were fixed by a stronger emotion than usual. But they had never been written down; no kind of journal appears in his archives. His famous rose-colored notes were mere 'reminders' for immediate use. The daily list of things to do gives no trace of what was actually done. However, this man who did not look back on his past, on principle and for lack of time, who did not clutter himself up with unnecessary papers, and who often moved house, kept substantial archives. No doubt it was their bulk that helped them cross oceans, and periods of time. There was nothing superfluous, they were part of his baggage. He knew the essential was there, in a folder that he said was green but which was pink – a confusion that an intelligent secretary was quick to decifer. His codes were always inexact; his memory rejected precision.

He had never been able to learn a single verse of Corneille, which was a handicap for his high school life. And later he made no attempt to keep figures or legal texts in his mind. He was surrounded by men with phenomenal memories, whom he could turn to as dictionaries. He made a sort of asset of not being the prisoner of absolute values so that, better than other men, he saw the relative values which are the only ones that nourish one's judgment. When it was a question of names and faces he did not need any prod to his memory. He registered everything living in his mind, and could recall it at will. He always took a few moments to reflect before he spoke with men he met, or who came to see him, prolonging the handshake as if he were trying to capture a current, or transmit one, while he looked at them quizzically, crinkling his eyes. It gave him time to recall their name and to place them; or if he was meeting them for the first time, to get an impression that he would never lose. This is the picture of Monnet that all kinds of people had, people who came up and talked to him in meetings or in the street, or who asked for a private talk – that he seldom refused. But he was also the man of action with a tough expression and abrupt gestures. Many people only saw this side of Monnet. It should not be lost sight of.

The papers he took round with him were his auxiliary memory. Through them he was able to unburden his mind of all the details of the affairs in hand, and to find the thread of the main idea if necessary. The letters and notes written and rewritten throughout entire days and nights were made up of a substance that challenged time. They did not dazzle with the brilliance of great political works. You could find no search for style in them, and the words were merely those in current use. From the first draft, form had been sacrificed to content. First of all you wrote down what you wanted to say, then you made sure it had been said clearly, but in no way brilliantly. This exactness did not exclude striking formulae, but only when the situation described, or the action you were proposing, required you to shake people's ideas up. Urgency, need, efforts, choices were hammered in. In any case, if Monnet wrote at all, it was because there was no alternative. The act of writing was so painful that he evaded it as long as possible in favor of the spoken word. Jean Monnet convinced very often through conversations, which were thought to be his secret weapon. But everything had to go through the written word and, at the start, reflection was only tentative. It was only by the effort of putting things on paper that one could judge the coherence of a line of argument which had seemed unanswerable in discussion. This test of putting things on paper was carried out mercilessly, and it seemed it could be endless. Then it was stopped as unexpectedly as it had started, according to a ritual that seemed capricious to the uninitiated, but was the very heart of the experimental method.

This man without any college diplomas was a great teacher of logic. He would not have been able to master events if he had not first mastered the advanced techniques of reasoning. He has not left us any course books; it was an applied science, implicit in its objective and performed through action. Besides, this science looked as if it were disconcertingly simple, seemingly no different from elementary common sense. 'He says the same thing a hundred times over, that's his secret', people said, and he did not deny it. He compared himself to his maternal grandmother, 'Mary who never stopped repeating'. But the same thing a hundred times, is something out of the ordinary, which is worth explaining. It was nothing like an incantation. Did the people who got tired of being reminded of a danger or a duty, want to stop talking about it out of discretion or out of resignation? Jean Monnet took a long time to form an opinion or to ripen a plan, and did not see why he should be less obstinate with other people than he was with himself in pursuit of the common interest. And then, does one ever really repeat oneself? Yesterday's arguments, tone or environment are not altogether identical to today's. The man you are talking to will have touched him indirectly, he will give in out of weariness. But above all the moment came when he would say, 'If Jean Monnet insists so much, it's because there is a real problem'. He would no longer be easy in his conscience.

Jean Monnet was too often right for people easily to disregard his warnings. He never disturbed people or their ideas for nothing. Many statesmen, from experience, became ready to trust him in fields where they knew he was watching things closely. These areas were usually unexplored, so that he was not taking anyone's place. 'There's not much competition in the affairs I'm concerned with', he would say. In fact some of his political friends knew they risked his taking them too far and, fascinated by him, began to keep their distance too late. As for his enemies, they had not waited before rejecting his logic and opposing his initiatives. It was they who had most accurately measured the force of his ideas and the contagiousness of his methods. They tried to keep him away from the policy-making centers and to shroud him in silence. They succeeded quite well. But quarantine is no use if the germ has already been lodged.

To deposit the germ was the advice Jean Monnet would have given to his heirs, if he had had any. No such have presented themselves, no doubt for the same reason he did not meet any rivals. But he did not think in terms of recommencements. He left no blueprints for inventing, contrary to what ambitious people look for in his *Memoirs*. His inventiveness depended on circumstances, it had taken root in particular surroundings, and developed by means of institutions which had richly developed the germ: it is at that stage that one has to continue the work begun. He did not say 'my work' or 'my message', because it would not have been logical to personalize action that could succeed only by becoming collective. On the contrary he had a knack for impersonal formulae that gave his ideas their own chance, and the maximum of autonomy to what he had created. 'It's important to continue what has been started and is now moving of its own momentum.' In private he would add, 'Count on me to look after it'. But he took pains to make it someone else's affair, someone more charismatic than he or simply better placed: the Churchill Plan, the Schuman Plan. He liked it to become an organization if possible: the Plan (for France's postwar reconstruction), the High Authority (of the Coal and Steel Community), the European Parliament.

If he wrote his *Memoirs* it was not from egocentricity, nor to justify his action, and even less to entertain or astonish, but to prolong his activity after he was assured it was within his powers. What publishers and ghost writers pressed him to produce was something different: a lifestory full of adventures and picturesque anecdotes. They knew he was no writer. Let him talk then, and those famous discussions that had stirred so many men and so many events could be arranged for publication. It took many years to correct this mistaken aim, and he refused all offers until he was reassured that the profound unity of his life could be set out coherently in a book without any literary artifice. It was at this time – he was eighty-four – that he discovered the thread that had linked his intermittent activities, the thread that, if one went back in time, joined together Europe and the modernization of France, union among Frenchmen during the war, the Program for Victory, the Allied committees of 1940 and those of 1914. Then he realized he needed to go further back, as far as Cognac where his destiny was really earthed. Memories of the family table revived elements that were missing in a picture whose perspectives were still unclear in his mind. At bottom, he was not sure he had led his life with any spirit of continuity. He justified the detours in his path by the sense of necessity which, in his eyes, had been his chief driving force. 'I had no choice', he often said by way of explanation. It was an insufficient one. When he had a better view of the overall picture and the chronology had been tidied up, he saw that he had always looked for the same thing: to unite people.

To unite them for peace, so as to use the resources of nature better, no doubt, if one considers the final aim. But he hesitated a lot before using such great words. He saw himself first and foremost as a practitioner. He did what was necessary to solve the crisis of the moment and for that, all he needed was the means. However, it is no accident if these practical means harmonized with moral ends that one did not always take time to spell out. True, one spoke of peace to the League of Nations, of freedom in 1940, of democracy in 1945, but it was all mobilization language that was muted once the crisis was over. You do not spend all your lifetime uniting peoples. 'And yet that's what we did', said Jean Monnet with astonishment when he took time to look back. 'Wasn't our method to make men meet each other, whatever the problem, so that they talked about the same thing and discovered their common interest?' It was when he had it proved to him that this method had always been his and that it could be applied between peoples as it could between smaller social groups, or between individuals, that he decided to write his memoirs.

III

It is difficult to take the measure of the man of action who spends his life adjusting his effort to the obstacles he meets, who goes beyond the limits of his nature, who gives way to certain passions and holds others in check. Sometimes you can define him by his ambition, which is a projection of his image of himself. Not being able to grasp this image directly, you guess its outlines according to what space he aims to fill, later on according to the void he filled, and finally according to the emptiness he leaves behind him. In the last resort you turn to the average opinion of him or the legend he left. Jean Monnet bypassed all these approaches and his biographers hesitate between presenting him as an economist, a diplomat or a politician, categories even less appropriate than calling him a Cognac brandy merchant or a Californian banker. If in the end we have to give up trying to stick a label on him, can we at least sketch his character in the light of the many testimonies people have written on him?

Paradoxically, it is the stories of the people who came closest to him that distort the most. His associates have memories of him that are both attractive and terrifying, that they exorcise through humor. They justify their being bewitched by describing him as a great sorcerer – an image that his opponents are very ready to accept. They all describe picturesque sides of his character – and always the same ones. The legendary circle is already closed and time can add little more, for want of new input or new unpublished personal eyewitness accounts. But the circle does not define the man, who was bigger and more complex. This is quite normal in a man who cared less about being a somebody than he cared about doing something. He would say to publishers who pressed him to fill his memoirs with attractive anecdotes, 'I tell the story of things as I saw them, take it or leave it. I've worked for the future, for the duration and I'll give a durable witness to it'. In private he added, 'Let's not write to please people like them. They only think of immediate success, and they're wrong. This book will only sell slowly'. And in fact there are not many intimate confessions in it. Yet this chronicle of a working life will perhaps give researchers their most valuable source on the man who deliberately effaced himself behind his work.

The results of Jean Monnet's work leave little doubt that it was inspired by rigour, optimism and generosity; and that is enough to be able to judge the man himself. If he had not been an essentially moral creature he would have chosen a different path and written a different book. Let us not regret that in his *Memoirs* he limited himself to telling the events that had a durable significance and did not give way to the temptation to create effects. That was his rule of conduct, and he did not think that the function of literature could be different from that of action. He only wrote when he was convinced that there was no better way left for him to act for Europe. Even if he had lived through a hundred picturesque adventures in Winnipeg, Shanghai and Algiers; even if he had met a hundred Pilsudskis, Roosevelts and de Gaulles, he would not have overloaded his story with them even for a publishing success. Nor had he, unlike so many writers of memoirs, any need to justify himself or settle accounts. His motive was much simpler: 'We have built up a method that has succeeded but is only at its beginnings. It must be useful to other people who are continuing along the same path'. At first he envisaged a methodical description of his method. But others made him consider that since he had already applied them many times, in dramatic circumstances, would it not be better to illustrate them in their setting of recurrent crises, the repetition of mistakes – and the permanence of the remedy? He was convinced and agreed to tell his story. He had to learn to speak of himself in the first person, something he had never done.

He spoke of 'we' and it was quite the opposite of a royal 'we'. He would have done nothing without a team, a team that widened in concentric circles, englobing all the actors in a collective endeavor. The document commonly known as the 'Monnet Plan' referred on every page to the thousand people who had contributed to its formation, and to the endless teams who carried it out. Nobody ever heard him say 'my plan' but 'our job', just as in Cognac people said 'our firm' because the stockholders should never be forgotten. By nature, authority wants to impose itself. Impatience often came into it, as Jean Monnet had seen with his father, J.G., who was excessive in his sudden short rages. They called him 'quick to fly off the handle' or to put it more poetically, impulsive. He had not put the world's burdens onto his shoulders. He got along well with his clients and visited them regularly, especially the Germans as he spoke their language. His son took after him in his sudden bursts of irritation (this was a strong word for Cognac) but he had not the same light-hearted temperament that soon got his father back on form. Besides, Monnet had chosen to take on responsibilities and face endless obstacles, that did not leave him time to calm down. Has anyone ever seen him relaxed? To many of his associates Monnet seemed a hard man, exacting, insensitive to other people's private problems and stingy with his thanks.

This reputation for tyranny is not without some truth, but it is ambiguous because it was given him by the men most closely attached to him, who might be suspected of making their dedication sound like heroism. It is true that ordinary men had trouble keeping up the pace he imposed on their teamwork. This rhythm was neither a natural one, nor society's norm. It was not beyond the physical or intellectual capacities of a well-chosen team. But it destabilized the men in it. They might be ready for any exertion but were reluctant to sacrifice their private lives, or to accept the effect on their psyche of the erratic hours they worked. Above all, the feeling of going round and round a fixed idea gave them a sense of giddiness. Their intellectual training had prepared them for a strictly linear dialectic with some carefully programmed arabesques, according to the university system they came from. They found it difficult to stay confined within the circle where Jean Monnet drove his thinking like a gimlet into the heart of reality. They did not always see that they were going deeper and that every written draft, even if it was repetitive, even each monotonous re-reading was progress. He was not one to go back to persuade himself, at the fifteenth draft of a document, that the first was still the best.

There was no fixed hour for these exercises, and above all no time limit. The people expecting the document would have to wait. 'Too bad if they get upset. What's important is that we should be satisfied with our work.' But whenever is one satisfied or literally, whenever have we done enough? There again the intuition of the moment comes into it, a responsibility impossible to share. Jean Monnet never made a decision under the stress of fatigue. If necessary he would go off home to bed, 'I leave you to get on with it, men. Let me have the document tomorrow morning, when I'll see more clearly'. You had to suppress your wish to rebel, because he was right. The power of decision needs its own hygiene. 'Seeing clearly' for him was a state of well-being to which he would have sacrificed all others. When things got too involved in his head he blamed the weather, and drank fizzy mineral waters that he had supplied to him from another continent. But often the trouble was less in himself than in the facts. Opening an office window could not improve the international climate. Then he would go to get more information at the epicenter of the storm or, better still, he went off to the mountains for solitary walks.

*   *   *

In the Cognac cellars you do not easily create VSOP brandy. You need to taste and spit out many a mouthful. When the time comes, you reluctantly decide to bottle and label it. When Jean Monnet wrote on a document 'final version' he was not jubilant, but resigned. 'Let's stop there', he would suddenly say. 'We're not going to do any more good now. On the contrary we risk spoiling everything.' More than most people, the ones from the Charente region are sure that the best is the enemy of the good. At least, they always remember this at the right time. But deep in their hearts they are not sure that if they worked a bit more and above all, let time do its work longer, the result would not be better. Perhaps the only real mystery of Jean Monnet was where he inherited his tense readiness for lightning decisions, disturbing the other side of his nature. There were no soldiers in the family and not even any hunters among his forebears, nothing except one grandfather who liked to fish. As a child he played at the Boer war in the garden of the house on the Rue de Pons. But that was the popular game of the time. However, his outstanding actions were born of instant initiatives, when a situation was at its most dramatic and could only be understood by a strategist's cool appraisal.

He was not interested in card games. No one ever saw him playing poker, trying to have other men believe he held cards that he had not got – nor chess either, pondering future moves. He only joined in games that other people had started, and almost lost, against superior forces. Most often they could see no way out, or had no means of forcing the only exit. The time for heroism or ruse had passed. Those who no longer hoped for a miracle were organizing themselves to submit. This scenario would repeat itself from time to time in our democracies, whether the opponent was an armed force, a dominant economic power, or more confusedly disorder, both material and emotional – suspicion, fear, crisis and abandon. The situation was deadlocked and Jean Monnet thought so, like everybody else. But he did not share the general discouragment and even less, the panic. This kind of situation stimulated his faculties. He did not say, 'There's always something that can be done', because it was no time for general remarks, but, 'This is what must be done.'

He did not wait to be called upon. He took the shortest paths to the power center, or whatever replaced it in moments of crisis. He found friends there in the entourage, not well-known, but men whose influence and coolness he had detected. He had already approached them some time back and together they had tried to master events and prepare some quick moves. They were linked by their common clearsightedness and their unsuccessful attempts to make themselves heard. Jean Monnet had never lacked men like these. He said he would never have been able to do anything without them and deeply valued them; but should we think that he had been lucky to meet them, or that he had the gift for finding them? Salter, Plowden, Rajchman, McCloy, Horace Wilson, Felix Frankfurter, Clappier and others who achieved at one moment in their lives a role in history because they risked all to see Jean Monnet's ideas tried out by the existing political powers which were otherwise bereft of imagination or resources.

How could this idea be summed up in a single page on a statesman's desk or a council table, instead of the minutes already drawn up to spell out defeat, or the abdication act already drafted? This kind of story is repeated many times and forms the stuff of the *Memoirs*. Jean Monnet recalled the surprising events of his career and then concluded, 'You see, all that happened quite naturally'. He possessed, in fact, the art of restoring the natural course of events by unexpected circuits. He did not face insurmountable obstacles head-on, but you could not say he went round them. He leaned on them, using them to build up a different structure where they no longer acted as a dead end but a point of departure. In this way the waste of allied resources became the decisive argument for political union. The desire for revenge could only be eliminated by the fusion of sovereignties, etc. It is what he called 'changing the context', a reassuring way of saying that he was revolutionizing structures and turning ways of seeing things upside down.

Ordinary common sense would say that he shifted the difficulty. And it is true that this great simplifier of ideas did not simplify other people's work. Those in government who took him to be a magician expected him to produce 'neat solutions' to the problems they offloaded onto him. But every time, he handed back to them another problem which dissolved the first one into a new picture that was bigger, richer in progress – but also in new requirements. For example, to drown German steel competition inside the European Community was a way of making men fall into their own trap when they had hoped for advantages without any sacrifice of their rights. Many people recalled that this man had the habit of widening the scope of his missions – he did this with Viviani, Clemenceau, Churchill and others – and we know some men who swore they would never entrust even the smallest job to him again. But it was too late. On the evening of 9 May 1950, it was too late for anyone to stop the process which the Community's creator was conducting, with or without a mandate. Only his atavistic caution and his experience kept his ambition and his influence within the limits strictly necessary to the success of his action.

'I don't recall ever saying to myself: I'll do this or do that with my life. Circumstances have decided. I don't know anything except events. I must say I've never found any lack of them. But to seize them, you must have prepared yourself well beforehand.' One can think this formula too simple, and indeed it would be too simple to advance any kind of political ambition. When you yourself want to be a figure on the stage of history, you have to provoke and manipulate events. But if you have no other aim than to prevent history from going off the rails and becoming murderous, it is enough to watch, and to intervene at the right moment. We can dream of a time where Jean Monnet's genius stayed unused because of a shortage of great events where he could reveal himself. For instance, where Salignac set up the vinegrowers' cooperative, and where his father led the mutual-aid associations. He might have been bolder than they in organizing the common good, but would he have been another Saint Simon, another de Lesseps? It is not impossible, supposing he might have witnessed some tragic social confrontation like Saint Simon, or like de Lesseps seen with his own eyes his export cargoes blocked by an isthmus of land. He was born intolerant of everything that sets men against each other, or whatever separates them and amputates their creative capacities. But he was not a knight errant. Nobody came to wake him every morning by reminding him, as the author of the 'Reorganization of European Society', Saint Simon, was reminded, that he had great things to do.

Let us not linger over this game of hypotheses in which he himself refused to get involved. 'Maybe', he would say, 'but that's not what happened.' On the other hand, everything falls into place if you add together what he called his pre-disposition – his allergy to obstacles and to wasteful mess – and the formidable challenge of the events that took place at the beginning of his active life. The clash of economies and the race to blockade that the war 1914–18 represented (a somber epic still to be described), could not but revolt a young intelligence just opening up to the incredible development prospects available to western society. Not only do men condemn themselves not to meet except to kill each other, but they also disorganize the entire circulation of goods within their own camp. Jean Monnet's aptitudes found in this fact his first decisive challenge. All he had to do was to communicate his overwhelming evidence. It is astonishing that nobody else was concerned about the question at the same time.

Our contemporary awareness of the weight of economic facts (no doubt itself another form of blindness) leads to a surprising question: if young Jean Monnet of Cognac realized, through reading the London *Times* and just looking out of the train window, as his father had advised, that the mobilization of war material was disorderly and wasteful, what were millions of other people doing, who seemed not to be interested in the fact? Perhaps they were thinking of their personal destiny and their national glory, or of their fiancée, their flag or their fear. But we can imagine too that some of them, either dazed or enthusiastic, watched the impressive comings and goings of freight trains and boats without for one moment doubting that all was perfectly organized by the powers that be.

Respect is always a religious sentiment. We should all still be seeing the sun revolving round the Earth if one single powerful mind had not dared to tackle the problem from the other end. Jean Monnet was one of those very rare beings capable of believing in what they see, as they see it. He did not belong with those who say, 'That's not possible, it would be too absurd', and so make absurdity legitimate. He did not know about the respect that freezes freedom of judgment and, if by nature he tended to take nothing for granted, events only reinforced his independence of mind. 'When you see a difficulty, never think that the people responsible are busy solving it. If you think it needs action, see to it yourself.' What is unbelievable is not that he acted this way from his youth but that so few others did, and that he was one of the few in any case who acted upon his conclusions – conclusions that were clear to everybody once the decision was at last taken.

Certainly at critical times there must have been examples of lucidity similar to his own, and even cries of revolt, that were so quickly silenced by optimism on one side and dejection on the other that one could hardly remember having heard them, when Jean Monnet could not stop himself from intervening against all good sense. If he was not then the only one to denounce the rise of perils that threatened his generation more than once, he was exceptional in thinking that the impossible must be done at once to avoid or overcome the perils; and that the most daring initiative was the most legitimate, without concern of hierarchies or formalities. At such times all his faculties were mobilized for action that would need the greatest coolness and clear determination in a context of general panic. He did not wait for proof before he intervened. He knew from experience that nothing was ever planned beforehand to face up to cataclysms, but the crisis had to develop before his advice was listened to. Even if he invented solutions to meet events out of control, it is not his genius for improvisation one should most admire, but his permanent readiness to deal with situations that had gone out of order.

He used to say, 'You can only create well in a certain amount of disorder'. He meant that you can only suggest new structures and put better ones in place when things are on the move, and this movement deeply troubles people. But in this he also was different from reformers who themselves create the disorder they require, to open up the road to their solutions. He had no liking and no leniency for deliberately painting things as black as possible. Unfortunately, misfortunes arrive by themselves, in their own time. You can see them coming, because they are the results of badly solved problems, and in no way due to fate or to people's ill-will. It was on the basis of this explanation that Jean Monnet had decided on his vocation, 'When I meet a problem, I have to solve it'. He would sometimes add, 'The urge is stronger than I am', but that remark, instead of enlightening us, brings us back to the mystery of the programming of the individual.

IV

Let us turn our backs on Cognac, as he did without any thought of a return, even though references to its microclimate and its flourishing well-tempered cosmopolitanism were later a major theme of his *Memoirs*. But a moment arrives when it is simpler to explain the man of action by his actions, and show the audacity of his endeavors through his accumulated experience. One day, the inventor of the European Community sold his shares in the family firm to some German wine merchants. If this fact contains a hidden symbol, it is not the one you would think. Cognac had adopted international free trade a long time before, and there was a Rue Cobden[1] there a century before a Place Jean Monnet. There was no need to exercise an economic nationalism, for it had never really taken root there. The truth lay rather in the recognition of an affective transfer. Houjarray became the family home, more full of memories than the house on the Rue de Pons. You need to release yourself from the past if it has ceased to play a relevant role. The man who in 1923 dared to sell the family stock of vintage brandy was quite capable of selling the business in 1960 without any regrets. The Monnet name continued but emptied of all its sentimental contents. Jean Monnet kept an eye on its reputation as long as he lived.

There was seldom any talk of morals with this very discreet man, or rather this man who was so extrovert in appearance that his interior life seemed a secondary part of his personality. The fact that his behavior was always very dignified could be seen as due to his character and upbringing. In any case, why look for the moral roots of respectability when it certainly is just a matter of social attitudes? Yet if you probe the depths you can discover the soul's quality. Jean Monnet had not the time to concern himself with his being, neither where it came from nor where it was going. Nobody could draw him out on this subject. His spiritual side was lived very intensely but never conceptualized. He detested mystery in all its forms, and no doubt had some secret arrangement with it. Metaphysics asked endless questions, so he kept away from the subject as far as possible; or he neutralized any display of it by a few summary superstitions like knocking on wood – a gesture he made every time he said, 'I think we're succeeding'. Other signs of exorcism were harder to detect, but we can be sure the only reasons for his hesitations before starting his trips, his capricious changes of time-table or means of transportations were to deceive fate.

His great tolerance for religious beliefs went further than his political liberalism. It was the tolerance of a man influenced by the women who had filled his emotional universe. The trio of mother-sisters-wife forced his respect for their piety, whether it was formalized or interiorized – or even institutionalized (his sister Marie-Louise was one of the founders of the independent Catholic Action). Like his father in Cognac he would go and wait for the mass to end at Montfort L'Amaury. To stay on his feet at the back of the church as some did when they arrived before the mass ended, has nothing to do with God, nor with society, but has to do with women. It was not a compromise, it was an attention. With Marie-Louise he had an extra link, the closeness that unites people with a gift for organization. Each of them was good at stirring up the hierarchies. Nonetheless it would be wrong to look for mysterious political interferences in their two careers, both of them using the same methods. The good relations that Europe has maintained with the Vatican developed along other paths. But the older brother and the younger sister followed each's respective activities with interest, pride and a touch of amusement.

Jean Fourastié started to be interested rather late in the spiritual qualities of the man whose intellectual rigor and capacities for vision he had measured and esteemed. Oddly, Silvia Monnet thought that Fourastié, the author of *What I Believe*, was wrong. She did not talk about her husband's interior life, but she recognized that at most his faith did not probe deeply. She would have had scruples about asking for extreme unction to be brought to him, if he had not said, 'I'm asking for it, not you', to reassure her. They had a religious marriage ceremony when they were free to do so, late in life. He preferred to dwell on the deep importance of his civil marriage in 1934, and on the international validity of the code of laws he had chose, after thorough investigation. It was the Soviet Code. What was involved was the dissolution of a previous marriage contracted by Silvia de Bondini according to Italian law, which did not recognize divorce. It would have been easier to go to Las Vegas or even, it seems, to Czechoslovakia. Yet despite considerable difficulties he took the side of the legal experts whom he had asked, 'In this field, which legal system is both the most accommodating and the most serious?' 'I wanted to have behind us the legitimation of a great country', he said. In Moscow they passed in a few minutes from the Divorce Office to the Wedding Room at the other side of a corridor. They remembered having seen flowers in the Wedding Room. The law officer who performed the ceremony said to Silvia, 'Never forget, madam, that according to our law you are a free woman'. Ambassador Charles Alphand was less optimistic. 'You won't be able to get out of this country easily' he warned her, because she had had to take out a Soviet passport before the ceremony. But this venture, one of Jean Monnet's riskiest, turned out well. It had cost him months of work, and a fortune, the just price for what was a great love, shared and lasting.

It is not straying into anecdote nor infringing the secrecy of private life to speak of Jean and Silvia Monnet as a couple. They themselves had so intimately linked their destinies that you saw them together at every decisive moment – but one needs to look at this fact more closely, because women know how to make themselves invisible when they feel a respect that is as strong as their love. Here, Silvia's influence could have gone unseen if he himself had not testified to it, and she would have been non-existent if he had not wanted her role acknowledged. Initiates were well aware of the importance of this, because the phenomenon of the complementary couple was frequent in the type of family oligarchy best illustrated by the Blums in France and the Roosevelts in the United States. You could not dissociate Jack and Ellen McCloy, Henri and Hellé Bonnet, Hervé and Claude Alphand. We have seen that never-ending work can break up couples if it is not integrated into family unity. Seen from outside, the wife's role was not at all apparent in the field where only the man's responsibility was involved. The entire history of the events of 1934 to 1979 could be told without showing the role of Silvia Monnet, because basically it was not really a deciding factor. She herself never claimed any part in the big decisions, and modesty was not the whole reason; one could clearly detect the limits the husband assigned to his wife's influence, and which she respected. Such a balance is rare, and difficult to maintain. But it was tacitly included in the conjugal pact.

What the outside observer saw went along these lines but was incomplete. One would have also needed to hear the telephone calls he made to his wife when he had only just left her, then several times from his office and finally only a few minutes before he went back home. Or the conversations at dinner, which he almost always ate at home. He would describe his day, tell her of his worries and his hopes and wait for her reaction. When he invited his colleagues out to his country home he insisted that Silvia should join in the discussions. He gave her his draft memoranda to read. But these attentions were given without any indulgence. She ran just as much risk as anybody of being put in her place. How many times did he tell her, 'You don't understand anything, you're getting us sidetracked', asking her to leave after he had called her in, 'Leave us to get on with our work now'. To avoid drifting and to stop the talk was his natural right. The most violent human attachment would not have made him change direction, and Silvia knew it. She would get up and protest, for form's sake, 'You asked my opinion and I've given it'. She would not have thought of persisting for one moment, or of getting vexed, because in fact her views had more chance than anyone else's of being considered. Never did this woman misuse her immense power. Her very forthright opinions often irritated his colleagues. But her vehemence came from her Italian nature which one tended to forget. He paid no attention to the style of speaking, but to what was said. He could say outright, 'I'm not listening to you any longer' and there would be no reprisals. Perhaps he had made it clear early on that he would not stand for any.

Two great personalities became linked by a vital need for complementarity. It is pointless to ask where the dominant force lay, without knowing all about fifty years of continuous and profound sharing. It seemed as if art, poetry and sentiments were on one side, and on the other infallible logic and willpower. But that would be to overlook that Jean Monnet himself was a poet of the earth. He soaked himself every day in the countryside, he smelled its primordial fragrances. They were the fuel for this creative imagination. Without many words he showed his enthusiasm at the changes of the seasons, or the persistent snows. From these morning walks he brought back small wild flowers that Silvia kept in the pages of books. He went further than she in simple and direct sensitiveness. She was the only one who knew his strong displays of emotion. She knew he could not stand sights that were too awful, and she kept him away from them. He had a horror of violence, suffering and illness, as much for himself as for other people, and refused even to hear about them. At the cinema he went out in the middle of the movie about the atrocious little girl who told lies. But on the other hand he took his daughters Anna and Marianne to see Westerns – he had rubbed shoulders with cowboys and trappers in his young days; and he liked justice to have the last word. He had no great pretentions to good taste, but trusted the judgment of the artist he had married.

But they were linked by something even stronger than their mutual enrichment. This was the challenge they had made together to the world when they had chosen each other in a single instant. He was twenty years older than she. She was the very beautiful young wife of an Italian business man. It all happened at a dinner party in Paris. René Pleven, another guest at the dinner, witnessed the meeting between them that was like a lightning stroke. Later a long race began that led them to Shanghai, to Moscow and to Washington, plus a great legal battle around a little girl who was born during a marriage that was theoretically indissoluble. Such ordeals either wear love out or make it strong forever. In their case they had an extra sequal – they isolated them from their native society and for a while from countries ruled by the Latin legal code. In other latitudes they found greater tolerance or more indifference, laws and customs that were more favorable to private happiness. They were protected from the temptations of the social round and installed themselves quite naturally in a world consisting of a few friendships, which they never left.

It seems clear that Jean Monnet was not destined to take root in the land of his birth. This Rastignac from Charente

who had not aimed to challenge Paris at the age of his first
initiations but had looked for them in London and then in
the far West; this man who had fought for the Alliance even
more than for the Motherland; who manipulated pounds
sterling, dollars, yens and zlotis oftener than francs; who
married under Soviet law – was he going to become a
cosmopolitan or a prototype citizen of a new world? He
never ran this danger. Not for an instant did he envisage
changing his nationality and though he owned Chinese
residence cards, British passports and American special
mission papers, if he thought in English and counted in
dollars, it was because all these were useful at a given
moment. Nothing changed his immemoriable peasant atavism, and throughout the world his friends were astonished
that anyone could doubt his strongly specific origins. 'Jean
Monnet? But he's a Frenchman!' they exclaimed when
people wanted to tell them he had lost his roots. When the
Americans became aware just before the victory of World
War II that their gigantic arms effort had been master-
minded by an unknown Frenchman, John Davenport outlined the first portrait of him in *Fortune* magazine under the
title, 'Mr. Jean Monnet of Cognac'. For months already, this
'great American' as the Gaullists mockingly called him had
only one driving aim: to give back life and strength to
France, soon to be liberated.

But it would be another mistake to think he had waited for
this moment to end an overlong absence, a sort of voluntary
exile, and to rehabilitate himself with his forgotten compat-
riots by some striking move. 'Rehabilitation', yes, but in the
sense this word was used officially by the Washington services
to describe the rebuilding of devastated Europe. He was
impatient only to see his mother again, and his sisters
Henriette Chaumet and Marie-Louise who remained the
magnetic pole of his life. The compass of this professional
migrant had stayed fixed on Cognac. Once his pilgrimage
was over he settled at the heart of his new workplace as if he
had never left. Gaston Malewski found a small private
mansion for this prodigal son next to the church of Saint
Clotilde. There, in a maze of awkward staircases and of
rooms either too big or too small, plans for the great rational

modernization of France were worked out. At fifty-seven,
Jean Monnet began a career as a top civil servant under the
orders of General de Gaulle.

The job was no less great than the ones he had carried
through in much bigger areas, and for economics of larger
dimensions. This entailed material reconstruction that was
unprecedented in the western world. From any reasonable
viewpoint it was a lost cause. Rationally, it was workable if it
was accompanied by intellectual reconstruction. With the
Monnet Plan, Descartes' *Discourse on Method* was to have its
first socio-economic try-out on a human scale. Marx had
misunderstood Descartes, who was distorted by being interpreted through German philosophy. Jean Monnet was intuitively saturated in Descartes, whom he had never read.
Every difficulty was divided up into its basic elements. The
French economy was reduced to a few primary numbers.
The work of each was linked materially and psychologically
to the others, and the whole was attached to an overall idea.
So France changed its outlook in a few years. The people
who run the country today still have a nostalgia for this age
of simplification. The method has not been lost. But which
amateur mathematician could now convert an infinitely more
complex mechanism into new primary numbers?

Above all, what system of persuasion could replace the one
whose secret Jean Monnet carried away with him? Neither
the magic of words nor an imposing presence, nor even the
power of money have possessed as much influence as the
slightly muted voice – insistent, certainly, but lacking any
special effects – of this man, shorter than most of the people
he could keep listening to him, willingly or not, in some
window recess. Sometimes his hands would be in his jacket
pockets, but oftener he would put them on your arms to
make you feel you too were the prisoner of necessity. 'Believe
me ... don't get it wrong ... there's no other way out.' Such
warnings, repeated a hundred times, never wore out. On the
contrary, they had been verified by experience a hundred
times. On the Rue de Martignac the talk was simple, 'Modernization or decadence.' Who would have seen that as a
choice? It was an injunction. Jean Monnet had always practiced the technique of the sham alternative. But before he
encapsulated his own thought and concentrated his willpow-

er he had tirelessly turned the problem over in his mind. 'I reflect for a long time and I convince myself. Once I am convinced, I act.' He expressed this same idea in other ways. 'An essential rule of conduct is first of all to know what you yourself think.' He never advocated a cause if he had not thought it out and won his own conscience over to it. That is why he could be seen immersed in long hesitations and tedious investigations. 'What's he getting at?' people asked for weeks. Then his logic seemed faulty and his imagination delirious, as Paul Reuter thought when we heard Monnet talk for the first time of a Franco-German power.

It was also on the Rue de Martignac that he himself drafted in his own hand the points where one can make out the barely organized germ of what two weeks later would be a new stage in European history:

> We must change the course of events. For that men's minds must be changed. Words are not enough. Only immediate action affecting an essential point can alter the present static state of affairs. Profound, real, dramatic and immediate action is needed which will change things and bring reality to the hopes that people are on the point of not believing any longer.

This key sentence sums up the thought, the method and the style of Jean Monnet. The thinking is global, the method is meticulous and the style effective. The purists would have a lot to say about the repetitions. If the author had his reasons for insisting on necessity and urgency, could he not at least have varied his words and phrasing? This was a minor worry for the man who had just written 'The cold war, initial phase of the real war ... In fact we are already at war'. It is no moment for looking up synonyms in the dictionary. Beside, there are no synonyms. Every word has a meaning, and only one.

One can clearly see the obscure procedures of thinking that was going to lead to unheard-of action. Jean Monnet by now had convinced himself, but had not yet got his plan of action. But if one must do violence to history in order to save the peace, this violence should be peaceable. A legal revolution, a democratic attack on national sovereignty, ideas that are apparently contradictory. But since there is no choice, the means must exist somewhere. His mind prowled round, getting closer. Others were doing the same at the same moment, with no contact between them, as one sees on the eve of all great scientific discoveries. A jurist was to provide the mechanism, or more precisely a constitutionalist. We should pay our respects to the sheer chance that sent Paul Reuter that way; but let us not forget that chance itself is also a means. 'In life there are only events' Jean Monnet used to say. 'We must use them to further an objective.' In his *Memoirs* he was more explicit about his method. 'Events that strike me and absorb all my thoughts lead me to general conclusions on what should be done. Then, circumstances control the moment and suggest to me, or bring me, the means. I know how to wait for a long time on circumstances.'

The time is May 1950. The waiting cannot go on any longer, deadlines follow one after the other in the West. Everyone is taken unawares, and it is Jean Monnet's moment. He has become a public figure. His name is known, though not his face nor his career. He is aware that fame is given only to politicians and he has hesitated over becoming one of them. In 1945 the Left would have found him a place. He talked it over with his wife, and they decided he would not go for a life of public platforms. It was then that he proposed his modernization plan to de Gaulle, who replied, 'Carry it out yourself'. He consulted his wife again but this time for form's sake. 'He offered me my own child, I could not refuse.' From then on he had to build a type of authority on the scale of his aims. His sense of economy was like that of the elegant physicist who created the grandest effects from the smallest machines. The *Commissariat du Plan* came last among the State's administrative expenses, and its head became part of no administrative hierarchy – a position that favored an uncontrolled reduction of his forces. The Schuman Plan slipped unnoticed into this mechanism, which was plugged into all the centers of political decision. It was to cost only a few sheets of paper and a few telephone calls. The technique of using limited power reached its highest point. 'It takes a long time to reach power', said Monnet, 'but very little to explain to those in power what must be done.'

In his sixty-second year his vitality was phenomenal. He

acknowledged, 'At that time I lived through a period of passionate activity'. He no doubt understood then that he had not yet really met his destiny. He had almost encountered it in 1940 when he thought up the proposition for a Franco-British union. But this was an almost desperate attempt in desperate circumstances. Already events had taken an uncontrollable turn. Exactly ten years later Europeans found themselves once again in a situation of extreme necessity. This time they were no longer the only masters of the game. The cards they held and that they had tragically botched in 1940 now belonged to the superpowers. Divided Europe would be a passive stake. United at the heart of a western world, Europe could again become an active factor for security and peace. But union between who, and up to what point? The only clear reply was one that nobody dared to formulate, resentments were still so sharp. First of all the other options must be raised.

In 1940 Jean Monnet sounded out the British, without any great illusions; but he still felt a certain regard for this universal empire that proudly outlived its time. His message was not well received, and later he would know it had not even been understood. The following year he returned to the charge, because at that time you needed to knock twice at the British door before starting out on an ambitious venture. Was it a gesture of friendship or a tactical move? It is difficult to know. The sequel was to show how strong the nostalgia for the City had remained in the gentleman Jean Monnet.

The German option was one of reason. It grew into one friendship, of the sort practiced by exceptionally upright men. Jean Monnet knew neither the country nor the language of those to whom he transferred the contract of union that the British had not been able to sign. His very first German contact was with Chancellor Adenauer. The minutes of their conversation written by the coldest of Quai d'Orsay diplomats is one of the most moving documents of our time. This meeting of 23 May in the Schaumburg Palace in Bonn was not only the beginning of a friendship between two men. It was the true birth of Franco-German reconciliation, and of the European Community founded on equality of rights.

V

It is hard to imgine Jean Monnet sitting in front of someone else's desk, with his document-case on his knees. He must have done it sometimes – he had no hesitation in presenting himself as a supplicant when he thought it worthwhile – but he usually arranged his working method and his position so that things happened, as far as possible, in the setting where his habits and his backup team reigned. It is one of the great secrets of power to get other people to come to you, and protocol, either written or unwritten, does not regulate all the difficult cases. In fact there are many situations that one can avoid by reducing one's vulnerable social surface to a minimum.

Jean Monnet possessed a great strength of indifference toward problems and people who were not within his sights at a given moment. He did not willingly enlarge his province. So as not to keep having to be a supplicant, in order one day to be more free to make insistent demands, he set up parallel hierarchies in his work center. Thus he was free from any formality, although he protected himself from obstructive closeness. If he was obliged to be dependent on some outside authority he made sure it was the highest one, not to be closest to the source of all power, but on the contrary, so that distance left him the maximum freedom of movement in the emptier spaces where things really happened. He used the interministerial telephone rarely, but turned it to his profit by making it his alarm signal to the people he harassed. Without either a great title or great office, he would always have been in an inferior position compared to the holders of political power, if both he and they had not invested him with a sort of status of variable geometry that gave him access to all levels. But he took little advantage of this and stayed on the outer edge of the public scene, not seeking to become familiar with public figures or to advise them on many matters. He was careful not to wear out his influence and not to waste his authority. He did not use the openings offered him to pass opinions to the top, if they were outside his own competence. These channels were reserved for useful communication – which might never occur or, on the contrary, that circumstances might soon require. He kept in touch with top-ranging contacts, never asking a small favor but being ready to pester endlessly when the moment came. At bottom he was never really completely at ease with the powerful. Though his path often crossed with theirs, he did not share their conceptions of action.

So it was with Churchill, whom he could only convince through the backing of a former, devalued Prime Minister, Chamberlain. So it was with de Gaulle, who pretended to see in Monnet nothing but a very ingenious fellow. So it was even with Adenauer who showed him friendship but did not put him at the level of a high official. Let us talk rather of his successors, and especially of Willy Brandt and Helmut Schmidt, who did not hesitate to have frequent meetings with the man the Elysée Palace never consulted. Let us talk also of John Kennedy, who one day called him the 'world's statesman'. A new generation of leaders, whose day might have been shortlived but whose goodwill and generosity are unforgettable, admired his work and listened to his lessons. Edward Heath was one of these – it was in friendship and confidence that he found a new path for Great Britain. One could draw a line between two types of democratic statesmen, equally respectful of parliamentary liberties but deeply separated by their concept of power: according to whether they though above all that they incarnated it, or whether they simply wanted to exercise it.

In Jean Monnet's eyes they all shared a common characteristic that he called egocentricity, meaning they were obliged to care a lot about their image, from which they drew a part of their strength. 'If you want to play a personal role' he would say, 'you must appear. The business of politics is linked to a certain way of presenting things. The statesman lives in a world of images. For him, to be somebody or to do something are not alternatives as my friend Dwight Morrow said. It's all one.' He was indulgent toward the professional distortion that could explain and even plan on illogical behavior. The subjective factor that was outlawed for himself and his close associates had necessarily to be accepted from these others. And this diagnosis once being acknowledged, the theatrical games of government leaders no longer surprised him. 'Let them say that. You'd say the same thing if you were in their place. What matters is what they're going to do.' On that point he was no longer so tolerant. When the verbal nationalism of a de Gaulle passed into action, he was suddenly no longer an amused spectator. 'I can't stand to hear that without reacting. Let's dictate a reply. We'll see later what will come of it.' That is when he started the counter-powers moving: the press, the Action Committee.

The Action Committee was Jean Monnet's homeopathy: with the political bodies in reserve he acted on the political bodies that were in place. The same men who had been and tomorrow might again be actors on the political stage and who were not subject to the limitations of the executive function, men who were directly responsible for the fate of millions of human beings and therefore dazzled and groping – these men when they came together far from the cameras, in a quiet place, controlled only by their consciences, became different. They were freed of the servitude of partisan action and brought back to a clear view of an essential problem. They could give free rein to their own natures, which were at bottom generous and favorable to positive action. At such moments Jean Monnet converted their egocentric strength into common resolution. He undoubtedly took a great deal of trouble, and was admired for the fact that no difficulty discouraged him, at an age when he had a right to a more restful life. But one should not forget that difficulty was his natural environment and that it reassured him about the consistency of his aims. To tell the truth, he had probably never been so happy as during the twenty years of the Action Committee, that he lived through as a free man, bringing his method to its point of perfection. He had plenty of time to discover the deep springs of parliamentary life and to analyze the common characteristics and the varied forms of European democracy. This latter experience, begun with the Assembly of the European Coal and Steel Community, completely reconciled him with the political world. He already respected the world of the labor unions. Friendship implanted itself through working together.

These meetings of representatives of political parties and workers' organizations looked impressive only on photographs. In fact they finalized, as one says, a lengthy prepared common text that Jean Monnet had traveled around negotiating for weeks with these bustling men, at times and places that suited them. Let us not restrain our admiration of this indefatigable traveler, who at eighty-seven went off alone by train to Bonn or The Hague (his last pleurisy almost took him by surprise in a sleeping car). But let us remember that he did not consider anything that was necessary as a tiresome chore, and particularly not journeys. From the time of Cognac he knew that nobody can represent the firm or the goods better than oneself. He would call the 'client' on the telephone: 'I absolutely must come and see you. Don't move, I'll come to you. Just tell me the day that suits you', and this approach left the other person no escape route. But if he did not hesitate to decide on a trip, if he was impatient to conclude the deal, when the moment came to move everything happened like a mini-drama. To the real difficulties of the journey he added imaginary ones which were, as we have seen, his way of outwitting fate. Until the last minute he did not know which of the plane or train tickets reserved for him he would actually use. He would decide on one out of the many in great commotion, but in fact kept to his old habit of traveling alone. Taxi drivers, porters and hotel doormen were his accredited guardian angels. They recognized through his way of requesting their services, and perhaps also by the good quality of his worn baggage, that he was a personality for their best consideration. His generous tips would confirm this impression.

The day when he was forced to accept that his strength would no longer take him where he ought to go and convince people, he decided to disconnect his network. It was not an institution. The Plan, the Community, the Council of Europe survived their founder but not the Action Committee, which was like a magnet to iron filings as long as the magnetism worked. His decision could have seemed based on pride but it was simply realistic, and everybody accepted it as evident. He tried to explain, without being even himself convinced, that the European Council which concentrated within itself all the power of action, made the pressure mechanism that had caused it to emerge no longer useful. If there is a degree of truth in this excuse, it should be looked for in the lasting influence of the method Jean Monnet taught to a whole generation of European leaders, who had learned to talk to each other beyond the frontiers on problems of common

interest. Is it not true that a majority of heads of state or
government at the Council were members of the Action
Committee and had seen there the patient development, the
knowledge and the mutual understanding that produce a
consensus? But on the contrary, who could deny that the
inventor's departure left the machine soulless, and that for
years the federative principle has been lacking in the construction of Europe?

The first portrait that made the French public aware of
him was entitled 'Jean Monnet, or the Optimist' and the
construction was Voltairian.[2] This Professor Pangloss who
had been seen at the epicenter of the century's great earth-
quakes, who had raised so many ruins, was admired for
finally returning home to cultivate his garden in the French
style. They still did not know him. He was not a providential-
ist. You could count on nothing, nothing was to be taken for
granted. He did not believe in the best of all worlds, but in a
world that was capable of being improved. The truth was he
believed nature was good but that people had trouble finding
their way around its complexity, and they added to it
through their own excesses and their endless taste for
intrigue. He agreed with a statement of Jaurés, which one
should not smile at, 'Everything is always very difficult'. With
this great truth of experience as a starting point there is only
one possible line of action: to work to simplify the problems.
It was, as we all learned, the most harassing kind of work, the
sort that everybody puts off until tomorrow, until one day
things are so inextricably mixed up that the problems have to
be resolved by violence. Through his lucid observation he
was able to see this day coming and to prepare himself for it.
His optimistic imagination did not doubt there would be a
solution. So his active pessimism prepared itself for a painful
effort, encountering a thousand obstacles. He did not accept
the expression 'to make light of difficulties' and in any case in
this field he was suspicious of demobilizing terms. 'I am not
an optimist' he would insist, 'I'm only determined.' In the
same spirit he said 'You have to work a long time to find your
luck.'

One did not always understand him when he used words
from the old magic deposit that he himself used in their most
positive sense. He defined luck as the meeting of a long-time

resolution and circumstances ripe for action. Optimism was the will to succeed, with its corollary of good sense, 'As long as you haven't tried you can't say a thing is impossible.' We have seen that the idea of a bet was not in his line of thinking. 'When you're involved in an undertaking you're not going to make assumptions about the risks of not succeeding.' He barred his door against Cassandras. He followed Antigone on her narrow path. But he did not stumble against obstacles. Then, he used his power of transmutation again. There was nothing magic in it but, like all magic tricks really, it was an unusual way of following the laws of physics: you only push against what resists. Popular common sense had discovered this long before; but Jean Monnet felt reassured because God – in other words someone well informed – had confirmed it to Ibn Saud in the desert.

To make use of obstacles is both a philosophy of action and at the same time, if one so wishes, a practical formula for daily use. For example, if some statesmen are vain egocentrics, then let's make our aims serve their need for prestige. In a wider perspective, since Franco-German rivalry is a threat to peace, let's transform it into a peaceful union. And to begin, let us convert our arsenals of coal and steel into common industrial wealth. It is always a case of Christopher Columbus's egg. This method, which attacks the very object of the difficulty and turns the center of gravity upside down is a masterpiece of dialectic. But the object can be too massive, or inert. So one must neutralize it by surrounding it, dissolve it or marginalize it.

This treatment was applied with a degree of success to European nationalism, which is fading little by little into a new framework. Its virtues have proved to be so rich that we must transcribe the formula as Jean Monnet set it down in his *Memoirs*:

It was at that time, undoubtedly, [1950] and that precise problem [of Germany] that I realized the full possibilities of an approach which had long been familiar to me, and which I had applied empirically in trying to overcome difficulties of all kinds. I had come to see that it was often useless to make a frontal attack on problems, since they have not arisen by themselves, but are the product of circumstances. Only by modifying the circumstances can one disperse the difficulties they create. So, instead of wearing myself out on the hard core of resistance, I had become accustomed to seeking out and trying to change whatever element in it was causing the block. Sometimes it was quite a minor point, and very often a matter of psychology.

No doubt to change contexts has been a common practice of the experimental method from the beginning of time. But to advance from empiricism to working by rules marks great progress. In this way Jean Monnet extended the political scientific work of Claude Bernard – whom he had not read, any more than he knew the *Discourse on Method*, as we have seen – although he applied it in his approach to reality. To attack a difficulty by dividing it into its irreducible elements did not discourage him. He preferred a patient dismantling of what already existed to the great abstract constructs that intellectuals like. Though he would warn his associates against endless analysis, he completely refused to listen to talk of synthesis. 'I've never understood what that word meant' he would cut them short. Once the parts were dismantled he would reassemble them in a new order, in a new basis. But first of all it was essential to make, as Descartes recommended, 'such complete lists and such wide reviews as to be certain that nothing was left out'. For this, his skill and patience were unrivaled. We have seen him putting these qualities to work in situations of such drama that there was neither time nor possibility of changing the circumstances; one could only face up to them. When the problem already weighed heavily and was impossible to get round, such as an ongoing war where the only choice left was to mobilize the maximum of resources, first of all one had to make out an inventory. This was an intellectual exercise that most civilian and military headquarters are incapable of. They have neither the patience nor the courage to face the truth. They prefer to launch the attacking armies until the stocks of men and material are used up. Then the inventory is made by subtraction. Jean Monnet's genius was to wage the war of numbers, to break down the establishment's resistance, to drive the services into their corners and then to compress the masses of data onto a single page. This way showed the true situation, and was eloquent in its simplicity. For those with a sense of responsibility, action flowed naturally from it. The history of the economic battle front where victory was decided between 1916 and 1918 still remains to be written. That of the 1941 Victory Program has not been a military secret for a long time, yet it is still the least-known episode of the war. The 'all out production plan' launched by Jean Monnet is not in the strategy manuals, although it was decisive.

No doubt a new generation of historians will acknowledge the role played by a small number of men, equal to the great commanders though with no military stripes and often with no mandate, who devised and built up the arsenal of the democracies. Which Nazi spy paid attention to these civilians, who constantly pressed officers for figures given with ill grace, that a few young statisticians mulled over day and night? What enemy intelligence service was interested in Jean Monnet, Arthur Purvis or Bob Nathan? Men like Albert Speer were unaware till the last minute that their gigantic plans would be overtaken by an invisible Frenchman, in the shadow of top bureaucrats who themselves lived in the shadow of Roosevelt. Besides, they would not have given ten dollars for the notion that a sheet of graph paper or a balance sheet like a hardware store's showed the gap that must be filled to save the free world. This sheet of paper exists. Jean Monnet brought it out occasionally from a vault, as if it were still a great secret.

This strongbox was almost empty. Its owner detested secrets. He believed there weren't any and did not want to know any outside the circumstances of war. He did not glory in the fact of having played an important role on these occasions, and preferred to remember the plans he was making at the time for the forthcoming peace. Among all the humanitarian and ideological reasons that motivated his effort to speed up the end of the war (Keynes estimated that he had shortened it by a year), his impatience to rebuild, reconcile and unite must be included. It was not enough to want to win the war but it had to be won quickly, completely and through an overwhelming superiority. He was said to have made the following statement, so out of line with his native moderation, 'Better to make ten thousand tanks too many than to be short of just one'. His hatred of war and his impatience for peace were immoderate. Rationality waited to regain its rights.

From these periods of violence and excess in everything he tried to retain cool lessons and useful experience, steering clear of the exaltation that filled and sometimes swelled the chief actors in the drama. On the other hand he dramatized the peacetime clash, to which he applied the same vocabulary and the same methods that had served to mobilize energies and resources in the dark hours of war. 'You'll never hear me talk differently' he would say, 'whatever the circumstances. It's the way I'm made.' He always used the serious and metallic vocabulary of necessity, and active verbs in common use but carefully selected, excluding all negative syntax. When colorful rhetoric went out of fashion his sober style was never outdated. On the contrary, under the firm rule and even monotony of a schoolmaster who mercilessly demanded that drafts be rewritten, it became the style of a generation of disciples. It would merit semantic study.

The Book of Genesis according to Jean Monnet would have gone as follows: 'In the beginning was necessity. Necessity imposed itself on men and things. It left them without choice. It generated urgency, that generated action, etc.' But how much happier and more imaginative Jean Monnet became when it was no longer his job to destroy the wall of brute force that the democracies' negligence had allowed to rise, with the spirit of domination and revenge laying the foundations. His task was to rebuild the world through common effort, by integrating the means through a system of equal rights. No longer face-to-face challenges but solidarity in action, which implied that each man understood his partners and that all points of view were harmonized. This method allows the greatest hopes, but ambitions had to be limited. Jean Monnet did not dream of universal immediate concord. We must speak of his philosophy of space and time.

VI

The space in which Jean Monnet's creative imagination

moved could be outlined on a map of the world: it was the region where parliamentary democracy operated and *habeas corpus* was respected. He did not dream of shutting it in on itself, but rather of increasing its influence by fusing its resources. His aim was for the civilized potential of a continent threatened with decline to be able to continue to develop, in the interest of all peoples. His ideas extended to universalism but he did not think that this was a useful dimension for action. He accepted the concept, though he did not care for it, that Europe had a message to spread, but first it should exist as a united whole. That this unit could make itself heard, or even survive, without close links – as equals – with the United States, he did not believe. He could not see any advantage in questioning the fact. For him North America and Western Europe were products of the same civilization. He did not burden himself with complicated formulas. 'Civilization' he would say, 'is liberty', and that excluded a lot of people. If he would not rest until Great Britain joined the Community it was because Britain had been first to demonstrate the most advanced models of public freedoms. If he involved all his energies to promote an association of equal partners between Europe and the United States, it was because both sides had the same concept of democracy and practiced it in the same way.

Those who suspect him of having given his allegiance to the United States can reread his exhortations to Americans, that were listened to during a favorable moment of history. 'Agree to deal with us as equals concerning our common problems. Together we could establish a balanced relationship with the Soviet Union and help the suffering world.' Kennedy believed him; but it was easy for his successor to reply, 'Who are you?' Europe did not decide to speak with one voice. Soon there was silence, and the Great Powers spoke to each other over our heads. Another generation of Americans came to power, that he knew less well. Kissinger respected him, but not as a partner in his chess game. The opportunity had passed. For lack of a better course, the Germans looked more attentively toward the East, as he had foreseen. The British did not think it to their advantage to make institutions with great resources work, contrary to what he had foreseen. In spite of all this, he did not lapse into pessimism. He would reply to those who were anxious, 'Do you have a different solution?' Nobody was to have one for a long time. He used the strengths he still had to maintain the Community's cohesion, and to give it what he thought was an effective level of authority. Then he wrote his *Memoirs*. But he never looked for a substitute to the European construction he had invented a quarter of a century earlier. This was not for any lack of opportunities: people proposed new East-West or North-South balances, or mechanisms at different speeds. He believed that European necessity would survive these ups and downs.

Without knowing it he was a great geopolitician in the most basic sense. This man of country stock did not doubt that men were modeled by soil and climate. For example, the French were as essentially diverse as the aspects of nature that surrounded them. He saw a source of human richness in this, but also contradictions and loss of strength. Our national French institutions were set up and they should be improved, to correct our tendencies to excessive individualism. He never abandoned this idea, and when he undertook to unite European peoples he met the same problem of diversity on another scale. In fact, if by some miracle the frontiers had been abolished, we should have had to try to govern more than 150 millions of individualists who were conditioned like the French by an infinity of varieties of nature. In 1950 the miracle did not happen and besides, it had not even been dreamed of. On the contrary: 'Europe will not be created in one stroke nor in one overall construction. It will be made through solid achievements that first build up a real interdependence.' Solidarities like these would place the amalgam where it would flow naturally. Less prudent and less realistic (but the circumstances themselves were unreal) was the 1940 proposal for a Franco-British union, 'One flag, one parliament, one people'. That miracle almost happened. The attempt, that only just failed, made the people who saw in it nothing but a desperate expedient, tremble in retrospect. This irritated Jean Monnet. 'It was a very serious proposal. Believe me, in a calamity one is serious. But don't ask me what would have happened. I can't argue in this hypothetical way about what didn't happen.' But he also added, 'Things would have happened that would have changed people's minds, changed the way the war went – and would have changed Britain's and Europe's future.'

Being a moderate federalist, unlike some of his associates, he did not dream of a European state, or a new European man. Our old continent was rich in its diversity, and it was this that perhaps distinguished it most clearly from the others. What was the point of calling for a European identity that risked being only the nationalism one wanted to destroy, on a different scale? So he became more and more hesitant on the Community's institutional objective. He did not make any declaration on either its final form or the length of time involved. These two notions left him rather ill at ease. 'There is no end to what we are doing' he would say, 'except death.' On the other hand he believed in human limits, which is not the same thing. He also distinguished between a fixed expiry date, which exhausted effort, and the mobile calendar that indicated the stages.

Nuances like these were in direct contrast to the subtlety of the lawyers which he, with his empiricism, could not do without for a single moment. But he kept them on the sidelines. He knew you cannot put things in order if you do not first of all put order into ideas and words. 'To envisage the final form of the European Community today, when we have wanted it to be a kind of process of change is a contradiction in terms. Anticipating the result blocks the spirit of invention. It's as we gradually climb that we'll get to see the new horizons.' He used images of the mountains, that he knew well, because he had no words to describe this future situation that reveals itself in stages, nor the progress created through going forward. One day he thought he had found a better comparison in the book of Thor Heyerdahl. This was about the raft that ventured onto the Pacific Ocean and could not turn back. At the same time a whole dialectic was being worked out around the 'point of non-return', and is still wrongly used in connection with Europe. But he was always brought back to the old concept of necessary choices and of priorities to be respected, because that was the meeting point of scarcity and urgency – situations where this crisis expert gave the best of himself.

Making choices one after another is not easy, but under pressure everybody has to make up their mind to act. It is quite different to foresee shortages, put needs in order of priority, share our resources, combine forces, space out problems in time; and all of this through perfectly democratic methods. You have to apply an advanced technique, that requires mastery of continuance. All this was called the Plan, and later it was seen as a burning need. Jean Monnet preferred to say that it was a living reality. He programmed its growth and its succeeding stages according to a scheme that he considered obvious, so long as an even more evident need had not appeared. Adaptability was also part of the program, so much so that at any moment he could say, 'We've gone wrong' or 'We've underestimated the difficulty'. Without calling the objective into question, he was not a prisoner of his plan nor of his pride. He spoke of Europe too as a living reality, but it belonged to another chapter of biology, fecondation. 'We've introduced a germ of change', he would say. 'Nothing will stop its development.' Since then the expression 'to conduct change' has been invented. That is exactly the job he assigned to the institutions of the Community and that they are carrying out more or less well. The living reality conceived on 9 May 1950 as the embryo of an organized being has resisted all attempts at abortion. It has grown, both huge and anemic at the same time, without losing the essential characteristics of the political body it should be and will be. But has enough notice been taken of the fact that its author left it only a few years after its conception?

At the end of his life he said, 'You know, I've always been a man for beginnings. When things are launched they inevitably become administrative. And I'm not gifted for management. I get bored'. He fought as long as he could against proliferation. He had even hoped that Europe would function with small numbers of personnel, who would call on the services of independent experts for consultation whenever necessary. He was as anxious to surround himself with competent people as to get rid of them when they had served their purpose. To sense the moment when men's work is going to be counterproductive is the privilege of the man who knows how to decide. In Luxembourg he was persuaded that it was easier to keep people on hand. The result was that you then had the officials without getting rid of the experts.

He found himself at the head of a heavy administrative machine whose exponential growth annoyed him. He left it for other reasons and not at the hour of his own choice. But for some time already he had been dreaming of a new beginning, with a team he would have a grip on. It was at 83 Avenue Foch in Paris that he achieved his masterpiece, the light and powerful apparatus of the Action Committee.

Almost seventy years of age, he abdicated a genuine, concrete and prestigious authority to go and operate, almost alone, the immaterial force of an idea. He willingly quitted a comfortable world to create a difficult enterprise. This enterprise has been excellently described,[3] but it still escapes the best observers because it does not enter the usual categories of politics, although it is nothing more than a way of activating existing political mechanisms. The men of the Action Committee had no other legitimization than what they held through democratic election in their country; and their power was what their party or labor union exercised on the life of the nation, modified by the coefficient of their personal influence within these formations. Theoretically the Committee was only a simple addition of forces, and further off there were also the wishes that the Committee expressed when they were taken up by the parliaments and the governments of the countries. Then was it not a pressure group among others? Jean Monnet did not understand the question. 'I'm talking to you about an action committee, that's pretty clear isn't it? Why do you always want to look further than what you've got in front of you? We come to agreement on resolutions – the word was not used by chance – that parties and organizations in power or in opposition pledge themselves to propose and defend in their own country.'

In effect, these men met in broad daylight in the normal framework of their political office. None the less the phenomenon was so unusual that it did not have time to become fixed into general habit, and it has not been copied. With three associates and two secretaries Jean Monnet stirred more political reality and animated more parliamentary life in Europe than an institution elected by universal suffrage has, that now mobilizes three thousand people. Were the times more favorable? Perhaps, although it has never been natural in any country for a majority and an opposition to proclaim their agreement on a project, and to put it through together. This however was seen to happen, and no political analyst has understood yet – but it is a job for a psychologist – how an old man managed alone to span the gap between an Italian socialist and a British conservative, a Dutch antirevolutionary and a German social democrat – and all these politicians on one side, from all the labor unionists on the other. The secret is simple: he brought them together on affairs that united them. But that explains nothing. Today an evident interest still unites these men, and it is still the same – they do not deny it either, in their general speeches. But the idea of forming a single committee, agreeing on a single line of action and above all pledging themselves to support it back home seems utopian to them. Also, nobody has come to suggest this to them again.

Communists were not members of the Action Committee. They had not been invited, though they had been in the Plan. Their attitude toward the European Community was extremely negative. Jean Monnet did not try to convince them. 'They are the most extreme conservatives' he said. 'Their rigidity of thought puts them outside the currents of progress. Discussion with them gets nowhere because they want to make you move without moving themselves. But when they find they're completely isolated . . .'. He did not bother to try to talk to the deaf nor to convert unbelievers. People like this he left to some future date, and got back to the persuasive force of present realities. He was less concerned with changing men's minds than with changing events, and in accordance with this method he only needed a small number of the latter to have an effect on a great number of people. To create situations that required a certain line of action was more economical and more dependable than to obtain undependable memberships. It was the same for governments as for the parties and for individuals. Jean Monnet did not think it was possible to convince the USSR favorably to see Europe being created; and the idea of meeting its leaders to try to alter their point of view – an art he generally excelled in – did not even cross his mind. 'They'll take account of us when we exist' he used to say. 'But to wait until their attitude to us develops, and to ask ourselves what they think about what we might do is the best way of making no progress.'

His philosophy on the size of the European Community is summed up in the following sentence. 'The Community is a collection of rules freely agreed to. Those who can't or won't observe these rules exclude themselves.' This principle left the door open which Denmark and Greece, restored to democracy, entered and that Portugal and Spain would enter. He saw no risk there of denaturing or unbalancing, but only of technical difficulties for which the Community would find solutions within its own mechanisms for adaptation. On the other hand he feared everything that weakened the internal coherence of the institutional system: all exceptions or privileged treatment. There could not be two levels of participation. 'The British will always ask for special positions, but one mustn't agree to discuss with them on such bases.' He thought it was in the interests of the candidates themselves not to weaken the Community by unequal rules. No doubt he sometimes regretted not having dared to begin by a real political pact between France and Germany. But since the only possible way at that time, and in any case the way that was chosen, was that of an economic Community with members equal in rights and duties, one had to continue on the same lines.

He did not have a great opinion of projects to reform the institutional mechanism, or of variable speeds or geometries, because they did not attack the cause of the problem, which was the lack of spirit of decision among the leaders. The system itself lacked nothing, as it included all the instruments of decision-making, if people wanted to use them. Jean Monnet discouraged those who talked of opening up a revision of the Treaties in order to strengthen them. 'Don't count on governments giving a hand to improve something which itself is a continual process of change. They are there to administer existing things, with administrations that want to keep what gives them their power. It's normal. If it were different there would be permanent revolution, which people would not tolerate. Change should come from outside the installed powers, when it is time.' External pressure, the choice of the time, were his affair.

The man for urgent moves was also throughout his life, as

we have seen, a man with endless patience. This capacity to move his thoughts according to two contrasted rhythms was essential to his equilibrium. Through it he avoided the psychological jolts that would have made the splendid continuity of his work impossible. If setbacks did not stop him it was because he saw them as chance mishaps that merely slowed down an ineluctable progress. His periods of discouragement were short – just long enough to change speed – and his controlled slowdowns took observers by surprise. They thought the reason was empiricism, or excessive optimism. While his entourage was still feeling the shock and starting lawsuits, he had already gone back to his natural pace of a peasant striding along a row of vines. 'We're in too much of a hurry' he would say. 'You don't change people's attitudes so quickly. It gives us a good lesson.' 'So what should we do now?' he would be asked. He would give you the astonished scolding look he kept for answering pointless questions. 'Why, keep going, obviously. What else do you want to do?'

If this was his reply during the last years of his life, it was not only because inventiveness and the strength to embark on new enterprises left him little by little. It was generally acknowledged that there was nothing else to do but to preserve one's gains while facing a crisis whose extent it was not yet possible to measure. Early on, from the first symptoms of disturbance in 1973 he had had a foreboding the torment would be long. 'We're living in a system that's grown too complex, with mechanisms that are too precise' he said in rare moments of discouragement. 'Don't fool yourselves; it may jam somewhere.' He was reminded of 1929 although he did not see a parallel between the two crises, the first being due to an identifiable accident that would be easy to repair today. But he pointed out too that progress in the instruments of control did not follow the increased complexity of structures any better now than formerly. He doubted the capacity of individuals to master a society that was becoming unforeseeably differentiated; and he saw the only salvation in establishing new rules administered by modern institutions. He would certainly have latched onto this objective if his years, which had been given him generously, had not at last weighed on him.

He saw age coming and guarded against it. If his entry into his career was a success, his leavetaking could serve as a model to all good men. He chose the moment to retire in the same way that he had decided everything, after long reflection and in agreement with the people close to him. One might have said he had exactly calculated the length of time and the strength that he still had left to complete his *Memoirs* and to see to their publication. He had no illusions about the continuation of his influence in the political world from which he distanced himself. 'Don't tell me that people will come to ask my opinion,' he said. 'I know very well it's not true. And it's quite natural. One man alone can't do anything. I have never been alone, contrary to what people think. I've always worked within a group, an outfit, an institution.' Essentially he was right. But after all, they came to see him; he was awarded great distinctions. He was able to know his grandchildren and his great-nephews better. Silvia surrounded him with immense devotion. He saw his *Memoirs* appear and heard how they were received. And knew he had said the essential about what he had done and what others would have to complete.

VII

On 20 March 1979 he was laid to rest in the little cemetery of Bazoches. There was a gray sky and the winter, so hostile to his chest, was endless. A few days earlier, on the morning he died, a sudden snowfall had covered the damp house he no longer wanted to leave, not even to live longer in Arizona or Egypt, where earlier he used to go to look after his health. A ray of sunshine broke through and lit up the tomb where they buried him. He had chosen the spot, at first in the shadow of the church in a corner traditionally reserved for the deprived. But he decided for the light. Shall we ever say often enough that he was the enemy of all obscurity? In the tomb next to his, Pierre Viansson-Ponté lies. Chance made them meet there, as they met on the wooded paths of Bazoches and in the official palaces of Paris. They had great esteem for each other, but their proximity in this small village never led them to greater intimacy than provincial wisdom prescribes.

On 26 August 1982 Silvia went to join him, worn out by giving him the extra strength he needed to leave his life and to remain in our view with the nobility he always had. She put everything in order, tried to keep the house, but persisted less against the difficulties because her spirituality did not attach itself to an earthly place. 'For me, Jean isn't there' she said, looking without any apparent emotion at his tomb. When she was sure the memory was maintained as he would have wished by the Lausanne foundation, she left Houjarray for the Roman climate of her childhood, where her brother Alexander lived.

A European institute with good intentions bought the house where the Community was invented and then endlessly reanimated. But except for a miracle, a bureaucracy will not be able and will not want to do anything with a lovely thatched-roof farm.

For his part, Jean Monnet believed in the permanence of terrestrial things and cared about their maintenance. He had thought Houjarray could be used one day as a reception center for young people. He was concerned to know where he might be at that time. For him his parents were indeed at Cherves-de-Cognac and he abandoned the idea of joining them there fairly late. As long as he could he went regularly to the little cemetery in Charente. He, who did not like either the idea or the trappings of death, went back quite naturally to visit the grave where he had taken his mother after he had given her all the happiness she could receive. He said to the guardian, 'Close the gate after me'. And stayed for hours in the paths of that poor garden, exorcised as it was in his eyes from all the malfeasance he would have suspected elsewhere. The link had never been broken between two beings who were secretly very close in their natures. Very close also in age, we should not forget: only nineteen years separated him from his mother. When he was sixteen a Bordeaux physician had taken them for brother and sister. She did not try to keep him near her, but he wrote to her every day. Later she welcomed Silvia as another daughter, with the reserve and discretion natural to her but also, without any doubt, with a nobility of heart capable of evoking deep attachment.

One should not feel compelled to decipher people's nature, nor even attempt to get through their protective envelope. Only their own kind can receive the signs that they allow to filter out. There is nothing left of Jean Monnet's abundant letter-writing to his family, and it is better this way. Let us just remember that this man who used other people's pens so often and who left no written draft of a speech or of a single article, is the same man who wrote a great deal, describing in the evening his journeys, his activities, his hopes and fears, in letters posted from Cairo, China, or entrusted to discreet messengers from Washington or London. All the letters were burned at Cognac at the time when the Germans established their headquarters in the family house. Precious archives went up in smoke at the same time, notably papers handwritten by Roosevelt. The rest, his correspondence with Silvia, she destroyed later. 'It's of no interest to anyone but us.' She was surely right because nobody more than she respected the image of Jean Monnet, and none has served it better.

When his mother died he did not feel the despair his family had feared. She had passed away gently when her hour came. Twenty years earlier, although he was less close to him, his father's death shook him to his limits, to a degree that those who knew his violence better than his sensitiveness had trouble imagining. This phenomenon is not rare among mature and experienced men. The death of the father, even if he were already distant, resounds like a cataclysm that one is never well prepared for. Of his paternal grandfather only a few anecdotes survive. This eccentric old man, who died aged 100, used to have the village dancing to the sound of his violin but left no great trace on his descendants. At least in memory, the maternal line was dominant. The Demelle family still seem living people, like characters out of legends, embedded with dignity into their modest dwelling on the Rue de Lusignan. They used to go to draw water from the well at the boundary of their district. Their daughter's impressive residence did not interest them. The family came to see the Demelles at their home. As long as they lived, Jean Monnet's first visit, whether he was back from London or Geneva with his rising prestige, was to see them. He never forgot their example, and the old man with his little Second

Empire beard, his round hat and workman's cloak, sitting upright in front of the fireplace, went on being a point of reference for Jean Monnet until he himself, in his old age, returned to a respected rustic lifestyle.

We have still a lot to learn about Jean Monnet, but let us not wait until unpublished documents appear to throw new light on his personality. Let us attempt instead to deepen the knowledge we have within ourselves, and through the witness of people who through his influence came to share his convictions. In this way we see him in dozens of books of memoirs, and we must turn to this source. But it is not unlimited, because these memorialists are busy looking at themselves and have only kept in mind the most spectacular, but also the most ritual, aspects of his behavior. It is certainly not without importance that the descriptions, even as far as the adjectives, agree. But where is the legendary aspect of the reconstituted image, in these late portraits? For want of a picture taken at the time how are we to see the young man arriving in Geneva, already provided with gifts that were to change the history of Europe before he even had that ambition? Was he merely restlessly active by nature? Louise Weiss remembers him: 'Sparks of genius lit lights in the hazel eyes of the diminutive Jean Monnet when, lively, mysterious and charming, he wove the web of influences that right from the start guaranteed a remarkable power to the League of Nations'.[4] The description would be even more valuable if it had not been written fifty years later. There were no contemporary ones.

So we resign ourselves to not knowing the man in his prime, ceaselessly expending his energies on refloating currencies, settling bankruptcies, making and losing money. Just as we must stop imagining the young dandy in a silk cloak caught sight of in London, the visitor to Hudson Bay wrapped in a fur coat, the bachelor keeping open house in his private mansion on Paris's Rue de Condé, the frequent visitor to the Chiang Kai-Sheks at their house on the Yangtze River. Only a few photographs exist, that show him sure of himself, his physique expressing his confidence. Everything was still potential. The times of greatness were not ripe. It was difficult to imagine them, because they could only be times of misfortune. Had Jean Monnet clearly seen that the

Versailles treaty, the Geneva setback and the rise of Nazism would mean a return to war? It is a fact that he kept his mind open to international action. His network of friends showed him not to be a man dedicated to his private affairs for a long time ahead. He was more occupied with his own affairs while he waited to be needed again to serve the general interest. When he said 'There are not small and great affairs, there are the affairs one is attending to' he was formulating a piece of advice that is valuable for every instant of life, but not for a life plan. Let us not play on words: he had one great plan, always to avoid mediocrity. By avoiding it, you can go very far.

When you quoted to him Montaigne's disturbing statement, 'Wherever your life finishes, the whole of it is there' he nodded his head. 'Perhaps, but I know that if I had not lived well beyond sixty' (knocking on the wood of his armchair while he said this) 'I'd have missed the essential'. There are many who witnessed this moment when he seized the essential, and detailed accounts of it are not scarce. As he possessed the art of making everything natural, we mixed his words and actions with the reality of his whole being and accepted the idea he was totally extrovert. He challenged introspection and depth psychology, so we thought he had matured and ripened his spirit for a long time. Nobody ever came to tell us the contrary. So they ordered a bronze sculpture of his head. Should we be astonished that it did not look like him? His portrait should be entirely redone. Unfortunately few artists approached him, and there are very few lifelong friends who have served him. He did not seek out the company of famous artists or writers he could easily have met. It was quite by chance that Saint Exupery met him in Washington – but this magician mostly fascinated Silvia and her women friends. Later he might have been seen walking in the Bois de Boulogne with Charles Lindbergh – but was this not chiefly because he was fond of his marvelous wife Anne, the novelist, daughter of Dwight Morrow? Only once did he follow up a pure caprice. He had just read in the paper that Arthur Miller was in Paris. 'Suppose we invite him to lunch?' he said to Silvia. 'But we've never met him.' 'I'd like to get to know him; call him on the telephone.' 'He'll think it's odd.' 'Why? Try, and we'll see.' The next day the writer was at their table. But Jean Monnet practiced this kind of *acte gratuit* very rarely. Silvia had to deprive herself of seeing a good number of artists who would have enriched her sensibility. Her compensations were rare and, among the many guests whose cool intelligence had to be endured, she never forgot Robert Oppenheimer's face, shining with the power of his spirituality. She made no mistakes on the quality of the spirit, and in this field she could have no complaints. Even in the austere circle where she had allowed herself by her own consent to be enclosed, to give her husband her moral support, she knew what beneficent genius was, for she had met Ludwig Rajchman, the little Polish doctor who quietly approached the powerful in this world, and then dedicated himself to abandoned children by creating UNICEF. They had no better friend, except perhaps John McCloy, Felix Frankfurter, Etienne Hirsch, Walter Hallstein and a very few others whose moral greatness sustained their strength of mind. Of moral greatness and strength of mind, do Jean Monnet's work and his *Memoirs* tell us enough? Must we consider unimportant what has not been recorded, either through modesty or lack of attention, and show him in a more human light? The impressions he took in and the traces he left on the long road of his life, from Cognac to Houjarray, passing through five continents? We have collected a few, before they are all effaced. A great many are still buried in men's memories. And this essay has no other aim than to incite those who have them to bring in their turn their own testimony forward.

NOTES

1. Richard Cobden was a nineteenth-century British writer advocating free trade.
2. *Réalités*, Paris, March 1946.
3. Fontaine Pascal, *Le Comité d'Action pour les Etats-Unis d'Europe de Jean Monnet* (Lausanne: Centre de recherches européennes, 1974).
4. *Combats pour l'Europe* (Paris: Payot, 1968).

The quotations on pp. 41, 49–50 and 54 are from Monnet's *Memoirs* (Paris, 1976).

2 An Unsung Hero of World War II

Robert R. Nathan

The victory over the forces of Hitler in World War II might have been delayed many months, with a great many more casualties, but for the brilliant talents and adamant determination of Jean Monnet.

The name of this remarkable Frenchman seldom appeared in the press or on the radio during the defense build-up prior to Pearl Harbor and the all-out mobilization in the challenging months in early 1942 just after the United States entered the war. Yet until Jean Monnet provided the leadership during the preceding year for setting much higher goals for American armament production, the prospects were dismal for the successful defense of Great Britain and Russia.

The outlook for the allied nations was discouraging when Japan attacked Pearl Harbor. The production of war material in the United States was accelerating but the level of output was quite limited and the production goals still modest. Monnet's talent and drive helped change all of this. The story of his role in relentless pursuit of higher military goals as a means of achieving large and growing increases in military production is historically significant. In Europe, the British and the Russians were on the defensive everywhere and in the Pacific the Japanese were extending their control wherever the Western powers had military bases or wherever access to the materials of war was critical.

Monnet was a man who worked quietly, effectively and close to those who had the power to make decisions and to achieve results. His effectiveness exemplifies the kind of leadership desperately needed today in solving some of the most urgent international and domestic problems.

Monnet was in England in May 1940 when France was overrun by the powerful Nazi forces. He was reputedly the man who proposed to Churchill that common citizenship be

67

offered by Great Britain to the French people to preserve their spirit of independence and will to resist the Germans. Whether that proposal would have been effective if offered somewhat earlier is speculative, but it was a dramatic and desperate move on the part of Churchill to encourage those in France who strongly opposed surrender and who wanted to continue the fight.

Later in 1940, after France's fall, President Roosevelt promised that, if elected, he would not send American troops abroad. That commitment was expressed even before the campaign in the late 1930s. There is no reason to believe Roosevelt was not sincere in promising to avoid direct American involvement. But, as the fate of friendly nations in Europe grew dismal, Roosevelt increasingly recognized that it was in America's interest to provide considerable arms to the surviving countries of Europe. In this effort, he faced strong opposition at home.

After the fall of France, Churchill sent Monnet to the United States as a high-level member of the British Ministry of Supply to seek prompt and massive increases in the flow of American weapons of war so that Britain could survive and turn the tide against Germany. It was late in 1940 when Monnet arrived in Washington. Not long after, I had the great good fortune of meeting him, although just where and when we met is not recorded.

He had heard of my work as Associate Director of the Bureau of Research and Statistics of the Defense Advisory Commission with special focus on military requirements. My earliest discussions with Monnet revealed his rigid concentration on one principle: American armament production was the most critical requirement for winning for war. In our frequent meetings he never suggested that active American military *participation* was essential for victory; but he repeatedly said that if the Americans could only supply the arms needed by the British, and later, the Russians, Germany could be defeated. He never wavered from this argument and its corollary that US arms production must be rapidly and massively increased.

EARLY PROBLEMS IN THE US DEFENSE MOBILIZATION

The National Defense Advisory Commission came into being in June, 1940. Its purpose was to strengthen America's ability to defend the country from aggressors. But it had no clearly articulated objectives, no strategic goals nor any policy guidelines. It had no clear operating responsibilities within government. It was, as its title said, only an advisory group. Yet it was somehow to plan and program for defense – whatever that meant.

The commission also had no quantitative objectives in terms of numbers of planes, guns, tanks or ships needed for that defense. Its organizational structure was a monstrosity and lacking clear decision-making authority. Finally, this group had as co-chairman William Knudson, an outstanding industrialist and President of General Motors, and Sidney Hillman, President of the Textile Workers Union. It was a strange combination. The rest of its members were businessmen and New Dealers. The commission started life with ridicule from conservatives, America Firsters and advocates of 'peace at any price'.

I was approached to join this organization by Leon Henderson, a member of the Commission with whom I had developed a close relationship over many years. He asked me to leave my job as Chief of the National Income Division of the Department of Commerce and join the commission staff as Associate Director of its Bureau of Research and Statistics, headed by Stacy May. Because my experience in national income studies was useful here and because I was distressed at developments in Europe, I agreed.

One of my first tasks was to bring together all relevant information on military requirements. Another was to analyze our productive capacity to determine where bottlenecks could be anticipated, assuming the economy became increasingly mobilized for defense. This work brought me together with Jean Monnet not long after his arrival in this country.

The task of projecting shortages of resources in a full-employment economy proved more feasible and fruitful in 1940–41 than trying to determine military requirements.

Based on the work done on national income at the Commerce Department from 1933 to 1940, and on rough assumptions of shifts in demand resulting from military needs displacing civilian ones, we promptly concluded that we needed tremendous increases in our productive capacity for aluminum for aircraft and copper for ammunition. We also foresaw a substantial expansion needed in the machine tool industry in an all-out defense mobilization.

Perhaps most distressing for the business community was our conclusion that mobilization would also require considerably more capacity for steel production. This industry, at the depths of the Great Depression in 1932–3, was operating at about 15 to 20 per cent of capacity. Even at the start of 1940 it was functioning at only about two-thirds of its capacity. When we concluded that at least 10 million more tons of steel capacity was needed for full mobilization, the industry adamantly opposed the plan, insisting that the civilian uses of steel could be cut back to allow expansion of the military requirements. But our analysis showed that even with severely curtailed civilian use, there would be a substantial shortage. President Roosevelt supported our view that more steel would be needed and even threatened that the government would build that capacity if industry refused. Finally, with many incentives to make expansion attractive to the steel industry, capacity began to expand before Pearl Harbor. Fortunately, our steel capacity in 1942 was already one-eighth higher than it had been 18 months earlier.

This analysis of requirements of essential materials under the 'full-employed economy' concept led to investments in new facilities, especially for expanding aluminum and copper capacity, and increased stockpiles of copper and other strategic materials needed from abroad such as rubber, nickel and steel alloys. Attractive incentives also encouraged large expansions in other industries like machine tools. So, even without data on large-scale military needs, the expansion of supplies of defense-related materials began in late 1940 and continued throughout 1941. This saved much time when it became essential to use scarce materials only for armament and essential civilian production rather than for the expansion of productive capacity of basic industries.

One of the important early decisions was to enact the

Lend-Lease legislation to provide our allies with war supplies, using the concept of loans or leases. It was a brilliant stroke because it helped to stimulate some increased military production for friendly nations and led to the initial conversion of some facilities from civilian to military outposts. Monnet's memoirs include the following interesting comments on Lend-Lease:

> The constraints of the Cash and Carry Law, whereby the British could take away only what they could carry in their own ships and pay for with their own cash, had to be bypassed by some device which only the President could initiate and impose. It was his responsibility: we knew that he was aware of it and was looking at a number of possible solutions. His indecision alarmed Churchill, who on December 8, 1940 decided to send him an impassioned letter ... Churchill appealed to the common destiny of two countries facing a common danger. Britain would bear the brunt of the human effort, he said, if America could supply the arms and aircraft and protect the convoys. 'You may be sure that we shall prove ourselves ready to suffer and sacrifice to the utmost for the cause, and that we glory in being its champions. The rest we leave with confidence to you and to your people, being sure that ways and means will be found which future generations on both sides of the Atlantic will approve and admire.' [Winston Churchill, *The Second World War* (London, 1948), vol. II, p. 501.]
>
> Roosevelt was deeply impressed ... The question was not so much technical as one of psychological presentation: how to make acceptable to Congress and to American public opinion his firm decision to give British all possible aid without asking anything in return? The solution he came to was Lend-Lease. Like the Marshall Plan eight years later, it was a simple idea, such as can only result from exceptional strength and exceptional generosity in a man and a people. In addition, Roosevelt had a genius for expressing his ideas.
>
> It enabled him, as soon as he was back in Washington, to persuade America to make a gift by presenting it as the hiring-out of goods that were never in fact to be returned.[1]

Monnet later went on to give both a profound and a very

personal account of the importance of these statements of
the American President:

> The alliance of the two great democracies was now
> cemented, and there was nothing to prevent the better
> endowed of them from using all its resources to strengthen
> its more exposed partner.
> 'The United States,' I said one evening to a group of
> friends, 'must become a great arsenal, the arsenal of
> democracy.'
> Felix Frankfurter interrupted, 'Very good,' he said; 'but
> promise me not to use that phrase again.'
> 'Why not?' I asked in astonishment.
> 'Because I think I can soon find a very good use for it,'
> he replied.
> A few days later, we listened together to Roosevelt's
> famous radio 'Fireside Chat' of December 29 [1940]: 'A
> nation can have peace with the Nazis only at the price of
> total surrender ... Such a dictated peace would be no
> peace at all. It would be only another armistice, leading to
> the most gigantic armament race and the most devastating
> trade wars in history ... We cannot escape danger, or the
> fear of danger, by crawling into bed and pulling the covers
> over our heads ... We must produce arms and ships with
> every energy and resource we can command ... We must
> be the great arsenal of democracy.' [Robert E. Sherwood,
> *Roosevelt and Hopkins* (New York, 1950), pp. 224–6; Ed-
> ward R. Stettinius, Jr., *Lend-Lease* (London, 1944), p. 69.]
> After our conversation Frankfurter had gone to the
> White House to slip that phrase into the speech, which
> Hopkins was drafting for the President ...
> The first great obstacle was gone: the verbal problem
> had been solved. It took three months of legal and political
> battles to get from words to deeds. But when words were
> the public's expression of a President's determination, they
> amounted to an international pledge, and they brought
> action in their train. Roosevelt used the magic of words
> with great skill.[2]

Armaments provided under Lend-Lease in 1940 and 1941
were important to Great Britain but still without a decisive
impact for its security, although they had an important

psychological impact there. In the United States, however, the quantities involved under Lend-Lease were far below levels needed to expand greatly our capacity to produce arms or to have a significant constraint on our consumption. Only after Pearl Harbor did appropriations and procurement levels result in an avalanche of planes, tanks, guns and ships. But it was the advance planning in 1941, to which Jean Monnet contributed so much, that effected the rapid and enormous transition from modest defense production to a phenomenal war output.

During the second half of 1940 and the first half of 1941, the major problem for mobilization planning was the absence of data on military requirements. The Army and Navy Munitions Board had been in existence for some time and it was charged with the responsibility for military planning, but no major strategy decision had been made as to what to plan for. When the leaders of the Munitions Board or the supply units within the different military services were asked what their requirements were, they responded 'Requirements for what purposes?' They questioned whether the defense mobilization was related to a ground war or an air war or a sea war and what magnitudes were to be involved, namely, whether plans were needed for an army of one million men, two million men or ten million men. Obviously, these were questions that the Defense Advisory Commission and other civilians were in no position to answer. Nor was there any basis for the military or civilian heads of the military departments to select one or several of these alternative goals.

Calculating requirements under a variety of assumptions was possible, but the political climate did not stimulate such an undertaking. It became extremely frustrating. Appropriations requested by the Department of Defense continued to be modest throughout 1940 and 1941. The magnitudes requested under the Lend-Lease Program were not enough to lead to a meaningful degree of preparedness for a major mobilization. Changing the name of the Defense Advisory Commission to the Supplies Priority and Allocations Board (SPAB), chaired by Vice President Henry Wallace, and then to the Office of Production Management under the leadership of Donald Nelson had little impact. Without much larger military requirements and appropriations, our preparedness for defense or war proceeded at a slow and moderate pace.

THE MONNET CONTRIBUTION

Jean Monnet said again and again that he had one overriding conviction: American military production was crucial to defeat Hitler and Mussolini. He struggled to pursue higher requirements. In retrospect, his single-minded focus may not sound like a great innovation, but it truly attacked the very heart of the problem of mobilizing America's economic power. Monnet stated repeatedly that his focus was not on how the United States might participate militarily but on the very challenge of how to get the British the massive quantities of airplanes, guns, tanks, and ammunition that the United States could produce. Yet the United States did not yet have the quantities of armaments needed to stop Hitler's advances. Such quantities could not come forth without far higher goals, multiplied appropriations, unprecedented levels of contracts with American industries, conversion of plants from peacetime to wartime production and lower levels of civilian consumption. The United States seemed to by trying to aid Britain without really over-exerting itself.

Great Britain was being battered from the air and its supply lines were under assault by German ships and submarines. It suffered from bombing damages to its production facilities. The outlook was dismal and the all-powerful United States was deeply concerned but only limitedly involved. Monnet saw the problem clearly. He struggled for a solution in all of his waking hours – and probably also in his dreams.

I saw Monnet very often in the early months and the summer of 1941. We frequently discussed the problem and a variety of alternative tactics for getting military requirements greatly increased and for accelerating the mobilization efforts of American industry. Convincing the Army, Navy, Air Corps and the Merchant Marine to ask Congress for huge appropriations was most difficult. They had no basis to justify much larger appropriations and would have encountered tough questioning and hostility.

Politically, it was also difficult for President Roosevelt in 1941 to call for all-out mobilization appropriations because of his campaign commitments a few months earlier to keep the United States from an active role in the war. Nor was it feasible for him to ask for huge increases in funding for Lend-Lease alone. The vociferous America First group opposed our getting involved to any degree, even with Lend-Lease. They contended that larger Lend-Lease supplies would inevitably lead to total United States involvement.

Deep concern about the fate of the democracies in Europe was prevalent among the intellectuals and among many other groups, but there was very limited popular support for the United States to accept increasing responsibility for supplying arms to Britain and Russia through a massive defense mobilization. Roosevelt had clearly expressed his determination to supply some of Britain's armaments – but that alone did not produce the higher levels of production. A vital link was somehow still missing.

Monnet viewed these problems with vast American experience. He had been active in US banking affairs since the 1920s. He had also worked with American military officials in 1938–9 when he negotiated aircraft contracts for the French government. In his early months in the United States in late 1940, Monnet expanded this US governmental network by meeting top officials in the War Department and even in the White House. He had already met President Roosevelt in 1938, and he renewed this acquaintance with a brief meeting upon his arrival in 1940. It was Monnet's remarkable capacity to influence important decision-makers, whether old or new associates, that led to his highly successful contribution to America's mobilization. He had an uncanny ability to determine who would be most receptive to his efforts and thus most useful in getting the results he foresaw as vital to the survival of the Allies. For example, Monnet developed a close and continuing relationship with Jack McCloy, Assistant Secretary of War and, earlier, an outstanding attorney in New York, who had been recruited to help with mobilization. McCloy became part of Monnet's growing network in the relevant agencies of Washington.

Monnet was an impatient man because he knew better

than most the grave jeopardy of Great Britain. He would not waste precious time with small talk or socializing. He was anxious to meet and talk with anyone who could help. He had an unusual ability to spot effective operators and would quickly discard those who were not in a position to help. He was persistent when he sensed an opportunity to recruit an effective supporter. But he had no time or energy for ineffectual or phony persons.

I particularly remember one dinner at his home on Foxhall Road on the edge of downtown Washington when he had eight or ten high government officials as guests. Leon Henderson was there. There was plenty to drink before we ate, good wines with dinner and Monnet's family brand of cognac as we sat afterwards in the living room. I recall Monnet commenting that good food and good discussion did not go together. The dinner broke up reasonably early; there had not been much serious discussion of policies or key issues of the day. Yet Monnet was at work. He watched everyone intensely and listened carefully to what each said and to how they responded to each other. Watching him was fascinating. His expressive eyes often revealed his inner thoughts. The conversation had wandered from the serious to the humorous and over many subjects. He had assembled a diverse group apparently without a specific plan or goal. Yet Monnet did have a goal, for he was trying to judge each person on his expressed views and on his interplay with the others. It was a fascinating mark of his single-mindedness to use such an innocent occasion for his own unique purpose. I saw Monnet more frequently during the late spring of 1941. Occasionally, he came to my office. Often I would go to his house. I never visited him at the Willard Hotel; and I am not even sure I was aware then that he had an office there with the British Supply Council.

Monnet was in his early 50s and was in excellent condition. He took long, vigorous walks in the morning to keep himself trim and energetic. Sometimes he would ask me to come to his house early in the morning and we would walk together in Rock Creek Park before breakfast. He would occasionally say – and emphasize with his gleeful eye and charming smile – that Rock Creek was his personal park because his backyard led directly into the parkland.

Actually there were only intermittent discussions during those walks. He did not like to walk slowly or to talk continuously. Rather, when he had an interesting idea he would stop or slow down, state his view and await a response. Then there would be little or no further conversation except when a new idea appeared and would, again, be briefly discussed. When we returned from walks or sometimes when I came just for breakfast he would be unavailable until after he got his massage from one of his house staff.

At the breakfast table he returned again and again to the problem of how to get the military establishment to produce very large requirements for production. I too had been frustrated by this problem but now I began to realize all that Monnet was doing to overcome it.

Monnet often told me about the individuals backing him in London, especially Tommy Brand.[3] Keeping in constant touch with him and others enabled him to keep up to date on the bombing destruction in England and what the British themselves were doing to increase military production at home and abroad. Despite the heavy bombing, the British production of arms continued, and even increased, but they desperately needed more American help.

One of the people Monnet worked with in Washington was Harry Hopkins, President Roosevelt's personal advisor and friend. Hopkins was named by the President after the 1940 election to visit Britain and assess the country's preparations and resolve as it prepared for the Nazi onslaught. Jean Monnet was one of those who briefed the envoy, according to Robert Sherwood's book *Roosevelt and Hopkins*. When Hopkins returned from London in early 1941, he had become an articulate spokesman for Lend-Lease. Monnet was, of course, working toward the same goal and concentrating on assessments of what the British needed in military supplies and how the United States could make and deliver them.

My work brought me together with McCloy, Bob Patterson, the Assistant Secretary of War, and Bob Lovett, another top defense official. McCloy was easy to work with and to discuss difficult issues with freely. He had a sharp mind and a good conceptual grasp of the problems of mobilization.

Patterson was a much more reserved and formal person but exceedingly fair and very competent. All three got along with Monnet and were supportive of his objectives. They shared with him the commitment to build up our industrial capacity. I do not recall anyone with whom Monnet maintained close contacts who was not supportive of those objectives. But even though they seemed to share his concern, there were limits to what they could accomplish until the White House established much larger preparedness goals and commensurate appropriations, contracts and the guiding policies and controls.

I remember Monnet telling me many times about preparing specific cables to be sent from Churchill to Roosevelt and then preparing the answers for transmittal to Churchill. Each side knew what Monnet was doing but they were so impressed by him and so supportive of his objectives that they went along with his unusual tactics. He met and discussed his goals with many top officials – anyone who would listen, in fact – but his principal and decisive strategies were confined to officials with the greatest clout and nearest to the seats of ultimate power.

Monnet always focused sharply on precisely what he was seeking and on what strategies would bring the best results. He often told me what he was doing and explained his purposes. Then he would tilt his head with a half-smile as though requesting a comment of approval. He derived an inner joy from each achievement. He had a wonderful way of twinkling his eyes and smiling a bit when some tactic worked well. Though he did not care for publicity about himself, he did have a healthy ego. He greatly enjoyed approval of his actions by those in whom he had confidence and close working relations. A subtle mannerism – a smile or a word dropped – led the observer to recognize a lively mind at work. He had an inventive intellect; he was always coming up with new ideas and policies in support of the basic goals of production to prevent Britain and eastern Europe from falling into the hands of the Nazis.

Over the years, when I discussed Monnet's activities and his conviction that the only way to save occupied Europe from Hitler's domination was through American production, the response on occasion has been skeptical. 'What was so great about that? It was obvious!' Yet it was not at all obvious in 1940–41. It was not easy to get a consensus that our production goals should be greatly increased. Roosevelt's 1940 campaign commitments that he would not get America directly involved in the war was widely quoted and supported. Those commitments were not in total harmony with his own deep concern over the fate of Britain and Russia. But increasing the arms flow alone did not provide a sufficient basis for total mobilization. It became crucial, therefore, to set goals around such mobilization under two difficult and not entirely consistent conditions: the goals must be realistic, comprehensive and drawn with careful measurement of the country's capacities; and yet they must be prepared with political sensitivity and in secrecy until events forced our country to act. There was a genuine impasse in production planning and Monnet was determined to break it.

THE DECISIVE MOMENT

A major break in this dilemma over larger military requirements came in the early summer of 1941 when Monnet's intensive and persistent efforts at the highest levels of authority in Washington and London began to achieve results. One key to this change was the freer flow of information between two capitals. Monnet was directly involved in this question and its resolution led to Roosevelt's successful efforts to determine total mobilization needs for the United States.

In utmost secrecy, President Roosevelt directed the civilian and military leaders of our armed forces to prepare the requirements which would be needed to win the war if our country became directly involved. At the same time he sent Averell Harriman and William L. Batt, respectively, to Britain and to the Soviet Union (which had just been attacked by Hitler), to get the requirements of those countries to achieve victory.

Once faced with the task of submitting requirements for victory for the West, the leaders of our military departments could no longer respond with questions about what kind of war might be fought. The dimensions of the war were now clear. Obviously, the military leadership faced a difficult task since there were many assumptions to be made about alternative strategies. But weighing such assumptions was the heart of military planning, and the commander-in-chief had not given orders to those in the best possible position to judge what armaments were needed to win.

I had the impression that some middle-level officers regarded this whole exercise skeptically, but the top military leaders took it seriously. Before long, the figures began to arrive. The magnitudes were staggering and the lists were endless. There was no scheduling of requirements over time and no indication of priorities of one category of armaments over another. The output would be limited only by the country's maximum productive capacity minus the most essential civilian needs. Once total requirements were agreed upon, a priorities system would impose order in delivery dates.

Once Monnet saw these figures, he was bubbling over with the joy of a loving father for a newborn child. He knew that the critical missing link in setting ambitious goals had been overcome. The first and essential step to large-scale mobilization had been taken. He had no desire to get involved personally in the complex task ahead of applying these schedules and priorities to the country's economy and industry. But he came to see me, or phoned me, often. He never wanted to deal with the procedures or assumptions of the detailed numbers. But he was a bit anxious about the production levels which would have to follow this planning. I kept him informed of our progress and explained the complexity of a job which still had to be kept largely secret although ultimately it would involve the entire country. Monnet never sought to follow exactly what we were doing with the masses of data. Yet his frequent presence made these twelve-to-fifteen-hour days, seven-day work weeks more bearable. He was anxious for results but he knew the planning had to be done well to succeed.

When these huge requirements were assembled in the Bureau of Research and Statistics of the Office of Production Management, it was obvious that order had to be imposed on production through schedules designed by both categories of goods and agencies. The Navy figures, for example, did not state that a given number of destroyers or fighter planes were needed in three months or three years. The aggregate figures supplied, whether of merchant ships, tanks, uniforms or basic training facilities (and no matter which military service) had to be placed in priorities related to both the war effort anticipated and the capacity of the still-civilian economy to transform itself into full mobilization.

We knew reasonably well, for example, how much total steel would be available in 1942 by months, quarters, and half-years; and the same was true for 1943 and 1944. We also knew the capacity of aluminium production and how much new capacity could be developed over what period. The earlier build-up of supply data, undertaken early in 1940, now began to pay off.

The development of a full-employment model of productive capacity of key materials for 1942, 1943 and 1944 proved invaluable when related to the military requirements. We included, of course, the data from the British and the Soviet military plans. Finally, we deducted what the country would need for the most essential civilian needs. We translated these requirements into total tons of steel, millions of pounds of aluminum and tons of copper – the essential ingredients of modern war. The resulting levels of vital materials were related to the next few years. We also priced the military requirements as a percentage of GNP. There had been some intelligence estimates that the upper limit of total national output that could be made available for military purposes was about 40–50 per cent.

The remarkable levels of war production actually achieved in 1942 and 1943 proved to be close to the goals to which Monnet had made such an important contribution in the fall of 1941. There was no computer program to make such projections and much of the work was based on assumptions and judgments which could not be tested. The result was the Victory Program which the President announced just after Pearl Harbor, and which proved to be both accurate in understanding our needs, and prescient in gaining that understanding before the actual events which propelled us into the war.

There were, of course, limits on how closely we could predict some needs. In the civilian sector, for example, we lacked the means to estimate accurately how much steel, copper, aluminum, wool and other materials would be needed to keep the economy functioning. Workers needed housing and clothes. Fuel was needed for their cars and, since new cars would not be built, parts to keep the old ones running. Only essential housing would be produced but how much could new ideas and techniques substitute for old methods and materials? How much scrap metal could be collected and processed? Monnet always urged the utmost austerity for civilians in any wartime plans.

As our requirements assignment neared its end, Monnet was both anxious and happy. His pride and confidence showed in his eyes and smiles in our frequent meetings at this stage of our collaboration. But we seldom dealt with the raw numbers. I do not know whether Monnet had top security clearance, but I did keep him generally informed of our major assumptions, basic techniques and how the measurements were proceeding.

One thing did concern him: the resulting numbers must be defensible but they must also be large! He was anxious for the results of the calculations since that was, to him, one more step on the road to production and victory.

Monnet, of course, did not know how or when these large numbers might be translated into actual appropriations and contracts and how they might serve the desperate and immediate needs of Britain and Russia. Since his mind always focused on the future, I am convinced he was thinking ahead to the problems of the Roosevelt Administration in getting the funds and converting the economy to full mobilization even while we were still assembling the numbers to make our case.

It was late September 1941, as I recall, when the armament production plan was fully matched to the total mobilization needs. Monnet was excited about the size of the 1942 output levels and the substantial increase for 1943, but he wanted assurance that these goals were as high as we could go. He feared they would be cut back. He was not ready to discuss even the possibility that excessively large requirements might be counterproductive.

Monnet's attention now turned to protecting and, if possible, enlarging these goals as they reached the top levels of government and eventually, the White House. I was never sure but I suspected that he may have influenced the increase of the requirements we had produced, sometime during the White House review. Lord Beaverbrook, the British Minister of Supply, was in Washington at this time and I was told by some White House people that he persuaded President Roosevelt to increase some categories. Monnet could well have played a part in that decision. He strongly believed that the larger the numbers, the greater the required effort and sense of urgency.

In his memoirs, Monnet states that he believed the goals as calculated could be increased by 50 per cent and that Roosevelt agreed. This was incorrect, since the goals were already very ambitious in relation to resources available. The figures that came back from the White House had been raised only modestly.

THE FEASIBILITY CONTROVERSY

On another critically important occasion – the feasibility of the goals – Monnet again revealed that he was much more concerned about goals being adequate than excessively high. Soon after Pearl Harbor, I expressed to him my grave concerns that highly excessive goals would almost certainly result in chaos in the armament industries. We would end producing less than the optimum numbers of planes, ships, tanks, guns and ammunition. He listened, but he preferred to take a risk by seeking higher arms production rather than settling for a lower, more secure number by being more cautious. We were not as far apart, however, as his memoirs suggest. Over the following months, he realized the importance of the feasibility question.

When one examined the details of Roosevelt's Victory Program, the levels were not substantially different from our earlier calculations. But to the people, and to American industry, they sounded far beyond what was possible. Actually they were largely attained, but their feasibility immediately became a critical issue.

Soon after Pearl Harbor, President Roosevelt established the War Production Board (WPB) with Donald Nelson as chairman. He was given the responsibility for mobilizing the nation's resources to win the war. The WPB comprised the heads of all the top government agencies directly involved with the mobilization. Nelson established the Planning Committee of WPB and named me chairman, with an eminent economist and a corporate leader as the other members. The Planning Committee soon found that setting annual goals was not sufficient to get the maximum output of armaments. Once Roosevelt announced the Victory Program, the armed forces requested staggering levels of appropriations. The military establishment was also not aware that chaos and waste would result without careful scheduling.

Early in 1942, the Planning Committee submitted a Feasibility Memorandum to Chairman Nelson. We pointed out that there seemed to be no coordination among the military agencies or even within an agency. Everyone seemed to want larger and larger appropriations and expanded orders with industry for their war materials. Each agency and each unit set its own targets and appropriations goal and each assumed its needs would get top priority. The result, unless controlled, would be excessive fabricating capacity, unrealistic scheduling of components and an end product far less than could be attained by targets that were both ambitious and feasible. Again, Monnet followed this controversy closely but without ever becoming involved in its details.

Donald Nelson accepted the analysis of the Feasibility Memorandum but others did not. One of his board members, General Brehon Sommervell, head of the Army's Service of Supplies, disagreed vehemently. Even with further discussion, he never agreed and never forgave the Planning Committee for intruding into his area of military responsibility.

I continued to see Monnet quite often, especially during this feasibility matter. He was still concerned that our scheduling efforts might not achieve the maximum output. He gave considerable thought to this key problem. Having devoted himself so fully to the goals issued a year earlier, Monnet understandably retained some fears of underproduction. I emphasized to him that the all-out efforts now by the military agencies contrasted with their reluctance in preparing mobilization goals before Pearl Harbor. But what convinced Monnet that our 'ambitious but feasible' plan made sense was the amazing pace of war mobilization and production which proceeded in a reasonably orderly manner. I am convinced that without the feasibility study this orderly pace would have been impossible, our production flow would have been lower, and waste and confusion much higher.

Monnet's contribution to formulating the Victory Program prior to our entry into the war has never been fully appreciated. It is clear today that the high goals established in 1940 would never have been expanded or attained without him. His combination of vision, total commitment, dogged adherence to very high goals and his extremely effective sense of strategy, maneuver and manipulation – all accomplished in the most selfless way – helped so greatly in America's total mobilization that it can be fairly called decisive. Jean Monnet was truly an unsung hero of World War II.

NOTES

1. Jean Monnet, *Memoirs* (trans. Richard Mayne) (New York: Doubleday, 1978) 159.
2. Ibid, 160–61.
3. Brand was a British official involved with expediting the arrival of US goods for the war effort.

3 Jean Monnet, the United States and the French Economic Plan
Irwin M. Wall

It would be difficult to overestimate the importance of Jean Monnet in the history of the postwar reconstruction of Western Europe. In many ways Monnet's ideas shaped the structure of the economy of postwar Europe, and consequently, determined much of its political evolution as well. Monnet's influence was not a reflection of any specific position he held. He was first, head of the French Supply Council, the economic purchasing mission that coordinated French imports from the United States to France under Lend-Lease. In January 1946 he became head of the Commissariat du Plan, a newly-created structure to oversee the rebuilding of the French economy, attached directly to the Prime Minister's office. From that position he later went on to assume the presidency of the European Coal and Steel Community. During the actual work of constructing the European Common Market from 1955–7 he held no official position at all, rather leading a pressure group, the Action Committee for the United States of Europe. Monnet was neither politician nor technocrat, nor a charismatic leader of the masses. His unique strength and importance lay in his personal convictions, a network of friendships and influence among the most powerful political figures in France, the United States, Britain, and the other countries of Western Europe, and his extraordinary power to persuade. Indeed, planning, not coercion, became the hallmark of Monnet's method of persuasion. And the French economic plan became a landmark in the history of postwar Europe, helping to shape the structure of the Marshall Plan, the European Coal and Steel Community, the abortive attempt to construct a European Defense Community, and the Common Market itself. There was a direct line from the Monnet Plan through the Marshall Plan to the Schuman Plan and the Pleven Plan. All of them were, in varying degrees, Monnet Plans. Planning was hardly original with Monnet; it was in effect built into the structure of postwar France. The experience of the 1930s, Vichy, and the Resistance, all pointed toward the necessity of planning. In the case of the 1930s, it was the negative example of the failure of liberal economics to bring France out of the depression, compensate for the nation's industrial lag, or manufacture heavy weapons in sufficient quantity to prevent the debacle of 1940. Planning ideas proliferated in the trade unions, a wing of the Socialist party, and among leading industrial circles. Léon Blum's second, abortive, Popular Front government in March 1938 included Pierre Mendès and Georges Boris, two fervent planners, in positions of importance.[1] Under Vichy, a technocratic, modernizing current of thought assumed great importance, and the Delegation Générale á l'Equipment Nationale, the Office Centrale de Repartition des Produits Industriels, and the Commités d'Organisation, all in different ways anticipated the postwar Commissariat du Plan.[2] Planning was included in the charter of the National Council of the Resistance, and one of the first acts of the Provisional Government in November 1944 was the creation of a Ministry of the National Economy under Mendès France. Mendès proposed a modernization plan for the economy, but it was obscured by the conflict over his accompanying proposals to force an exchange of bank notes and freeze bank accounts in the spring of 1945 in a radical effort to forestall inflation. The thrust of his plan was also too daring for economic liberals in that it would have integrated a policy of nationalization of key industries, that is to say structural reforms of the economy, with a strong dose of deflation and austerity, in order to give the state the economic leverage for a coherent industrial policy.[3]

Mendès' defeat, in which Monnet played a role, left a vacuum which Monnet was able to fill. Monnet reaped the heritage of all the previous efforts at planning of the 1930s, Vichy, the Resistance and the Provisional Government. He was close to the economic liberals, René Pleven and René Mayer, who had engineered Mendès' defeat, and neutral on the question of nationalizations. Monnet was above all a pragmatist and a critic of bureaucracy.[4] His genius was to propose a politically acceptable vehicle for the reconstruction of a neo-liberal capitalism via the use of the state.[5] This enabled him to construct a formidable political consensus around his plan so that all could see in it what they wished: French nationalists, concerned about security *vis á vis* Germany; French Communists, curiously suspicious of Socialist schemes for extensive nationalizations and desirous of placating the peasantry and petty bourgeoisie; and the Americans, in search of a coherent way in which to assist the Europeans to take their place in a new-world system of free trade and convertibility of currencies.

From the outset the Monnet Plan assumed extensive financing from the United States. There was nothing extraordinary about this: postwar plans in all European countries did so.[6] There was every reason to believe that American programs like Lend-Lease, and US-financed programs like the United Nations Relief and Rehabilitation Administration, would continue into the postwar period; without them, clearly millions of people would starve. All the European countries, including those of what was to become the Soviet bloc, lined up in Washington to receive reconstruction loans from the Export-Import Bank, and later the newly-created World Bank. The Soviet Union also looked forward to an enormous reconstruction loan from the United States, variously projected at different times between one and six billion dollars.[7]

In November 1944, Monnet established a French import program designed to continue in effect through 1 January 1946. Most of France's needs, 50 per cent of food and agricultural imports, 25 per cent of coal and other raw materials, and 90 per cent of finished goods were expected to come from the United States.[8] The aid was intended in the short run to enable France to assume its place alongside the Anglo-Saxon powers in the final defeat of Germany, but Monnet was clearly looking into the postwar era as well. The cost of this program, calculated into the Lend-Lease accords signed on 1 February 1945, brought the French debt to the United States to $2,575,000,000, for which Monnet hoped to receive a loan at 2.735 per cent interest payable over thirty years. And Monnet estimated that the Lend-Lease agreement gave France 22 per cent less than requested; the Americans pared his demands down by 40 per cent in the area of heavy transportation equipment, locomotives and railroad cars, and would provide no airplanes at all. Technically, Monnet noted that whatever was not covered by loan funds was offset by French 'reciprocal aid' to American forces on the ground in France; financially, 'We do not get anything for nothing'. French independence was fully preserved. But the American negotiator, Emilio Collado, saw the situation somewhat differently, anticipating that the French would be able to pay at most $900,000,000 of the total loan, if that, and initially would be able to make no interest payments at all.[9] Thus both sides in the negotiations early understood what Monnet made the central tenet of his postwar activity: France would modernize, and the United States, one way or another, would provide much of the financing.

The war's end, however, brought an abrupt cancellation of Lend-Lease shipments. The Russians interpreted this as a hostile act directed against themselves, but the British and the French were equally upset. General Alphonse Juin protested that the French occupation zone of Germany was rendered useless at the stroke of a pen, and French ambassador in Washington Henri Bonnet was urgently instructed to make inquiries.[10] But Washington understood it could not cut the lifeline of its allies. An immediate short-term credit of $400 million was granted to the French in order to permit shipments already in the pipeline to continue, and a supplementary 'lend-lease takeout loan' of $550 million was negotiated by Monnet in December 1945. Lend-Lease shipments were thus allowed to continue as originally projected. Moreover, the British were able to contract a huge treasury loan from the United States of 3.75 billion dollars on advantageous terms, and it seemed reasonable to suppose that Washington would prove equally generous with regard to France. Monnet, at least, had similar ambitious plans for the United States to finance French reconstruction, for as he told American embassy economic officers Livingston Merchant and Ivan White, in the long run the Americans must recognize that 'France was just as important as Great Britain' in the world-wide scheme of things. It was only by means of a loan of such dimensions, Monnet warned, that France would eventually be able to take its rightful place in the world system of free trade and exchanges so fervently hoped for by Washington; otherwise, 'France will modernize within a closed economy'.[11]

It is in this sense that Monnet's commitment to Washington in exchange, that France would join in international negotiations for the purpose of arriving at a general agreement on trade and payments, must be viewed. The French agreed that the purpose of such an agreement must be '. . . the reduction of tariffs and other barriers to international commerce plus the elimination of all discrimination in commerce, payments and investments'.[12] France did commit itself to the goals of free trade and convertibility of currencies in the postwar era. But Washington had first to agree to French demands that bilateral negotiations take place on the totality of French needs, and the Americans accepted the premise that only after a long period of reconstruction, or 'convalescence' of the French economy, would it be possible for Paris to consider the lowering of trade barriers. Nor must one see in Washington's plans for free trade and the 'open door' simply a projection of American imperialism. Similar objectives were shared by most European statesman in power in the postwar era. High French officials like Hervé Alphand, Guillaume Guindey, and Jean Monnet had come to believe that protectionism was in large part responsible for the previous French economic history of stagnation, and they had convinced prominent politicians, even Socialists like Léon Blum, of the virtues of larger markets of continental and international dimensions.[13] It was the common consensus of statesmen as well that the trade wars of the 1930s had contributed to the world depression and that autarchy was the policy of the fascist dictatorships, unsuitable for democratic countries.[14]

After Washington had agreed to negotiations on the totality of French needs, Monnet authored his memo to Charles de Gaulle, suggesting the formulation of an economic plan and the establishment of a government agency to implement it. As one of his last acts before resigning in January 1946, de Gaulle issued the executive order establishing the Commissariat du Plan. Unquestionably the formulation of a plan was in part designed to impress Washington with the dimensions of French needs and at the same time to convince American negotiators that their aid money would be put to good use. Referring to the Blum-Byrnes accords signed between American and French negotiators in Washington in May 1946, Monnet argued that 'The plan has made possible the accords; the accords will permit the execution of the plan'.[15] Monnet accompanied elder-statesman Léon Blum to Washington in March 1946, and it was Monnet who conducted much of the actual negotiation, while Blum handled the ceremonial aspects of the trip. Monnet placed great importance upon winning the endorsement of American negotiators to the principle of the plan, announcing his success in this aspect of the talks on 30 April: the Americans say the plan is viable, he cabled Paris, they saw 'no reason why the French people cannot achieve the goals fixed in the plan'.[16] This in turn allowed Monnet to argue that the French government was morally bound to execute the plan, since it had been the condition upon which the Americans had premised their generous aid package.

Monnet felt constrained to make these claims for political reasons; in fact the importance of the plan in the success of the negotiations has been greatly exaggerated, as has the role of the agreements in the implementation of the plan. First, the plan was hardly ready when Monnet arrived in Washington; it consisted of little more than a series of projections of desired levels of French production in several industries over the next four years, and an estimate of the imports necessary to achieve them. The earliest date on an actual text of the plan itself is November 1946, well after the Blum-Byrnes negotiations were over.[17] Secondly, the negotiations were not a success for the French, despite the favorable light Monnet tried to put on them in reporting on the results of his trip in Paris. The Ministry of Foreign Affairs was deeply disappointed; Blum himself, upset over the course of the talks, appealed directly to Secretary of State Byrnes, and then to President Truman. Failing to obtain satisfaction, he considered returning to Paris for further 'consultation', but Monnet convinced him to make use of his plenipotentiary powers and sign.[18]

Washington in fact declined to finance the anticipated

French deficit, or the Monnet Plan, in its outline form, over the next four years. The Blum-Byrnes agreements brought the French only a $650 million loan from the Export-Import Bank, not a Treasury loan of billions as was granted the British. To be sure, the Lend-Lease debt was canceled, and the terms for shipments since the war consolidated into a new loan; Paris also received the benefits of war surplus goods left by the Americans in France. The French were given the additional hope of support for a loan of $500 million from the World Bank when it began its operations a year later. The title could thus be 'dressed up' to look like close to two billion dollars.[19] But only the $650 million represented 'new money'; the Lend-Lease follow-up loans represented goods already consumed, and the $500 million from the World Bank was only a possibility, not a promise. $650 million was barely enough to get the French through a very harsh winter in 1946–7, while the imposition by Washington on Paris of a virtually free market for American film exports as an additional condition of the accords, caused a nasty backlash against the agreements in French public opinion.[20]

In fact the failure of the negotiations was foreseen when Blum and Monnet left for Washington. On the one hand the State Department had concluded that given the climate of Congressional opinion, which had made even the British loan doubtful, nothing similar could be offered the French; they would have to apply to the Export-Import Bank like everyone else. Monnet was unable to convince Washington that Paris was as important as London. But more than this, the climate of American-French relations was deteriorating over French opposition to the American goal of reconstructing Germany. The French had since mid-1945 been using the 'veto power' granted them in the Potsdam agreements to block the establishment of centralized services among the four occupational zones of Germany, on the grounds that the creation of a central postal service, or even the inter-zonal organization of trade unions, pre-figured the re-creation of a centralized German state.[21] The State Department hoped that Blum would bring French concessions with him to Washington, which might make the negotiations easier, but instead there was a noticeable hardening of the French position in Paris. In this respect, moreover, the Monnet Plan did not help the negotiations, for even in its skeleton state it was recognized in Washington as one of the main props of a French plan to displace Germany as the industrial center of Europe. Frances M. B. Lynch has argued that international objectives as well as domestic goals characterized the Monnet Plan from its inception; the plan was designed to enable France to compete in the international economy, and to become a major steel producer based on unrestricted imports of German coal.[22] The French-German relationship was to be reconstructed, based upon a continued French voice in the control of the Ruhr. French foreign policy aims were no secret in Washington, and did not change after de Gaulle resigned: France demanded detachment of the Rhineland, internationalization of the Ruhr, and economic integration of the Saar, and French negotiators in Germany kept up unrelenting pressure on the Americans and British to consent to increased shipments to France of German coal. The attachment of the Commissariat du Plan directly to the office of the head of the Provisional Government can in itself be seen as eloquent testimony to the importance the Monnet Plan held in both domestic and foreign French economic aims.[23] The French production target in the Monnet Plan was 12.7 million tons of steel in 1951, while Germany was to be held to the agreed-upon figure of 7.5 million tons, and 20 million tons of coal were to be imported annually to France from the Ruhr. Monnet intended France to be *'le premier maître des forges en Europe en 1950'*.[24] In Washington, the press complained that in granting the French their loan the Americans were underwriting 'a French plan to try for Germany's former steel markets in Europe'.[25] Monnet cited French military security as a justification for the plan's emphasis on heavy industry,[26] and this explains the coalition of both nationalist and Communist opinion around its objectives. During 1947 France and the United States were to argue bitterly over American plans to raise the levels of steel production contemplated in Germany. Ambassador Henri Bonnet, in asserting the French position, told Secretary of State Marshall that 'France did not believe that European steel production should be on the same pattern as before the war. Under the Monnet Plan there was provision for a considerable increase in French steel production which France felt should to that extent replace German steels'.[27]

The Monnet Plan's emphasis on six basic sectors of the economy, to the virtual exclusion of some others, was another troubling aspect of it for Washington, which believed firmly that deprivation of the masses was the primary ingredient fueling the strength of Communism in the postwar period. In 1947, Washington became wedded to the idea that flooding Europe with consumer goods was the best way to struggle against Communism, and this became a basic goal of the Marshall Plan. The Monnet Plan deliberately postponed consumer goods, placing priority on heavy industry.

Its most conspicuous failing, from the American standpoint, was its lack of provision for affordable housing. During the Blum-Byrnes talks, Secretary Byrnes remarked that he was greatly impressed with the French demonstration of their financial needs, but surprised that so much of the French program of imports was devoted to heavy industrial goods. This part of the package, he said, should be subjected to careful 'screening', and could be 'substantially reduced'.[28] The Americans were ready to pay for essential foodstuffs and raw materials for the French, but they were not yet ready to finance ambitious plans for economic reconstruction and modernization. Monnet was undeterred, however: coal, steel and cement products, he argued, came first; premature emphasis on inexpensive housing would act as a drain on economic growth.[29]

Early in 1947, American commercial attaché Ivan White warned that the overall economic and financial situation in France remained in disequilibrium, jeopardizing the success of the Monnet Plan. In White's opinion, France could modernize, or achieve financial stability, but it could not do both at the same time. The nation had a chronic food deficit, yet a high rate of consumption by the urban rich and the farm population; the French food crisis would not exist, said White, 'in a system of perfect distribution'. As it was, the impact of the scarcity fell entirely on the urban salaried classes, who received only 70 per cent of the share of the national income that had been theirs before the war. With the food crisis, White said, the execution of the Monnet plan, with its heavy emphasis on investment, operates as a continuing disruptive force on the social and political structure of France. . . . The question arises as to whether a democratic form of government can be evolved and consolidated during the next few years on the basis of the foregoing situation.

White feared that the Monnet Plan would not accomplish the basic goal of weakening the hold of the Communists on the working classes and strengthening democracy. He called for an alternative emphasis in French economic planning on food production and light industry, which would demonstrate the concrete benefits of American aid while raising living standards.[30]

Another American concern voiced by White, which was also on the minds of American negotiators in 1946, was the financial situation in Paris, which was characterized by rampant inflation. Inflation was as certain a path to political instability and Communism as the lack of consumer goods and housing, from the American standpoint. The Americans were sympathetic to the early plans of Mendès France to deal with inflation; the Belgians had forced a currency exchange and frozen bank notes as Mendès wished to do, and the Americans urged that course on the French. The Americans welcomed the Gouin government in January 1946, following de Gaulle's resignation, because André Philip, the new Minister of Finance, was pledged to a Mendès-type program.[31] Monnet had opposed the Mendès France program in 1945; his liberal concept of planning allowed for neither the extensive state control of the economy Mendès envisioned, nor the structural reforms required to achieve it. The Americans regarded the French tax system as regressive and antiquated, requiring radical overhaul; but the Monnet Plan did not address this question.

On the other hand Monnet insisted on absolute priority to investment in the basic sectors of the economy, and the devotion of external grants and loans in their entirety to such investment. Monnet was not an economist, and it does not appear that he concerned himself with issues of financial stability as they related to his plan until after his American visit in 1946. In August 1946, Monnet engaged the services of Robert Nathan, a New Deal economist whom he greatly respected, to evaluate the plan during its formative stage. Nathan's general conclusions were favorable, but he warned Monnet that for the plan to succeed French workers would need to work forty-eight hours per week, and purchasing power would have to remain low. He also pointed to the danger that the plan would lead to the creation of a strong inflationary spiral because of its absolute prioritization of massive state investment in the absence of sufficient resources.[32] Only after Nathan's critique did Monnet concern himself with issues of financial stability, and even then his general attitude was never to give priority to financial questions; money was a tool to be used in the interest of economic growth, and financial stabilization must never be allowed to take priority over modernization. It would be a 'fundamental error', Monnet wrote in 1947, 'to believe that French stabilization is purely a budgetary and financial question. . . . stopping inflation must be associated with economic expansion to increase total resources. . . . Modernization and stabilization go together, not one without the other'.[33]

Given the extensive American criticism of the Monnet Plan, and their initial refusal to finance it in 1946, one may legitimately wonder how the plan ever came to succeed. But Monnet's genius as a statesman was to look beyond momentary failure and to perceive reality over the long term. His immediate reaction to Blum-Byrnes was to revise downward the investment projections of the plan and separate the year 1947 from its long-term goals. Monnet could see the crisis of 1947 looming, but he retained the conviction that the Americans would come to see that the reconstruction of Europe and its insertion into the world economy, under the leadership of a resurgent and modernized France, was in their own interest as well as the interest of Europe. In the meantime he would bide his time, argue that the loan of 1946 was sufficient to get the plan started, and look to the promised World Bank loan and as yet unforseen forms of assistance to take care of the future. In a fundamental respect, Monnet anticipated the Marshall Plan. The text of the French modernization plan, submitted to the French government for its consideration in November 1946 and adopted in January 1947, not only anticipated future American financing, but stipulated that the 'counterpart' of external loans and grants in French currency be consecrated to internal investment.[34] Before the Marshall Plan was even thought of, Monnet had anticipated (if not suggested) one of its most extraordinary and effective features.

The idea of 'counterpart' became one of the most imaginative and useful aspects of the Marshall Plan in the eyes of contemporaries.[35] American aid monies were in effect used twice; first in the purchase of American goods and commodities essential to sustenance and growth, but second through the establishment of a special fund in local currency by the recipient nation through the sale of those goods to the population. Thus a special 'counterpart' fund in each Marshall Plan nation was available for internal use by the recipient government. The Marshall Plan further stipulated that 5 per cent of the counterpart fund be made available to finance the expenses of an American 'Mission' in the recipient country, the purpose of which would be to oversee the use of the rest of the aid monies. For there was to be no American aid without strings attached; Congress wrote into the Act what it perceived to be insurance that its aid monies would be put to good use. In fact, recipient nations were forbidden to use the counterpart funds without the express authorization of the Marshall Plan Mission. This provision of the law initially raised significant fears of American interference in the internal affairs of the recipient countries, but Washington could not be dissuaded, and all had to live with these terms.

Monnet insisted that the French government establish from the outset that counterpart funds in France would have one use, and one use only; to finance the Monnet Plan. He was aided in this determination in that the Americans were on record as having approved the Monnet Plan in its broad outlines in 1946; they could not easily, therefore, object to the devotion of Marshall Plan aid to its achievement. In May 1947, one month before Secretary Marshall announced his intent to establish a coordinated aid program for Europe, Jean Monnet wrote to Minister of Finance Robert Schuman to suggest the establishment of an autonomous fund from which to finance the six basic sectors of the French economy given priority in the Plan: coal, electricity, steel, cement, transportation, and agricultural machinery. Monnet was unsucessful in his bid to get his fund established independently of the treasury, but he did win acceptance for the provision that the allocation in francs of the counterpart of foreign loans be devoted to the fulfillment of the plan. 'By devoting the product in francs of these loans to the financing of essential aspects of the plan, we give concrete justification for credits requested and we reinforce our position in subsequent negotiations.'[36] And as Monnet predicted, the Americans eventually agreed to remain bound by this restriction as well. Whereas in both Britain and Italy the bulk of the counterpart was devoted to reduction of the national debt, in effect 'sterilized', in the parlance of the day, to prevent inflation, in France all of the counterpart went to the financing of the Monnet Plan. Marshall himself, moreover, was more impressed with French determination and overall conceptualization of the uses of aid, than he was dissuaded by the specific weaknesses his staff found in the mechanics of French planning. In search of a coordinated European response to his initiative, Marshall himself characterized his plan as somewhat along the lines of the Monnet Plan, 'but on a much larger scale involving several countries'.[37] And initial American hopes for the establishment of the Organization for European Economic Cooperation as the linchpin of an economically-unified Europe centered around the appointment of Monnet as the first President of that organization, a post he eventually declined.

Monnet immediately recognized in the Marshall Plan the means with which to finance the Monnet Plan, but he also recognized its dangers. On the one hand he deplored the division of Europe into Eastern and Western blocs that the Marshall Plan created or solidified. Monnet was apolitical, and one of the more interesting characteristics of the launching of his plan was the way in which he was able to rally Communist support as part of his formidable national consensus around the plan. Francois Billoux, the Communist Minister of Reconstruction and Urbanism from 1945 to 1947, agreed with Monnet's policy of postponing the construction of inexpensive housing, while implementing the government's expensive program of compensating those private property owners who had suffered damages due to the war. Communist policy from 1945–7 was to postpone the satisfaction of working-class salary demands in the interest of increasing productivity and production: *'produire d'abord, revendiquer ensuite'*, 'produce first and make demands afterwards'. The Communists further did not dissent from government policy to make good the losses of those whose property and homes had been destroyed during the war, an aspect of their anxiety to appeal successfully to the French petty bourgeoisie. Monnet regretted the expulsion of the Communist ministers from the French government in May 1947; on 1 July 1947 he wrote to Schuman expressing his fears that the Marshall Plan might force a break with the USSR, turning the plan from an economic program of aid into a political weapon. Monnet urged the government to do everything possible to avoid such a break, particularly during the June 1947 tripartite French-British-Soviet meetings aimed at forging a European response to the Marshall initiative.[38]

Monnet also perceived a second unwelcome consequence of the Marshall Plan: that a fundamental aim of its originators was to make the reconstruction of Germany palatable to the rest of Western Europe, especially France.[39] The consequences for France would be, and were, an inevitable adjustment of its German policy in the sense of accommodating American wishes. But here again, Monnet warned that France must at all costs keep control of the Ruhr; the German industrial heartland must not be allowed to become the mainstay of a remilitarized Germany, but rather an *'actif européen'*.[40] Monnet thus continued to stress the importance of integrating the Ruhr with the projected growth of the French steel industry, a concern out of which he developed the Schuman Plan for an integrated European Steel and Coal Community.

In 1951, Communist leader Benoit Frachon attacked Jean Monnet as *'le plus américain des américains francais'*, 'the most American of French Americans'.[41] But as the PCF had earlier recognized, the Monnet Plan was designed to establish the basis for an independent and powerful France, and it served to bend the Marshall Plan to that end. Monnet recognized the situation frankly in a letter to Georges Bidault on the occasion of the signing of the bilateral agreement with the United States implementing the Marshall Plan:[42]

> We are going to depend on this country [the US] to a great extent as much for the maintenance of our economic life as for our national security. This situation cannot continue without great danger. We are today 'the stake (*lenjeu*)'. We must transform this situation quickly into one of independence and collaboration.

One of the issues in the bilateral treaty was the perceived 'humiliation' of France having to submit its proposed expenditure of aid monies to the United States aid mission for prior approval. But Washington had already sacrificed much of the power over the French economy it hoped to gain from its control of the counterpart by its prior acceptance of the terms of the Monnet Plan. On 2 January 1948, Bidault had insisted, at Monnet's urging, that Washington agree to the consecration of its counterpart funds to the investment goals of the Monnet Plan. Washington initially refused; it intended to see its aid monies used for housing, roads, and land rehabilitation, large projects that would strike the public imagination and which could be adorned with plaques indicating that they were built thanks to the assistance of the American people. The French adamantly refused to consider cuts in the Monnet Plan, however; projects under way could not be abandoned without enormous wastage, they argued, and the Americans were told that any interference with the plan would cause the most undesirable, if unspecified, social and political consequences in France.[43] Washington finally accepted the French view; counterpart funds could be devoted to the Monnet Plan on condition that the French agree to undertake financial and monetary stabilization. The American Secretary of the Treasury, John Snyder, was bitterly opposed to granting his concession to the French, but Monnet enjoyed the confidence of key American officials such as David Bruce, head of the Marshall Plan Mission in France, and William Tomlinson, American Treasury representative in Paris, and this helped Paris in making its view on this crucial issue prevail.[44]

The result was that the Americans could not urge cuts in French expenditure for investment without being charged with causing the failure of the Monnet Plan and interference in French internal affairs. Richard Bissel, and ECA official, noted that it was impossible to ask the French for reductions in their investments, despite the fact that these were 'in excess of the amount which the French economy can support at the present time without inflation . . .'.[45] Despite two years of often acrimonious negotiations between the American aid mission and the French government, Washington never succeeded in changing the parameters of the Monnet Plan, or in forcing the expenditures its aid officials wished to see the French devote to housing, hospitals, and schools. In 1950 the issue reached a crescendo, with Washington threatening to cut American aid altogether unless the French increased their expenditure in these areas. The French government did eventually agree to put aside a small amount of US aid for housing and the development of tourism.[46] But the Korean War intervened, and American concerns rapidly shifted from the construction of French housing to the building of the French military potential.

Thus did the Marshall Plan in France become an auxiliary to the Monnet Plan in achieving the reconstruction and modernization of the country. In 1952 Monnet left the Commissariat du Plan to take over the presidency of the European Coal and Steel Community. The second French economic plan was formulated by Monnet's collaborators, and planning became institutionalized in French economic life. It is common to ask, but not particularly meaningful to attempt to answer, the question of the extent to which the Monnet Plan may be regarded as a 'success'. In answering such queries one is reduced to a kind of cost accounting, comparing original projections with actual results. Any such effort is fruitless. The plan did not achieve its original projections in any of the six basic sectors; but its genius was in its flexibility, and the projections were always changed from year to year to take into account changed and unforeseen circumstances. The plan was consultative and non-coercive, moreover. While it stimulated growth by channeling investment into some areas, it did nothing to discourage private investment in other areas that were not of particular early concern.

The major successes of the Plan were achieved in the

growth of the French electricity industry and railroads. The plan was also somewhat successful in reorganizing, modernizing, and stimulating the growth of the French steel industry.[47] The automobile industry took off under its own steam, however, and far outstripped the plan's early projections; and the plan bureaucrats did not attempt to prevent it from doing so.[48] Potentially deadly if it were a bureaucratic edifice, John Sheahan wrote, the plan succeeded in avoiding that pitfall; it raised industry's targets, but then ceased to constitute a plan in the sense of controlling results. It was 'decentralized decision-making with a promotional push'.

Philippe Mioche is the only scholar to have studied the specific committees of the various industries that convened in 1946–7 to draw up and implement the plan. The record of these were mixed. Electricity in France has continued to be a conspicuous postwar success as a nationalized enterprise. Monnet won the cooperation, on the other hand, of private steel producers in the consolidation of many small producers into a few, the introduction of two ultra-modern strip rolling mills imported from the United States, and the formation of a new corporation, Sollac, in which most of the existing companies purchased a share, to finance the modernization. The Monnet Plan contributed to the establishment in France of a powerful, modern steel industry. While Monnet worked hand in hand with the steel producers in the formative stages of the plan, however, he completed the modernization of their industry through the injection of foreign competition by forming the Coal and Steel pool over their heated opposition. The Monnet and Schuman Plans thus constituted a coordinated link in the successful modernization and transformation of the French steel industry. Agricultural machinery was added to one of the basic sectors of the plan as an afterthought in response to pressure from French farmers; in effect, its committee was not successful in formulating a cooperative approach to economic modernization, and France relied to a great extent on imports to fulfill its early tractor needs. A weakness of the plan was its failure in the machine-tool industry. It was not regarded as one of the basic sectors; the dispersed nature of production made cooperation unobtainable from so many small producers; and agreement could not be reached on a proposal to establish a new, large, national enterprise. The consequence was reliance on American imports and the sacrifice of supremacy in machine tools over the long-term to Germany and the United States.

There were eighteen committees in all created to study specific aspects of the Monnet Plan. All brought together representatives of industry, labor and consumers, and the Communist-directed CGT worked with management and the Commissariat in the formulation of the final results. Such major successes as the plan achieved, argues Mioche, came from its lack of political definition and thus the early consensus around it, the heritage of a pre-existing tradition of and disposition toward planning, and of Jean Monnet's leadership and personal conviction of the eventual receipt of American aid.[49]

A more sustained critique of the Monnet Plan was offered by Warren Baum, whose study was based upon personal experience as a US aid official in France. The integration of the committees was the weakest link in the planning process, Baum states, and there was no study of alternatives to the targets set forth, the possibilities of increased consumption, or the effects on inflation. Inflation was in effect built into the plan, and French governments achieved their precarious social stability from 1945 to 1950 by the progressive log-rolling of concessions to the demands of interest groups, thus precluding any escape from the wage-price spiral. Marshall Plan counterpart funds were immediately released into the economy in the form of investment, thus further fueling inflation. Meanwhile, the French government continued to protect, through tariffs and other concessions, archaic economic practice of vast numbers of the peasants and petty bourgeoisie, even as it modernized. There was thus no plan 'in the sense of a set of specific and internally consistent goals combined with a set of policies and controls to make sure that the goals can be achieved'.[50] Thus, what was a strength of the Monnet Plan for Sheahan was a drawback for Baum.

It is impossible in the present context to explore thoroughly the many strands of development of both the Schuman Plan and the European Defense Community. For present purposes it must suffice to show the continuity of both with Monnet's overall design and his attempt to harmonize his policies and hopes for France with the reality of American power and influence. The continuity of the Monnet and Schuman Plans was apparent not only in Monnet's perception of the need to open up the French steel industry to foreign competition, but also in his early realization that the strength of French steel depended upon German coke, and that French security depended upon continued access of France to the Ruhr and restriction of German sovereignty there. In exchange for abandoning controls on German steel production, France was conceded a place on an international authority for control of the Ruhr, under the terms of the London agreements of 1948. With the return of the Federal Government of Germany to partial sovereignty in 1949, however, the Germans applied for equal membership in the Ruhr authority, while German steel production by-passed French output in the same year.

In responding to American pressure in favor of European unity, the French attempted to secure tariff agreements with the Benelux countries and Italy; for a time the diplomacy of Europe was characterized by the proliferation of suggestive names like Fritalux and Finebel for the new European entity. But these schemes foundered on the reluctance of Washington to support any arrangements which failed to integrate Germany in the new Europe. French policy was thus at an impasse; and the Schuman Plan was Monnet's creative answer to a way out of the French difficulty.[51] Monnet was upset at the central place Germany was assuming in the Cold War, disturbed by the growing German drive toward a new European industrial hegemony, vexed at the failure of French efforts to cooperate with Great Britain in the European unity effort, and fearful that the growth of separate steel industries meant German superiority in production, a renewed arms race and the spectre of war. Franco-German relations were stagnating, and Washington made frequent suggestions that the Ruhr Authority needed to incorporate French and German steel industries together to be viable. Finally, Foreign Minister Schuman was 'in need of an initiative' for impending tripartite meetings with Great Britain and the United States on 10 May 1950 in London, while renewed French efforts to secure a kind of directorate of the Big Three, in the form of Premier Bidault's suggestion of an Atlantic 'High Council for Peace', had failed to find an echo among France's partners. The Americans insisted on some measure of European supranationality and wanted France to take the leadership.[52] Monnet's suggestion of a pool devoted to a single but basic industry combined pragmatism and vision; limitation to a single pair of products, coal and steel, greatly simplified negotiations, while success in so basic an industry was bound to provide a stepping-stone for future construction of a united Europe.

Although Dean Acheson's initial response was guarded – he feared the creation of a huge international cartel in Monnet's proposal – American influence was of importance in Monnet's initiative. Not only had US Ambassador to England Lewis Douglas, and High Commissioner in Germany John J. McCloy, both called for an extension of the Ruhr Authority to France and the Benelux countries, but George Ball, who had become close to Monnet through his work as a lawyer for the French Supply Council, proposed a framework modeled on American regulatory agencies such as the Federal Trade Commission. Hence the genesis of Monnet's suggestion for the creation of a 'High Authority', a term denoting a regulatory body quite alien to the European historical experience.[53] Ball made suggestions to Monnet on the creation of the community's institutional framework and the use of American anti-trust legislation as a model for the deconcentration of German coal and steel cartels in the Ruhr as preconditions for the successful negotiation of an accord.

Thus Monnet, as in the original Monnet Plan, won American agreement and backing through the personal support he enjoyed in Washington and the discriminating use of American expertise and models, in the elaboration of a project which, it should be stressed, responded essentially to French security considerations. Schuman was able to affirm to Gaullist Michel Debré that none of the controls enjoyed by France over the German steel industry would be sacrificed in the institutional framework of the Schuman Plan. Monnet became President of the European Coal and Steel Community following its ratification, and successfully negotiated a large American loan as one of his first actions. Once again he successfully used American pressure and support to accomplish a fundamental French security objective.

The Korean War intensified American concern over European military security. The poor opinion in Washington of the condition of the French army led to increased pressure for rearmament, and on 22 July 1950, Dean Acheson circulated a memo to all the NATO allies requesting information on the nature and extent of the increased defense effort they proposed to undertake, requesting a reply by 5 August.[54] Monnet prepared a project memorandum for the French government which became the basis of its reply to the Americans. Rearmament, Monnet said, must be a collective enterprise, not simply a juxtaposition of independent national efforts. It should involve supranational organisms of control; a common defense fund; equal contributions by all the allies based upon their capacity to pay as determined by per capita national income; and equality of burdens, to be guaranteed by internationally stable currencies tied to the American dollar.[55] Monnet's plan was adopted by the French government and proposed to Washington; it was all the more attractive because it would permit 'the full utilization and cooperation of the Atlantic Community without rearming Germany independently'.[56] The Americans, however, were not impressed, seeing in the French ideas a transparent scheme to 'spread their inflation' among all the allies, collectivize the cost of the Indochina war, and make the United States underwrite the military budgets of all the European states.[57]

The continuity in Monnet's response to the latest American challenge was striking: the search for supranational solutions, the breadth of vision extending beyond Europe to the Atlantic Community and the world, the quest for American support, and the attempt to harmonize American, European, and French national interests. These considerations had worked brilliantly through the triptych of the Monnet, Marshall, and Schuman Plans. But these were all civilian economic programs in which Monnet's appeal to statesmen to transcend nationalistic considerations could, in the immediate postwar era, fall on receptive ears. The period from 1950 to 1954 was dominated by military issues; NATO, European rearmament, the Korean and Indochina wars. International solutions were by definition more difficult to find. To be sure, the Americans had succeeded in securing

United Nations support for their Korean effort, which appeared initially to be a defensive response to a flagrant act of military aggression from the north. But the Indochina conflict was more easily assimilated to the struggles over decolonization than the Cold War, and Washington had consistently interpreted it in that light, arguing that only when Paris was prepared to grant genuine national independence to Vietnam would it be possible to separate the issues of Communism and national independence, and fully support the French effort. Monnet's position was weakened by his failure to question the French colonialist consensus over Indochina; his attempts to internationalize the conflict there foundered on the growing opposition to the war in France, which ultimately led to unilateral withdrawal under an old nemesis, Pierre Mendès France. And the continuation of the Indochina conflict contributed in turn to the failure of Monnet's next great suggestion, the European Defense Community.

The Korean War occasioned a minor panic in Europe during the summer of 1950, leading inexorably to the conclusion within NATO, that given the weakness of the French army and the lack of soldiering manpower as compared with Soviet forces, the rearmament of Germany was necessary. Monnet's suggestion for a common NATO defense budget was designed in part to provide for a German contribution to the common defense effort without allowing for the re-establishment of the Wehrmacht. In August 1950, support developed in Washington for the concept of a European Defense Force which would include Germany, allowing for the creation of German military forces under joint European command within NATO. The idea was proposed by Lewis Douglas, who, it will be recalled, originally suggested the extension of the international authority of the Ruhr to encompass the coal and steel industries of France and the Benelux. But the notion was very much in the air in 1950; similar ideas were articulated by Winston Churchill, Paul Reynaud, André Philip, and others; David Bruce, now Ambassador to France, rallied to the idea on 9 August, John J. McCloy on 11 August. On 2 September, Acheson instructed Bruce to press the idea on the French government.[58] On 14 September, both British and Americans pressed the need for some form of German rearmament on the French, and on 15 September the suggestion was brought to the council of the NATO alliance, where it quickly won the support of all the members of the alliance except France. Paris was isolated.

In an internal note the French Foreign Ministry characterized the problem it faced in terms remarkably similar to the challenge that had brought forth the Schuman Plan. A totally negative French position on German rearmament created the risk that 'German rearmament will be accomplished despite us, almost against us'. France must not challenge the principle of German rearmament, but rather prepare 'means permitting the retention of sufficient control on the part of the French government over German rearmament'. This could only be accomplished 'in the framework of a collective organization in which France would participate and play, by the nature of things, a determining role. . .'. As in the case of the Schuman Plan, France would try to use the American pressure and involvement in Europe to achieve its own specific aims.[59] The Schuman Plan was designed to save the Monnet Plan which in turn had been meant to establish French industrial dominance in Europe. The European Defense Community was designed to preserve a preponderance of French military power in the face of the inevitable rearmament of Germany.

Monnet himself established the link between the Schuman and Pleven Plans, both of which he had authored: the Pleven Plan would solve the problem of German rearmament 'by the same methods and in the same spirit as ECSC . . . it proposes the creation, for common defense, of a European Army under the authority of the political institutions of a united Europe'.[60] Washington was initially suspicious of the European Defense Community plan, seeing in it a cumbersome and unworkable scheme that would only serve to delay the creation of a German army. The American fears proved to be extraordinarily accurate. The complexity of the treaty as it was eventually negotiated went beyond the comprehension of most of those legislators and opinion-makers who had to pronounce upon it. And during the protracted, four-year struggle to negotiate and ratify it, no progress could be made at all toward the rearming of Germany.[61] Not least among the many ironies in the struggle over the treaty's ratification was that it became more and more attractive to the Americans as it became less and less desirable to the French. The struggle over EDC eventually tore the French nation apart, as nothing had done since the Dreyfus affair. It went down to defeat in the French National Assembly in 1954, and left Monnet disillusioned with and embittered against the subsequent drift of French policy. Monnet recognized the danger that continuation of the Indochina war represented for EDC's ratification; to the extent that the French were engaged in Asia, they were in danger of their European defense contribution being inferior to that of Germany, which made a joint army impossible. Monnet's answer was to seek to shift the Indochina burden to Washington.[62] But the Americans would only pay for the war; they were not inclined to fight it. And as French dependence on Washington increased, the resolve necessary for so unprecedented a step as a European army waned. In retrospect one may also conclude that the proposal for a European army was premature, impossible of realization in an age of intense nationalism. It had to follow European economic and political integration; it could not precede them. But one can only admire the audacity and boldness of vision of the man who proposed it. It remains in the direct line of Monnet's brilliant, and mostly successful attempts to balance and harmonize French interests, American pressure, and the aim of European unity. And if it is one day realized, the role of Monnet in its creation will surely not be forgotten.

NOTES

1. See the discussion in Richard Kuisel, *Capitalism and the State in Modern France* (New York, 1981).
2. It should be noted, however, that Vichy's planning was authoritarian and bureaucratic, while Monnet's system was consultative and consensual: see Henri Rousso, 'Le Plan, objet d'historire', *Sociologie du Travail* (March 1985), 239–50.

3. Phillippe Mioche, *Le Plan Monnet: Genése et Elaboration* (Paris, 1985) 47–52.
4. Henri Rousso, op. cit., 242.
5. Francois Bloch-Lainé et Jean Bouview, *La France Restaurée 1944–54: Diologue sur les choix d'une modernisation* (Paris, 1986) 76–89.
6. Alan Milward, *The Reconstruction of Western Europe, 1945–51* (London, 1984) 38–62.
7. See Thomas G. Paterson, *Soviet-American Confrontation: Postwar Reconstruction and the Origins of the Cold War* (Baltimore, 1973).
8. Archives Nationales (Paris) (hereafter AN), F60, 921, Memorandum by Jean Monnet, 10 November 1944.
9. Harry S. Truman Library (Independence, Missouri), Clayton-Thorpe File, Subject File, France, Box 2, Collado to Clayton, 1 February 1945.
10. AN, F60, 921, telegrams of 15, 18, and 20 July 1945.
11. US National Archives and Records Administration (NARA), State Department, Decimal File, 1945–9, 851.51/1–1546, Caffery to the Secretary of State, 15 January 1946.
12. Ministére des Affaires Etrangéres (MAE), A 194–5, 25 February 1946.
13. Michel Margairaz, 'Author des accords Blum-Byrnes: Jean Monnet entre le consensus national et le consensus atlantique', *Histoire, Economie et Société*, 3 (1982), 439–70.
14. A 'Yellow Book' of documents published by the French government on the eve of the Blum-Byrnes negotiations stated that 'the increase in the movement of exchanges is one of the essential conditions of international security and the re-establishment of world prosperity. This policy, in which the government is resolutely engaged, is the only one that conforms to the vital interests of France. It is opposed to autarchy, which would put France outside the circuit of world exchange and not only would preclude the growth of the standard of living of the population, but would risk its rapid reduction.' MAE, 194–5, 25 February 1946.
15. Fondation Jean Monnet pour l'Europe (Lausanne, Switzerland) (hereafter FJM), AMF 4/5/2, 23 May 1946, 'Notes pour le rapport au gouvernement sur les negociations conduites par M. Blum.'
16. FJM, AMF 4/8/137, 30 April 1946.
17. Mioche, *Le Plan Monnet*, 128–33.
18. Jean Monnet, *Memoirs* (trans. Richard Mayne) (New York, 1978) 253.
19. NARA, 851.54/4–946, 29 April 1946, Memorandum by under-Secretary of State Dean Acheson to George C. Marshall.
20. For the 'pessimistic' interpretation of the Blum-Byrnes agreements see Annie Lecroix-Riz, 'Négociation et signature des accords Blum-Byrnes (Octobre 1945–Mai 1946) d'aprés les Archives du Ministére des Affaires Etrangéres', *Revue d'histoire moderne et contemporaine*, XXI (July–September 1984), 417–48. Lacroix-Riz argues that despite the often 'humiliating' terms, France was constrained by the accords to enter into a Western bloc dominated by the United States.

I have agreed with Lacroix-Riz on her negative assessment of the agreements, but contested her conclusion that France joined an American-dominated bloc: see Irwin M. Wall, 'Les accords Blum-Byrnes, la modernisation de la France et la guerre froide', *Vingtiéme Siécle*, 13 (January–March 1987) 45–63.

21. See John Gimbel, *The Origins of the Marshall Plan* (Stanford, Ca., 1976), 41–9. Also Irwin M. Wall, *L'Influence américaine sur la politique francaise, 1945–1954* (Paris, 1989) 79–94.
22. Frances M. B. Lynch, 'Resolving the Paradox of the Monnet Plan: National and International Planning in French Reconstruction', *Economic History Review*, 37, 2 (May 1984) 229–43.
23. Various other motives figured in this decision, however: for instance, the desire to keep economic planning away from the control of the Communists, who headed the economic ministries, and Monnet's own allergy to the traditional bureaucracy.
24. Mioche, *Le Plan Monnet*, 249.
25. FJM, AMF 4/8/217, *The Washington Post*, 19 May 1946.
26. See Monnet's letter to Robert Schuman in *Jean Monnet–Robert Schuman, Correspondance 1947–1953* (Lausanne: Fondation Jean Monnet, 1986) 26–8.
27. NARA, Matthews-Hickerson File, Microfilm Reel 10, Bonnet-Marshall conversation, 21 July 1947.
28. NARA, 851.51/4–106, 10 April 1946, Byrnes to Caffery.
29. Mioche, *Le Plan Monnet*, 155.
30. NARA, 851.51/4–847, 8 April 1947; 851.51/4–2247, 16 May 1947, Ivan White to Secretary Marshall.
31. Quai, MAE, B Amérique, 119, Bonnet to Paris, 28 January 1946; NARA, 851.51/2–446, 4 February 1946 Ivan White to the Secretary.
32. Mioche, *Le Plan Monnet*, 139. Robert Nathan was kind enough to confirm the essential aspects of his critique of the Monnet Plan in a telephone interview with the author, 23 August 1989.
33. Quoted by Robert Frank, 'Contraints monétaires, désirs de croissance et reves européens (1931–1949)', in Patrick Fridenson et André Straus, *Le Capitalisme Francais, 19e et 20e siécle: Blocages et dynamismes d'une croissance* (Paris, 1987) 229.
34. The earliest text of the plan may be found in AN, F 60, 922.
35. See Harry Price, *The Marshall Plan and its Meaning* (Ithaca, N.Y., 1955).
36. *Jean Monnet-Robert Schuman Correspondance*, Monnet to Schuman, 12 May 1947, 28.
37. Foreign Relations of the United States (hereafter FRUS), 1947, III, Western Europe, Marshall Plan, 12 June 1947, 249–51.
38. FJM, AMF 14/1/1, Monnet to Schuman, 1 July 1947.
39. An interesting confirmation of a sort of the work of John Gimbel, *The Origins of the Marshall Plan*, op. cit.
40. FJM, AMF 14/1/4, 27 July 1947.
41. Benoit Frachon, *Au Rythme des jours: Retrospective de vinqt années de luttes de la CGT*, T.I., 1944–54 (Paris, 1967) 433.

42. AN, 457 AP 21, Papiers Georges Bidault, Monnet to Bidault, 18 April 1948.
43. NARA, Agency for International Development Files, ECA, Office of the Special Representative, Country Subject Files, France, Box 18, 'Report on Interim Aid, July, 1948'.
44. Gerard Bossuat, 'Les risques et les espoirs du Plan Marshall pour la France', *Etudes et Documents* (Paris, 1989) 213.
45. NARA, AID Files, ECA, OSR, Country Subject Files, France, Box 18, 28 December, 1948.
46. See the discussion in Chiarella Esposito, 'The Marshall Plan in France and Italy, 1948–1950: Counterpart Fund Negotiations', (unpublished dissertation, State University of New York at Stonybrook, 1985). Also, Irwin Wall, *L'Influence américaine sur la politique francaise*, op. cit.
47. See Jean-Pierre Rioux, *The Fourth Republic, 1944–58* (Cambridge, 1987) 180.
48. See the discussions in John Sheahan, *Promotion and Control of Industry in Postwar France* (Cambridge, Mass., 1963), and Warren C. Baum, *The French Economy and the State* (Princeton, N.J., 1958).
49. Mioche, *Le Plan Monnet*, 218–49.
50. Baum, *The French Economy and the State*, 23, 58, 346. The quote appears on p. 346.
51. Annie Lacroix-Riz, 'Credits américains et coopération européene (1949–1954)', in Patrick Fridenson et André Straus, *Le Capitalisme francais, 19e–20e siécle: Blocages et dynamisme d'une croissance* (Paris, 1987) 327–53; Alan Milward, *The Reconstruction of Western Europe*, 391.
52. Raymond Poidevin, *Robert Schuman, homme d'Etat, 1886–1963* (Paris, 1986) 249–72.
53. George Ball, *The Past Has Another Pattern: Memoirs* (New York, 1982); Papiers Jean Monnet, Dossier G. W. Ball, AMG 10/6.
54. FRUS, 1950, III, Western Europe, 22 July, 1950.
55. FJM, AMI, 4/2/3, Memorandum-Project by Jean Monnet.
56. AN, F60 ter 415 (1), 'Note sure le financement du réarmement', 31 July, 1950; also see memoranda of 16 and 19 August, 1950.
57. FRUS, 1950, III, Western Europe, 28 July, 1950, 152.
58. FRUS, 1950, III, Western Europe, 3 August, 1950, 182; 8 August, 1950, 190; 11 August, 1950, 206; 16 August, 1950, 213; 2 September, 1950, 261.
59. Archives Nationales, F 60 ter 415 (1), Note of 18 September, 1950. One can only speculate as to whether Monnet was the author of this note. But its link to his proposal of a European Defense Community is apparent. Monnet wrote in his *Memoirs* that he informed Pleven that 'we must resolutely oppose America's present policy', p. 345.
60. Jean Monnet, *Memoirs*, 346.
61. See Edward Fursdon, *The European Defense Community: A History* (New York, 1980). Also Irwin Wall, *L'Influence américaine sur la politique francaise, 1945–1954*, op. cit.
62. On 1 February 1952, Monnet wrote to Schuman that Indochina was

costing France 400 billion francs: 'It is exactly this amount that we are going to ask of the United States in order to permit us to make our contribution of 14 divisions to the defense of Europe.' The Indochina burden must be shared, Monnet said, in order for France to pull its weight in Europe. *Jean Monnet–Robert Schuman Correspondance*, op. cit., 129–30.

4 Gray Eminence
Richard Mayne

He had his back turned when I first saw him – a stocky figure in an old brown overcoat and a gray broad-brimmed hat. He had just come in, and was speaking on the telephone. His voice was dry, husky, and quick.

'*Très bien*, and don't forget the chicken for eight o'clock.' Then, picking up the receiver again: 'Get me Adenauer.' Waiting for the call, he turned to greet me. Under the hat, his face was ruddy. His eyebrows were raised over hooded, twinkling eyes. He had a small clipped mustache. He looked faintly Chinese and very like a peasant. '*Comment ça va?*' His handshake was firm and friendly.

We were standing in an old-fashioned apartment on the Avenue Foch in Paris, overlooking the Bois de Boulogne. The ancient elevator creaked; so did the parquet flooring. The double doors were glazed and covered with lace curtains. In such a setting, telephones seemed as incongruous as typewriters, steel desks, and filing cabinets. The place might have been requisitioned by some occupying force. In a sense it had, for these few crowded rooms were the headquarters of a multinational political group whose aim was to transform Europe. Its members were the non-Communist and non-Gaullist parties and labor unions of the six countries then forming the European Community: France, Germany, Italy, Belgium, The Netherlands, and Luxembourg. Its title, a touch rhetorical, was the Action Committee for a United States of Europe. Its work was practical, thorough, and effective. Its founder and president was post-war Europe's gray eminence, Jean Monnet.

At that time, in 1956, Monnet was sixty-seven, and looked about fifty-five. He was already a legend. 'Mr. Europe' was one of his press nicknames; 'the father of Europe' was another. He demurred at both. 'Don't you mean grandfather?' he asked an interviewer. He disliked metaphors: but this one was apt. Parenthood takes two; and Monnet believed in collective action. His role was that of catalyst. In 1950, he had persuaded Robert Schuman, the French foreign minister, to propose the Schuman Plan for a European Coal and Steel Community. To some, coal and steel seemed technical. To Monnet, they were raw materials for war which could now be used to secure the peace. A mere five years after World War II had ended, Monnet was proposing that former enemies join forces – that France and Germany 'place the whole of Franco-German coal and steel production under a common High Authority open to the participation of the other countries of Europe'. Soon, France and Germany were joined by Italy, Belgium, the Netherlands, and Luxembourg. Monnet chaired the conference to negotiate a treaty, and became the first president of the coal-steel 'High Authority'.

This, in his view, was only a beginning. Some weeks after launching the Schuman Plan, Monnet had proposed to René Pleven, the French premier, the Pleven Plan for a European Defense Community with a supranational army. As things turned out, it was too much too soon. In 1954, bitterly attacked by the extremes of both Left and Right, the Defense Community treaty failed to pass the French National Assembly. With it, a further project collapsed – the draft treaty for a Political Community, worked out by Europe's parliamentarians.

At that point, many feared that the whole enterprise of uniting Europe would come to a halt. But Monnet was not easily discouraged. Within a few months, leading Europeans were discussing what they called 'the relaunching of Europe'. By this they meant two new proposals from Monnet – although, as usual, he was promoting them through powerful intermediaries: the Dutch foreign minister, Johan Willem Beyen, and his Belgian counterpart Paul-Henri Spaak. The first plan was for Euratom, an Atomic Energy Community to control the peaceful applications of nuclear technology. The second was for the European Economic Community, the so-called Common Market.

By now, Monnet had left the High Authority and was recruiting his Action Committee. Month after month, while governments discussed the new projects and parliaments debated the eventual treaties, the Action Committee maintained its pressure. When the new Communities began, it kept in close touch with their executive bodies, smoothing out political problems, suggesting useful initiatives, and helping to ensure parliamentary and trade-union support. Behind the scenes, Monnet worked assiduously to initiate equal partnership between the European Community and the United States; he also, despite many setbacks, at length succeeded in enlarging the Community to include Britain, Denmark, and Ireland. His last political achievement before he died in 1979 at the age of ninety was to persuade the Community's governments to turn their regular summit meetings into a permanent institution – the European Council. Privately, Monnet saw this as a provisional government. One of its first acts was to confer on him the title of Honorary Citizen of Europe.

Such is the traditional story. It smacks a little of the pious *image d'Epinal*. 'If a united Europe is created in our time', wrote Theodore White, 'then Jean Monnet will probably be revered centuries hence as its patron saint.' Perhaps he will. But he was more complex than many saints or than most hagiographers; and even if he had never pioneered the uniting of Europe, his role in world events would have earned him a place in history. By the time that he was president of the European Community's first executive, he had reached an age at which others contemplate retirement, and he had already pursued an astonishing career.

In two world wars, Monnet made a crucial contribution to the cause of the Allies. In the first, while still in his twenties, he persuaded the French Prime Minister to stop Britain and France bidding against each other for scarce supplies; and he was put in charge of their joint efforts. After World War I, he helped to promote the League of Nations, and became its Deputy Secretary-General. He left to rescue and reorganize the Monnet family business, then became an international banker and adviser to governments. In Sweden he helped to liquidate the Kreuger match empire: in Shanghai, he raised capital for the Chinese railroads. Along the way, he contracted a runaway marriage.

As World War II approached, Monnet secured for France much-needed American aircraft, later allotted to Britain. In 1939, he was once more appointed to coordinate Anglo-French supplies. In 1940, with France on the brink of capitulation, he persuaded de Gaulle and Churchill to back his abortive plan for a Franco-British union which would have kept her in the war. Soon afterward, he went to Washington – as a British civil servant, with his French passport endorsed by Churchill himself. He coined President Roosevelt's slogan 'the arsenal of democracy', and played a key part in the subsequent Victory Program. In Algiers, in 1943, he managed to reconcile de Gaulle and General Giraud, preventing discord and possible bloodshed in France. As a member of de Gaulle's provisional government, he proposed and then headed the postwar Commissariat du Plan. He was involved in the Marshall Plan; and in 1951 he was even recruited by NATO's Atlantic Council as one of 'three wise men' – another was Averell Harriman – to assess the economic effect of the Western Alliance.

Monnet's multifarious activities earned him innumerable tributes. Lord Keynes believed that he had helped to shorten World War II by a whole year. Konrad Adenauer called him 'a true man of peace'. For Willy Brandt he was 'a wise counsellor'; for Edward Heath 'a constant source of inspiration'. Dean Acheson described him as 'one of the greatest of Frenchmen'; and the United States diplomat Robert Murphy, who once clashed with Monnet, nevertheless thought him 'in many respects more remarkable than de Gaulle'.

De Gaulle's relations with Monnet were sporadic, but more friendly than some people supposed. In 1953, attacking the project for a European Defense Community, de Gaulle lampooned Monnet – without naming him – as 'the inspirer' of 'supranational monstrosities'. A few years later, I remember, Monnet turned from listening to de Gaulle on the radio and exclaimed, '*il est fou!*' But this was a momentary outburst. When the General died, it happened to be Monnet's birthday; and he frowned with real pain at any tasteless allusion to 'birthday presents'. When I asked him whether de Gaulle had helped or hindered the uniting of Europe, Monnet was silent for nearly half a minute. Then he said: 'I think both'.

They had first met in the dark days of 1940. One evening in June, de Gaulle and his aide-de-camp Geoffroy de Courcel came to dine in Monnet's London apartment. When they arrived, Monnet was still in his office. In his memoirs he described how his wife Silvia had welcomed the General, then asked how long his mission in London would last. 'I am not here on a mission, Madame', de Gaulle replied: 'I am here to save the honor of France.' In conversation, Monnet added a piquant detail. Madame Monnet had been sitting on one side of the fireplace, de Courcel on the other. Standing between them, tall and austere, de Gaulle drew from his pocket the text of his next day's broadcast to France. But, instead of giving it to Madame Monnet, he passed it to Courcel, who had to get up, walk round, and hand it to her. It was a gesture worthy of a head of state.

That night, Monnet told me, he came to the conclusion that de Gaulle was at least as concerned for France's postwar future as for the urgent task of winning the war. This may have been hindsight. Then and later, the two men certainly talked at length about what should be done. When Anglo-French union proved impossible, de Gaulle set up his French National Committee in London as the new 'legitimate authority of France'. Monnet, as he wrote later, would have preferred 'a less dramatic attitude and a less personalized form of action': he feared that the London committee, under British protection, might alienate support in metropolitan and overseas France. When at length he decided to leave London for the United States, he received a note from the General. 'Our fundamental aim is the same', de Gaulle wrote, 'and perhaps together we can do great things.'

The chance came again in 1943, when Monnet was in Algiers – officially to advise General Giraud, but in fact to prevent a clash between him and General de Gaulle. On 30 May, de Gaulle arrived from London. That night, at his villa, Monnet talked privately with him. 'His character', Monnet noted,

> had not changed since I had seen him in London in 1940: it was the same mixture of a practical intelligence that could only command respect, and a disquieting tendency to overstep the bounds of common sense. He was by turns intimate, using his undoubted charm, and distant, impervious to argument when carried away by patriotic honor or personal pride. I agreed with his analysis of things, but only up to a point: beyond that point I could no longer follow him in his bursts of egocentricity.

Monnet worked with de Gaulle on the Algiers Committee

of National Liberation – 'the central authority of France', it claimed; later it became the provisional government. But before long, at his own request, he returned to the United States to secure further supplies for France. After the liberation, he divided his time between America and Paris; and it was in Washington, in August 1945, that he proposed to de Gaulle the idea of a French economic plan. 'You speak of greatness', he said, 'but today the French are small. There will only be greatness when the French are of a stature to warrant it.' He concluded: 'Everyone must be associated in an investment and modernization plan.' The General agreed. 'That is what has to be done', he declared, 'and that is the name for it.' And it was – although most Frenchmen came to call it the Monnet Plan.

On 21 December 1945, General de Gaulle signed the decree establishing the Planning Commissariat. A month later, he resigned. Never again were he and Monnet to work together. Only once, after the General's return to power in 1958, was there even the hint that they might do so. Monnet described it to me years later, when I asked him how he had felt on hearing that de Gaulle had died. I myself was torn, I said: I couldn't help feeling a certain regret.

Monnet thought for a moment, then said reflectively: 'Ah, yes, he wasn't a great statesman, but he was a great man. He found France in the abyss; he pulled her out . . . You know, I made a mistake. I ought to have talked with him, tried to convince him.'

'While he was out of office, you mean?'

'Yes. It was a mistake. I might perhaps have been able to convince him. He understood our affairs very well. He got the point.' Monnet paused. 'But delegating authority – for him, that wasn't possible. For him, France was himself. So, to delegate part of national sovereignty, that wasn't possible; it would have been giving up a part of himself. It wasn't to be done – he couldn't. It would have been giving part of his own flesh.'

'As in *The Merchant of Venice*.'

'Yes. He couldn't do it. But I ought to have tried. I was wrong.'

It was then that Monnet mentioned their later meeting, at an official reception, when de Gaulle was president of

France. 'I suggested to him how he could become president of the European Republic. He could announce a referendum, get himself elected for two years, and then it could be Adenauer's turn.'

'What happened?'

'He asked me to go and see him. I explained the idea. He called in members of his staff. But he didn't do it: he couldn't. Then, at the end, we were alone, and he said to me: "Would you like a more active life?" He was asking me if I'd like to work with him. So I said,' – and here Monnet chuckled – '"You know that I'm interested in only one thing – Europe." And he said: "Yes, that's it." But I didn't do it. Perhaps I should have done. I don't know.'

'Do you think it might have worked? You sold him the French Plan. Perhaps you could have sold him Europe.'

'Perhaps. But I don't think so.'

He was almost certainly right. Knowing Monnet, I could hardly imagine a greater contrast than with the tall, aloof, formal, eloquent, and solitary de Gaulle. One Frenchman who worked for them both at different times declared: 'With the General, you feel like the least intelligent of men. With Monnet, your intelligence seems to grow.' It did, because he challenged it. For many, de Gaulle was an oracle: Monnet was eager for discussion – with heads of state or doormen, on equal terms. De Gaulle, steeped in history, was skeptical of progress. Monnet, the advocate of change, knew little of the past and detested changes in his own environment; but he had a profound sense of the transformations wrought by time. The very way he pronounced that word in English – 'It takes ta-a-ahm' – was a talisman of patience.

De Gaulle, for all his hopeful rhetoric, was surely a pessimist. Near the close of his life, he told André Malraux: 'The question is no longer whether France will save Europe, but to understand that the death of Europe threatens the death of France.' As they went to the door, the General shook hands and looked up at the first stars emerging in the night. 'For me', he said, 'they confirm the insignificance of things.'

In Monnet's eyes, life was too precious to be insignificant. The world was full of trouble. People were poor, hungry, maltreated; violence threatened peace. One man alone could hardly alter things, nor could one nation. It would take collective effort, and time. The real difficulty was knowing how to begin. And having begun, continue; even setbacks could be helpful, provided that one learned from them. To be discouraged was self-centered and pointless in the face of the facts – 'necessity', as Monnet would say. Twice I happened to talk with him after the failure of important ventures. On one occasion I asked: 'Are you disappointed?' 'I'm never disappointed', he answered – in a disappointed voice. Earlier, when de Gaulle had just blocked Britain's first bid to join the European Community, I remarked: *'C'est déprimant'*. Monnet looked up quickly, blinked, and said: *'Non: c'est attristant'* – then went on discussing what to do next.

With America overshadowing the Western world, de Gaulle sought greatness for France in an independent Europe of sovereign nations – *l'Europe des états*. Monnet liked and respected American virtues, and his feelings were returned. He loved France, more deeply than some people realized; but saw her future best assured in a Europe united enough to be an equal partner of the United States. This made some commentators describe him as a federalist: but he himself was sparing with the term. Like 'the United States of Europe', 'federalist' was a useful slogan to help a whole generation discard old habits of thought; and for a time Monnet certainly believed that Europe could be united under a supranational government. Twenty years later, he privately admitted: 'At the beginning, we were wrong.' What had emerged in the European Community was what he called 'a permanent dialogue' between the national governments and the central common institutions: the Commission, the European Parliament, and the Court. That dialogue, in Monnet's view, was part of a civilizing process whereby nation-states were coming to accept the supremacy of law, as fellow citizens do. It was the fulfillment of his old maxim: 'We are not forming coalitions of states, but uniting people.' His favorite anthology was Robert Bridge's *Spirit of Man*; and one of his favorite quotations was from the Swiss philosopher Henri-Frédéric Amiel:

Each person's experience starts again from the beginning. Only institutions grow wiser. They accumulate collective experience; and, because of this experience and wisdom, people who accept common rules find that while their own nature remains unaltered, their behavior is gradually transformed.[1]

From Monnet, such literary allusions were rare. His peasant appearance was not wholly misleading, for he came of solid, prosperous, peasant stock. Born in Cognac, the home of brandy, on the Charente River midway between Angoulême and the Bay of Biscay, he had grown up in that quiet, staid, rather somber town, its walls still blackened by the microscopic fungus which thrives on alcohol fumes. All around lie the vineyards. The brandy-grape area of the Grande Champagne, as Monnet would point out, is no bigger than 250 square miles, yet it grows more than a hundred different varieties of grapes. 'Isn't it clear', asked Monnet, 'why the French are such individualists?'

Wherever his work took him later in life, Monnet usually sought a home outside the center of town. Even in the miniature city of Luxembourg, when he was president of the European Coal and Steel Community's High Authority, he took a house at Bricherhof overlooking meadows and woods. When he worked in Paris, he lived nearly thirty miles away to the southwest, at Houjarray, in a stone-floored farmhouse with a view across the fields to the forest of Rambouillet. He was alarmed at one time when he heard that Brigitte Bardot planned to buy a house nearby; but it turned out that she too was intent on peace and quiet. Most other neighbors were farmers. One of them owned a field adjoining Monnet's property, making it an awkward shape. Monnet's predecessor had tried to buy the field, but its owner had refused to sell. 'So long as I have this bit of land', he said, 'I can say *"Merde!"* to anyone.' Faced with this same refusal, Monnet bought a better piece of land elsewhere in the village and offered it in exchange. The bargain was struck instantly. Like had dealt with like.

Every morning, wherever he was, Monnet rose at seven, put on sturdy brown boots, a thick pair of trousers, a sweater and scarf, a hat, and an old dun-colored 'windcheater', and stumped off on a walk, usually alone. 'That's when I work', he explained. Walking with him could be unnerving. He would take one's arm, then stop and turn about, lost in thought. Conversation might become a spasmodic monologue. Others, too, could be disconcerted by Monnet's early-morning habits. Once, at a hotel in London, he went for his walk in the park while the night porter was still on duty. When he came back in his country clothes, the day porter could hardly believe that this humbly dressed figure was one of the hotel's guests.

As a boy, Monnet had briefly wanted to be a boxer. I once asked him why: was it because boxing was a conflict tamed by rules? He was tempted by the plausible answer; but he typically thought it 'too intellectual'. At school in Cognac, he had disliked academic study, and had never gone to a university. At the age of eighteen, when he went to North America as a salesman for the family brandy firm, his father had advised him: 'Don't take any books. No one can do your thinking for you.' In Paris, Monnet's room was full of books, many of them donated and inscribed by their authors; but he was no great reader, except of newspapers. Nor, unlike de Gaulle, was Monnet a fluent writer. He scribbled notes continually, in rapid 'debased copperplate' handwriting on small pink memo pads; but they tended to peter out in half-sentences linked by dashes. As he once told me, 'I can't write but I know how to correct.' He certainly did. One crucial draft I helped to work on with him – a European policy statement eventually adopted by the twenty-one political parties and fourteen labor unions of his Action Committee – went through 140 versions. Nor was Monnet a polished public speaker. He described de Gaulle, admiringly, as '*un grand acteur*'; but his own small voice was unsuited to oratory. Its huskiness bothered him: to improve it, he went to such Alpine spas as Challes-les-Eaux. On a platform, he looked flushed and ill-at-ease.

But he always heeded the rest of his father's parting advice: 'Look out of the window, talk with people. Pay attention to your neighbor'. As a traveling salesman in tough, remote frontier towns, Monnet acquired Anglo-American affability. Speaking French, he was often hard, cool, and aloof. When he switched to English with a faint American accent, his personality seemed to change: he would grin and chuckle, become one of the boys. '*Nous ne sommes pas des enfants de choeur*', he was fond of saying – roughly, 'we're no angels'; and in British or American company he could sound piratical and racy. In Washington during World War II, he confessed, he read crime novels by Peter Cheyney, and borrowed a saying from their hero Lemmy Caution: 'Whenever I don't know what to do, I get into trouble'. There was even a hint of fascination in the way he spoke of Ivar Kreuger, the finally fraudulent Swedish 'match king'. I was hardly surprised when a British diplomat, in private, called Monnet 'an adventurer'. Another thought he looked like 'a mixture of gangster and conspirator'.

Monnet's scapegrace nature emerged in stray remarks. Invited to preface a friend's book, he asked a colleague to prepare a draft. 'Nothing could give me greater pleasure', it began. 'Nonsense!' said Monnet. 'I can think of forty things.' One spring day in 1973, the Action Committee was meeting in the Berlaymont, the steel, glass, and concrete headquarters of the European Community's executive arm. As I guided Monnet through the labyrinth, I gestured at the rows of offices and the functionaries hurrying to and fro. 'Isn't it odd to think that all this was once just a piece of paper on your desk?' Monnet's eyebrows rose. 'Yes, it's extraordinary.' Then, with a smile: 'It's appalling.' In his crowded Paris office, on another day, he found me ankle-deep in books, papers, and box files: the contents of a cupboard had collapsed. I pulled a face at the mess, but Monnet grinned. 'Nothing ever gets done except in disorder,' he said.

He was only partly joking. Order could mean habit or tradition. Fresh thought would often start in perplexity – trying out countless approaches to the same crux. Monnet's intentness was infectious. When he embarked on any venture, it was because he saw it as the most urgent task in the world. It might involve great labor, long argument and investigation, regardless of the time of day. Sometimes, it meant working all night. Accordingly, when Monnet was due to catch a plane, his secretary took the precaution of booking him on several alternative flights, often in the names of colleagues or friends. A reporter who had known him as a young man at the League of Nations – 'short, quick, mysterious, with great charm and a sparkle in his brown eyes' – noted how even then he ignored office hours and administrative routine. Dossiers piled up on his desk unread: he preferred to talk with his informants, assessing them, weighing their words, checking one against another, plying them with questions which more bookish people would have called Socratic.

It was a banker's method. Monnet lived frugally. With any meal, he took no more than a small glass of wine. As he grew older, he gave up smoking and barely touched even brandy. 'If I were condemned to death', he once told me, 'I'd ask for *this* as my last meal.' 'This' was a plate of cold canned sardines, with butter, French bread, and *haricots verts*. Yet, despite his simple tastes, Monnet was also at home in the world of first-class travel and chauffer-driven limousines. For official occasions, he wore dapper dark-blue suits made for him by his London tailors. At luncheon in his Avenue Foch office, his own chauffeur served as a footman. On visits to London, he enjoyed roast beef and the solid, mahogany-and-leather atmosphere of old-world hotels and restaurants. On the way to Simpson's-in-the-Strand one evening in a rather slow taxicab, he looked through the window at the razzle-dazzle near Picadilly Circus, all fast food and one-arm bandits. '*C'est horrible tout ça!*' he exclaimed, with distaste and nostalgia in his voice.

Monnet's years as a merchant banker had marked him in other ways too. Many of his closest friends came from the same profession. English banking terms like 'swap arrangement', 'bond issue', or 'line of credit' might suddenly crop up when he was speaking French. And at crucial moments he would demand 'a balance sheet'. How many aircraft could the Allies muster in World War II, compared with the enemy? At the time, astonishingly, no one knew. When the facts were assembled, the need for action was clear.

Most of all, Monnet had a banker's flair and discretion. He inspired confidence, and knew in whom to place it. People in all walks of life, including such statesmen as John F. Kennedy, would consult Monnet as they might a banker or lawyer who was also a family friend. 'I don't know why', he said, with not quite genuine bewilderment: 'I always say the same thing.' But they knew that secrets would be safe with him; that he would leave them to take the decision and the credit; and that any advice he gave would be honest and worth considering – even if they finally rejected it. He was not always right or successful, as he freely admitted. One example was his suggestion to Lyndon Johnson that Israel and her Arab neighbors be encouraged to work together on desalinated water supplies – a variant of the Schuman Plan for the Middle East. The United States never took up the idea; but, as Monnet pointed out, 'Unless you try, you'll never know if you might after all have succeeded.'

Persistence was a quality that Monnet had inherited and learned. The maturing of brandy took constant patient attention. So did international understanding. Monnet used to smile when recalling that his maternal grandmother had been known in the family as 'Marie la Rabâcheuse' – Monotonous Mary. 'I think she had only a few simple ideas', he said, 'and to those she held fast.' He remembered her example when he was in China, confronting a wall of polite delay. An old friend advised him: 'Don't try to understand the Chinese; you never will. Just stick to what you want, and make your actions conform to your words.' Monnet heeded the advice – so well that Chiang Kai-shek detected 'something Chinese' about him. 'Don't waste your time speculating about what other people "really think,"' he insisted. 'Look at what they do. Decide on your objective, then think out how to reach it.'

On Monnet's desk, tucked into the corner of a photograph of his daughter, was a bent picture postcard of the primitive *Kon-Tiki* raft, on which Thor Heyerdahl and his companions had crossed the Atlantic. In 1954, when Monnet's plan for a European army was facing a crisis, he took a whole day off to spend with Heyerdahl. 'Those young men,' he said, 'chose their course, and then they set out. They knew that they could not turn back. Whatever the difficulties, they had only one option – to go on.'

To the end of his life Monnet went on pursuing the goal of international peace. He was not always solemn about it. One day in London, we were lunching at his favorite hotel. He had just succeeded in another effort of persuasion, this time involving the prime ministers of Britain and France. He was pleased and expansive. 'You know', he said, 'the world we live in is very complex. We can't solve problems by tackling them head-on. We have to change their context. We have to find the point where a change can be made – a change that

will go on by itself and change other things too. Once we find
that essential point, everything else follows. It's difficult.' He
laughed. 'That's why we worked for six months on this
business. When I showed it to our friend in London, he said:
"All great ideas are simple." That paper we had the other day
– it was good: it went into all the details. But it wasn't
convincing. To convince, you have to be simple. It's easy to
have ideas. What's difficult is to get people to act on them.'

A waiter appeared. 'Would you care for a sweet, Sir?' 'Just
a coffee', we both said. 'Decaffeinated', Monnet added.
Another waiter brought a trolley full of trifles, *gâteaux*, fruit
salad, and *crème caramel*. 'I'm tempted', I said. 'So am I', said
Monnet. 'When you see them, it's different.'

Three other memories remain. At Monnet's eightieth
birthday party, friends from many countries gathered at
Houjarray. I looked across the table at Monnet, sitting with
Etienne Hirsch, his assistant and successor on the French
Plan, and later president of Euratom. Different as they were
– Hirsch the Jewish engineer, Monnet the Charentais entre-
preneur – the two of them nonetheless looked like cousins:
both short and compact, no longer young, both with clear
bright eyes, both smiling. Hirsch raised his glass and stood
up. 'To Jean', he said. 'Without him, some of us might not be
alive.'

Monnet's last political act was to publish his memoirs. At
his request, I translated them. As I wrote, I could hear his
voice in my head, virtually dictating the text. He was pleased
with the outcome: Madame Monnet thought it 'more like
Jean than the original'. He asked me to go and see him, in the
familiar farmhouse sitting-room, surrounded by his wife's
paintings. It was quarter of a century since his first book, *Les
Etats-unis d'Europe ont commencé*, had helped persuade me to
join his cause. Now Monnet was frail, and could no longer
read; but he talked as in the past. We both knew that we were
saying good-bye. As I rose to leave, he took my hand in both
of his – and then amazed me. '*Je vous donne ma bénédiction*', he
said.

Not long afterward, on 20 March, 1979, Monnet's family
and friends gathered once more, in a small country church-
yard near his home. They came from at least two continents. The Federal German Chancellor had attended the

funeral service; so had the President of France. At first, the hymns and prayers had seemed incongruous, as if the Church were claiming Monnet for its own. His sister worked for the Catholic hierarchy, and he had greatly admired Pope John; but, with colleagues at least, he had seldom spoken of God, or death, or eternity. Yet, on reflection, there was justice in the claim. What had been Monnet's secret? His wisdom? His patience? His great intelligence? His persuasive skill? Underlying them all, it seems to me, was something simpler and more mysterious: moral and spiritual strength. In the end, it was Monnet's goodness that made him unique.

NOTE

1.   Monnet quoted Amiel on this point in his *Memoirs* (New York, 1978), 393.

5 Jean Monnet and the European Coal and Steel Community: A Preliminary Appraisal
John Gillingham

On 9 May 1950 French Foreign Minister Robert Schuman – reading formally from a text inspired and drafted by Jean Monnet – proposed to pool the heavy industries of his nation with those of her neighbors in order to form what would later be called the European Coal and Steel Community (ECSC).[1] In April 1951 negotiations for the proposed organization concluded. Its executive organ, the High Authority (HA), began operations in August of the following year. Monnet served as President of the HA until June 1955 when his resignation, initially submitted in November 1954, officially took effect. The ECSC was Monnet's greatest accomplishment: it set in motion the process that transformed Europe from a continent historically divided by nationalism into an emergent civilization formed by common economic institutions and animated by a common political spirit.[2]

Jean Monnet had learned from experience during World War I, long before most of his contemporaries, that for France, Great Britain, and all other European countries, international coordination of economic and political policy was a prerequisite for national survival; without it economic growth would be stifled, war would become likely, and dependence on external powers inevitable.[3] Though Monnet must often have been deeply discouraged, he never despaired: neither the protracted nightmare of Depression, nor the drift towards war, nor defeat, destruction and collapse caused him to give up hope that for Europe an age of peace, progress, and prosperity was within reach.[4] The American production miracle during World War II strengthened this conviction: where we had mobilized our economy for war, however, he would mobilize those of France and Europe for peace.[5] The French Plan de Modernisation et d'Equipement founded in 1946 was the first step in this direction, the coal-steel pool proposed in 1950 the second.

Neither the Schuman Plan negotiations nor the ECSC developed as intended, however. Though in his lifetime already known as the 'Architect of European Unity' – a sobriquet that must have made the outwardly modest man blush – Europe was not built according to Monnet's blueprints; the ECSC looked and operated differently from what he had in mind and was of only limited value in further European construction: as a model it was rejected by the statesmen who organized the European Economic Community, or Common Market, in 1957. Yet Monnet deserves singular credit for having made the breakthrough from an unhappy past into a new and better age; he was the indispensable link between Europe and the United States at a time when an ancient civilization needed the aid and guidance of a young one.[6] Without him the unification process would have started later, been slower, perhaps never even have begun.

When France proclaimed to an astonished and excited world, her readiness to pool the nation's heavy industries with any and all European powers, the unprepossessing but magnetic man of the Rue de Martignac had by then also already demonstrated through the operations of the Commissariat du Plan that his nation need not be forever trapped in the Malthusian outlooks and structures that had retarded growth between the wars: industry *could* be re-equipped and the latest technologies introduced. At the same time, modernization required more than re-tooling plant and introducing the latest technologies; closer and better forms of cooperation were needed between the state and private enterprise, new European markets would be opened, and businessmen taught to look to the future instead of the past.[7]

These considerations mandated a freeing up of trade and finance, and therefore also staunch support of the European Recovery Program (ERP) sponsored by the Marshall Plan. Though skeptical that a collective body like the US-sponsored Organization for European Economic Cooperation (OEEC) could act decisively to cut down the maze of laws and enactments carefully planted, and for decades nurtured and trimmed to protect the economies of Europe, Monnet stood out as unique among leading European statesmen in his steadfast support of the American attempt.[8] The simple truth was that to modernize industrially France needed a liberalized Europe.

A huge, dark threat nonetheless clouded the prospect: liberalization would inevitably result in the economic revival of France's conqueror and tormentor. Protection from the ex-Reich (and especially the coal and steel industries of its economic heartland) was a readily understandable French obsession, and security the main concern of France's foreign policy after World War II. Its formulators were highly intelligent men, who after 1918 had discovered the futility of pursuing a purely negative policy of threats, sanctions, and military force. Nor did they imagine that Europe could be rebuilt economically and politically in the absence of a Germany; the French never considered anything like the Morgenthau Plan. Yet France could do little on her own after 1945; the nation was weak and discredited, needed time to mend, and depended on the United States for survival.[9]

FRENCH POLICY ON GERMANY

The overriding objective of France's policy towards Germany was to gain time until it had recovered economically and politically. Both the foreign office and the French military government in Germany therefore did their utmost to perpetuate Allied Four Power control over the defeated enemy while at the same time using their veto power, along with other means at their disposal, to make it as ineffective as possible. This approach generated more smoke than fire: contrary to the case first prosecuted so vigorously by the historian John Gimbel, division between the US and USSR, rather than disagreements within the emerging Western alliance, were what blocked and ultimately prevented German reunification. The policy of obstructionism was sometimes counterproductive as well. It indirectly caused shortages of Ruhr coal that impaired the recovery of the national economy and further deprived France of a voice in the management of the Ruhr after the formation of Bizonia by the United States and Great Britain in January 1947. Yet French *Ruhrpolitik* was consensual supported by Foreign Minister Bidault, the foreign office, and Monnet himself. If French men and women were unanimous about any one single thing, it was to keep the Germans on a short leash.[10]

The most decisive change in France's policy towards the people east of the Rhine during the five years after the war was not the Schuman Plan but an order of Foreign Minister Bidault in January 1948. It came in response to the announcement of a joint US-UK plan to restore control of Ruhr mines and mills to German owners; to the French the action of the bizonal partners meant that the end of the occupation was in sight. Bidault therefore ordered all government representatives to stop exploiting the ex-enemy and start treating him like a future friend: the time had come, he said, to begin the work of reconciliation. The new departure was first evident at the official level in complicated integration schemes drafted by the diplomats of the Quai, and manifest as well in orders issued by Monnet and other senior officials to institute interministerial cooperation with German counterparts. Of at least equal importance in the long run was the attempt begun at the same time to restore private business contacts.[11]

The Locarno Treaty of 1926, which ushered in the era of Franco-German cooperation that ended abruptly during the depression, had a durable economic counterpart in the International Steel Cartel (ISC). Also formed in 1926 but renewed in 1933 with governmental encouragement, operational during the years of rearmament, and perpetuated in a new guise under the wartime occupation, the ISC had forged strong bonds between the steel producers of Lorraine and the Ruhr long before VE-Day. After 1945 all German cartels were officially abolished and international agreements became null and void. At the same time, the occupation governments were no more able than their predecessors during and before the war to dispense with the valuable administrative services of the old coal and steel syndicates; though officially proscribed, they lived on. In the Ruhr, as well as in France, the foundations for a revived West European steel producers' union remained intact.[12]

German producers nonetheless had a very insecure existence. The Allies remained pledged to a variety of policies which, though contradictory, all threatened to eliminate the smoke-stack barons. Among them were nationalization, decartelization, and, worst of all, the campaign for dismantlement, which began in November of 1947 and would continue in high gear for twenty-four months.[13] While it was running, however, French producers started trying to restore contact with their old cartel partner. Ruhr industry was willing to meet them at least half-way. Long before the Schuman Plan announcement German managers had developed plans to resurrect a modified version of the old Western European heavy industry cartel, at one point proposing that as a first step towards its formation the French take over the giant Ruhr steel producer, Vereinigte Stahlwerke.[14] Unless, however, the Allies relinquished the power to decartelize German heavy industry, set limits on its production, and nullify its future investment plans, a return to business as usual could not have begun. Though the sharp downturn on steel markets of late 1949 brought cartelization into the limelight for the first time since the war, discussion of the issue was premature.[15] An industrial restoration was impossible until the controls overhanging the mines and mills of the Ruhr had been lifted.

It was difficult for any of the Western Allies to restore normal diplomatic relations with the ex-enemy. The Soviets had little to do with the problem; tricked into rejecting the Marshall Plan, they were not invited to the London Conference of 1948 at which the United States, Great Britain and France agreed upon the general structure of the West German state, and more particularly set up a new International Ruhr Authority (IRA) to govern the industries of the coal-steel complex. IRA was ultimately supposed to develop into a common agency for Western European heavy industry. Disagreements, between the Allies and new Adenauer government, as well as conflicts among themselves, nonetheless prevented IRA from developing into anything more than a paper organization. It was a wholly unsatisfactory basis for settling the Ruhr Problem.[16]

The Saar Problem also remained unresolved. This secondary area of coal and steel production had been incorporated into the French customs zone after 1918 and remained there until in the plebiscite of 1935 its German-speaking population opted with near-unanimity for the Nazi Reich. After 1945 the French, their *amour-propre* wounded, were intent upon administering the region indefinitely, while the young and untried federal government, installed in Bonn in June 1949, insisted equally on a policy of the Saar's return – *Heim in die Bundesrepublik!* – in a desperate effort to establish its credentials as protector of German national interests.[17]

Against this background the French Foreign Minister Robert Schuman, a man of the Franco-German border committed deeply to reconciliation, made the first official trip to Bonn in January 1950. Vainly attempting to rally domestic support behind his policy of *détente*, he demanded that Germany cede France a fifty-year lease over the disputed territory, in return alluding only to future concessions. The meeting broke up in frosty disaccord. Chancellor Adenauer's blundering attempt a month later to convey goodwill by telling the American journalist Kingsbury Smith that West Germany wanted to merge and form a single state with France only increased the distance between the two: Marianne recoiled with shuddering horror to the overeager and inept suitor.[18]

The French and Germans could hardly have acted by themselves: Bonn and Paris had to make policy over Washington. Uncertainty and confusion in the American capital were behind the lack of improvement in relations between the two Western European nations. Though for five years the United States had been goading the statesmen of the collapsed civilization to overcome the ruinous nationalisms of the past and enter some form of economic and political union, we lacked both method and means. While speaking interchangeably of integration, unification, and federalization on the abstract level, our policy really aimed at the hopelessly remote objective of organizing a European customs union.[19]

Nor could we imagine European unification taking place without Britain, even though the UK stubbornly refused to play the federalizing role cast for it in American policy. The British wanted nothing less than to be catapulted into the brave new technology-driven world of open markets and competition envisaged by the progressive businessmen, lawyers, and economists who made foreign policy for the Truman administration, and nothing more than to trick the Americans into restoring the easygoing ways of the late-empire. Every right-thinking crown subject would, more-over, have considered obscene the mere suggestion that their heroic island nation was but one component in a pan-continental entity called Europe. Without the British, 'integration' was stalled: no American policy-maker believed that the French could ever become strong enough to control the Teutons or hold their own in any purely continental institution. Even though the September 1949 pound de-valuation shook Washington's confidence in the British, Washington's many subsequent entreaties to Foreign Minis-ter Schuman to take the initiative in dealing with the ex-enemy were half-hearted, as were the French responses to them: no cabinet was willing to deal one-on-one with Germany.[20]

Only Monnet was in a position to engineer the Schuman Plan. Many other men of distinction – French, German, Americans, and British alike – had previously advanced the European coal-steel pool as an idea for overcoming the historic antagonism between the two great continental pow-ers, but he alone had the clout to make it a reality.[21] In the years when the United States first confronted the responsibi-lities of world power, Monnet was the European Americans most trusted. No other foreigner has ever exercised compa-rable influence over the external policy of the United States.

While Monnet struck Americans as being incorrigibly French, he seemed almost deracinated to his countrymen, a member of some European sub-species of international operative that took root and grew in the atmosphere of Wall Street and Washington. Monnet had been well-connected in New York investment banking since the late 1920s, but his experience in the world of bond underwriting, mergers and acquisitions, and receiverships – though it versed him well in the uses and misuses of money – was a mere preliminary to that gained in wartime Washington as a member of the British purchasing commission and influential unofficial advisor to the American government.[22]

Monnet watched in fascination as after 1940 an economy, immensely powerful but not yet completely out of the depression, was mobilized to perform feats of production far grander than anything predicted in even the most optimistic forecasts. He analyzed key decisions and methods of operation, carefully observing how a handful of able and far-sighted men directed the energies of this mighty machine into the manufacture of arms and equipment needed for victory, and from everything he had seen, the well-placed war-manager from overseas concluded that the American example could be applied to Europe: on the banks of the Potomac Monnet became convinced that US production methods could revive and renew the economy, society, and politics of a weary, discouraged, and failing civilization.[23]

On the Potomac Monnet also met, or renewed friendships with, the makers and shapers of the postwar era. His list of close associates reads like a *Who's Who* of the Washington policy-making establishment. It included figures from the inner circle like Harry Hopkins and Felix Frankfurter as well as from journalism like the Grahams, Walter Lippmann, the Alsop brothers, and James Reston. Monnet was also close to key future American foreign policy makers like Dean Acheson, John Foster Dulles, Averell Harriman, John J. McCloy and David Bruce. And through them he met, or would soon meet, many of the bright young men fast rising to the second echelon of policy-making, whose influence would be felt through the 1960s and beyond, among them Robert Nathan, George Ball, Robert Bowie, William Tomlinson, Walt and Eugene Rostow, and McGeorge Bundy. Binding these men to Monnet, and Monnet to them as well, was a common, if never completely articulated vision of the future, of a revived Europe re-fashioned along American lines.[24]

In dollar-hungry postwar France Monnet was the man who knew best how to loosen pursestrings in Washington. To secure Lend-Lease assistance, de Gaulle vested Monnet as head of the French Plan, then a dormant agency, with commissarial authority. In February 1946 Monnet negotiated the Blum Loan, which kept the economy afloat for the next twelve months. In the next two years he managed to secure a disproportionate amount of Marshall Plan money for France. These flowed directly to the investment projects sponsored by the Commissariat du Plan, which ultimately depended for funding on neither Parliament nor the powerful inspectorate of finances: the tapline to Washington made Monnet a sovereign power within France.[25] Though this much resented status invited accusations of high-handedness and collusion with foreign interests, it enabled Monnet to act decisively through well-placed and favorably-disposed individual policy makers, and to avoid the delays, compromises, and general immobilization that often resulted from working through bureaucratic structures and following official procedures. Or as *Variety* might once have headlined it, 'RESENTMENT REARS AS RED-TAPE REMOVAL RUNS RAMPANT'.

THE SCHUMAN PLAN

No more accurate account of the immediate origins of the Schuman Plan will probably ever be written than the somewhat melodramatic descriptions provided in Monnet's *Memoirs* of a trip to the mountains spent pondering Europe's destiny, followed by a return to Paris where he and a select group of associates carpentered relentlessly at the Rue de Martignac to shape the odd blocks, boards, and beans of issues and ideas into a simple, serviceable, and solid construct.[26] Contrary to politically-inspired contemporary allegations, the proposal for the coal-steel pool was neither cabled from Washington nor inspired by the Pope, and no more promoted sedulously by evil cartellists than put into play as a Communist ploy. Though ideas for a coal-steel pool may long have been in general circulation, the Schuman Plan bears the distinct imprint of Monnet's approaches and methods.

This was evident in the announcement itself, a public relations coup of historic proportions. Timed so as to pre-empt the 10 May 1950 opening of the tripartite London foreign ministers' conference, at which the Americans were ready to demand an accelerated phase-out of German occupation, the French Foreign Minister spoke neither to diplomats nor heads of state but directly to the public. His message was as dramatic as it was simple: France was willing to sacrifice national sovereignty for the common good, and thus invited her neighbors to join a venture that would end ancient rivalry, prevent war, and lead to a brighter future. Now was the time, said Schuman, to cast aside old differences and begin negotiations without prior conditions and in a spirit of equality. At the very moment of its announcement the proposal for a European coal-steel pool became an established part of the context of events, a force for change, and a myth. The word Europe would never quite sound the same again.[27]

Many Americans were initially suspicious of the Schuman Plan as concealing a scheme for a new European supercartel, yet doubts and fears about its wisdom soon retreated before the conviction expressed by Averell Harriman in a cable from Paris that

> the proposal may well prove most important step towards economic progress and peace of Europe since original Marshall [Plan] speech [of 5 June 1947] ... It is first indication of bold, imaginative, concrete initiative on part of European country in attacking two basic problems ... integration of European economy and conclusive alignment of Germany on side of West with minimum political and economic complications.[28]

Secretary of State Dean Acheson played a crucial role in gaining American acceptance of the Schuman Plan. Informed of the planned announcement in time to block it, he immediately advised President Harry S. Truman, who supported him without hesitation, to stand unequivocally behind the French proposal, adding that the antitrust division of the Department of Justice should be kept from intervening.[29]

American support did not, however, mean US participation in the treaty negotiations, which began on June in Paris. For years the United States had been pleading with the nations of Europe to integrate their economies, and now that France had seized the initiative a US presence would have been counterproductive. Nor was there thought to be a need for one. The United States hoped to act through Monnet. Secretary of State Acheson as well as Director of the European Recovery Program Harriman were trusted allies; US High Commissioner in Germany John J. McCloy an intimate friend; and US Ambassador to Paris David K. E. Bruce a fond admirer.[30] Relationships at the working level were even closer. An intense, tireless, and intellectually-formidable young official of the Department of the Treasury named William M. Tomlinson was the chief unofficial link between the Rue de Martignac and the Place de la Concorde. At the US embassy 'Tommy', as Tomlinson was known to his friends, directed a special 'Working Group on the Schuman Plan Proposal', whose staff of economists and management specialists tracked the negotiation on a daily basis and acted as unofficial advisors to Monnet. In Bonn Professor Robert Bowie, who was General Counsel to the US High Commissioner, also kept closely in touch with developments in Paris.[31] Yet none of this was tantamount to US direction of the coal-steel conference; our policy was to remain in the background until needed by Monnet.

There was another reason why the United States deferred to the Frenchman. The 9 May 1950 proposal had much in common with New Deal thinking, as represented, for instance, by such associations of progressive businessmen, lawyers, economists, and production specialists as the Committee for Economic Development. John J. McCloy once called the Schuman Plan a Tennessee Valley Authority for Europe, a hardly complete but still insightful description. Like TVA the Coal and Steel Community was conceived as a program for economic expansion anchored in a key sector of industry and governed by means of a strong central authority through a code of business conduct restricting powers of private industry: it was to be an agent of political reform as well as economic progress.[32]

The importance of the New Deal model was evident in both the position papers prepared for the 9 May 1950 announcement and the so-called *document de travail*, the French constitutional draft for the coal-steel pool that would to serve as the basis for negotiations between the representatives of France, Germany, Italy, and the Benelux countries – 'The Six', as they were soon calling themselves. From the preliminary papers emerged the concept of a strong executive authority, whose primary function would be developmental and which would act by enforcing a code of industrial good conduct. While seeking the advice of unions and other 'constructive elements', the new directorate was to regulate business through competition, pricing and investment policy, and conduct joint buying and selling; as such it was intended to operate in a manner opposite to that of cartels. Where they existed to protect profits the new High Authority (HA), as the central agency was to be called, would encourage productivity; where private producer arrangements operated secretly, it would use open covenants; and where they were run by private managers in the service of private interests, it would be an agent of the public weal.[33]

These ideas took concrete form in the *document de travail*. Monnet wanted the centerpiece of the French draft, the High Authority, to be a muscular directorate acting collectively on the majority principle with executive power concentrated in a *primus inter pares*, the President. The new body's jurisdiction was to be subject only to a court to which governments might appeal and a parliament with limited powers of interpellation. Committees representing management, consumers, and labor were to advise the new directorate upon request but lacked statutory authority. New regional producer organizations, whose composition was not specified, were to act as transmission belts for the directives of the High Authority and provide the information it needed to operate.[34]

As for the economic provisions, the contracting states were to assign board regulatory powers to the High Authority so as to enable it to create a 'special market' (*marché unique*), 'pool production', and eliminate 'all privileges of entry and exit, tax equivalents [or] quantitative restrictions on the circulation of coal and steel within the area of member states'. The HA was further vested with specified powers in order to abolish 'all subventions or aids to industry ... all means of differentiation between foreign and domestic markets in rates as well as coal and steel prices [and] ... all other restrictive practices'.[35]

There was no precedent in European tradition for an institution based on an economic philosophy that resembled neither state socialism nor the approach preferred by the businessmen of the Continent, which was to espouse the politics of economic liberalism on the one hand while practicing what in Germany was known as industrial self-regulation on the other. Under industrial self-regulation business kept the conduct of its affairs in its own hands, could call upon the state for needed assistance, and would in general support the government in power as long as either profitable or necessary. Like their American counterparts, European businessmen objected strenuously to anything smacking of state dictation, or *dirigisme* as the supposed vice was known in France. The accusation would be leveled at Monnet and his work *ad nauseum*.

Monnet had deliberately excluded representatives of both French ministries and producers from the preparations from the Schuman Plan and also maintained this policy during the Paris conference, which was in session until April 1951. The coal-steel negotiations did not come before the cabinet even once in 1950, and in most ministries Monnet encountered heavy opposition.[36] He had long since made an enemy of the French steel industry, even though it would owe its long-term survival largely to him. In the late-1940s the planning commissariat financed, organized, and helped construct two of the giant continuous wide-strip rolling mills that manufactured the product needed to construct automobiles, and without which no large-scale steel industry could have remained competitive. This support won Monnet few friends: to the tradition-minded men of the *Comité de Forges* he remained a usurper harboring plans for cold socialization.[37]

The *Chambre syndicale de la Sidérurgi francaise*, the cartel representing the interests of the French steel industry, took a contradictory position with regard to the Schuman Plan. It was for rapprochement with the Federal Republic in general, supported all measure facilitating the flow of cheap German combustible to Lorraine, and approved wholeheartedly of 'the resumption of relationships with foreign steel interest'.[38] The iron-masters nonetheless offered to cooperate only on terms unacceptable to Monnet. Bewailing the high costs resulting from war and occupation, the incomplete state of the modernization program, a lack of liquidity, and the weakness of links to domestic manufacturers, they insisted that their industrial associations be represented at the conference proceedings. Monnet rejected this demand outright. French steel would remain a determined and bitter enemy.

The men of the Ruhr shared their French colleagues' suspicions of what in German was called *dirgismus*, but viewed the Schuman Plan as an opportunity to slip the noose hanging around their neck since 1945. Shrewd enough not to count on a commutation of sentence or simple reprieve, they grasped at once that the Schuman Plan's emphasis on equality was something to be earned rather than granted, a continuation of French *Ruhrpolitik* by new means rather than a break with it. The business manager of the German steel producers' association, the *Wirtschaftsvereinigung der Stahl-und Eisenindustrie* (WVESI), thus warned in a position paper drafted shortly after the 9 May 1950 announcement that the French could be expected to force Germans to consume additional low-grade French ore, increase energy costs, and 'suppress the greater dynamism which, even after World War II, our works manifest by comparison to the French'.[39] Though also expecting Monnet to block construction of a continuous wide-strip rolling mill in the Ruhr, he concluded that the coal-steel talks would result in the resurrection of the old Western European heavy industry cartel and for this reason counselled participation in them.

Chancellor Adenauer responded to the initiative of the French Foreign Minister with alacrity, officially regretting to the press only that it had not come twenty-five years earlier. The Chancellor had in fact received prior notification of the 9 May 1950 announcement and during a visit to Bonn he readily agreed to exclude occupation issues from the impending coal-steel conference, raised no objections to the Frenchman's veto of his first two nominations for chief German negotiator, and even adopted Monnet's recommendation of an obscure Frankfurt law professor named Walter Hallstein for the post.[40]

The Chancellor was no starry-eyed idealist. Regarding the Schuman Plan as German's main chance, he was confident that time was on his side, and feared only that in trying to move too fast the Federal Republic could rekindle the smoldering resentment of its neighbors. Adenauer thus stood above the broil of the coal-steel negotiations, and while mouthing Euro-platitudes let the industrialists of the Ruhr wage battle in the trenches. To Hallstein fell the inevitable task of acting as mouthpiece for high-minded official policy, while at the same time representing the material interests of German coal and steel during the Paris conference.[41]

Beginning on 20 June 1950 at the summit of European

diplomatic accomplishment, the negotiations followed a tedious, meandering downhill path which by fall had led to
swamps of bureaucratic maneuvering in the national self-
interest. The inglorious descent was due in part to the
inadequacy of Monnet's constitutional draft. Even with its
faults the *document* was a highly sophisticated text – shaped
by a powerful institutional logic and informed by complicated and original economic theory, much of it difficult to
grasp. To understand the literal meaning, not to mention the
implications of something as abstruse as the price policy
worked out by the Monnet team was intellectually exhausting. Months of thought and discussion were needed to work
out technically and politically satisfactory solutions.

Nonetheless, the *document de travail* was governed by
contradictory principles and framed by unrealistic objectives.
According to Article 17, for instance, the High Authority was
to 'eliminate the falsification of competitive conditions' while
at the same time equalizing wage and working conditions
throughout the community and 'assuring identical delivery
conditions for coal and steel at the point of departure from
mine or mill'. The pricing policy denoted in Article 25, to cite
another example, forced the High Authority to aim at
several targets simultaneously: protecting consumers against
discrimination and producers against 'disloyal' practices,
assuring the steady expansion of markets and outputs, and
'guaranteeing the spontaneous allocation of output at the
highest level of productivity'. The wage policy set forth in
Article 26 had a similar pie-in-the-sky air about it: the High
Authority was to prevent wage cuts during slumps, eliminate
'exploitative competition', assure 'coal and steel workers the
highest standards of living compatible with economic equilibrium' and at the same time introduce 'wage equality'. Finally,
the enumeration in Articles 28 to 30 of an array of broad
powers authorizing the High Authority to impose manufacturing programs upon firms, steer investments, recommend
changes in customs duties, banking roles, and transport
tariffs as well as fine wrongdoing producers, fueled fears of
encroachment and usurpation.[43]

Preoccupied with the German Problem, Monnet also made
little provision for protecting the interests of the lesser
powers among the Six, and to avert a breakdown of the

negotiations he had to cut special deals with each of them. Apart from tiny Luxembourg, Dutch cooperation was the easiest to elicit. Economically, they were at the mercy of West Germany and had no ultimate choice but to accept decisions made in Bonn and Düsseldorf. Monnet pacified them by attaching a Council of Ministers representing the interests of the contracting states to the High Authority. The Belgians presented the author of the Schuman Plan with a much more difficult problem. A traditionally free-trading nation straddling Great Britain and the Continent; a country beset by a chronic dispute between Flemish and Walloons; a political enterprise with an acquired expertise in slipping others the check, Belgium was in a position to demand a high price for cooperation. This was secured after months of intense negotiation by means of a special deal for the nation's decrepit coal mines, on which the German collieries agreed to pay a 2 per cent tax on turnover.[44]

Special provisions also had to be made for Italy, the odd man out among the Six. Geographically separated from the Western European coal-steel complex, only semi-industrialized, lacking raw materials, and generally uncompetitive, the Italians were clearly a special case, and they gained a preferential ore supply arrangement, subsidies for the importation of coal, and special tariffs and quotas to protect the steel industry. Though required to prevent massive dislocation, Italy's deal, like the one for Belgium, made a mockery of the equality principle and eroded the substance of the community. To survive, the coal-steel pool would need either core or axis; it would have to be built around West Germany or Germany linked with France.[45]

The Germans had no counterpart to the *document de travail*. This was no mere oversight. Because the Allies still forbade the Federal Republic from opening a foreign office, the coal-steel negotiations were the new nation's first opportunity to represent itself at a diplomatic conference. Even so, participation was predicated on prior agreement to conduct discussion within the context of the Schuman Plan idea. Monnet, in other words, set the agenda, organized the conference, and chaired its sessions, in addition of course to heading the French delegation. The Germans would have to get their way by working behind the scenes.

Bonn's basic working paper for the conference, though drafted in response to the French *document*, contains the gist of an alternative to Monnet's design for the coal-steel community. Its guiding purpose, while preserving at least a modicum of public supervision, was to restore the old international cartels. The Germans therefore hoped to weaken the High Authority as an institution by strengthening the Council of Ministers, assigning the proposed High Court broad powers of review, and empowering the General Assembly to monitor its activities. They also advocated curtailing its powers of intervention: it should not set prices, establish manufacturing programs, engage in long-term planning, finance new investment, or in any real sense enforce rules of fair competition. The German draft assigned powers stripped from the High Authority to producer associations, which by cleverly re-defining the term 'regional groups' turned what Monnet had designed as mere transmission belts into policy-making centers for industry. In the German draft the Ruhr, not the High Authority would run the community.[46]

Unlike the French, the Germans were united by a national consensus embracing the government, the ministries, industry, the unions, and much of the Social Democratic Party. Supporting the Paris negotiators was cumbersome but powerful institutional machinery operated jointly by representatives of public and private interests; it relentlessly ground out an endless stream of analyses, studies, statistical surveys, position papers, memoranda, and assorted think pieces. On 8 August 1950 a diplomat attached to the German delegation reported that 'the French *document de travail* has become outmoded in every single point as a result of the recent negotiations and remains of mere historical value'.[47] This was wishful thinking on the Germans' part; still, the Germans' Fabian strategy was effective. Instead of ending in August, as Monnet had originally hoped, the negotiations dragged on for months. When they ended the following April the variegated terrain of the French draft had been reduced to a largely featureless rubble.

On 25 June 1950 an unexpected event in the distant corner of the world changed the course, and possibly the outcome, of the Schuman Plan negotiations. The North

Korean invasion across the Thirty-Eighth parallel enmeshed the United States in a so-called police action fought on a very war-like scale that it would twice come perilously close to losing, and which eventually took the lives of 54,246 American servicemen. The events in East Asia not only shifted the fundamental emphasis of American policy in Europe from economic cooperation to mutual security, but brought about a sudden and dramatic improvement in the status of West Germany. The young nation would soon be invited to join the North Atlantic Treaty Organization (NATO), which had been created only a year earlier to protect Europe from German revival. The bombshell fell on 12 September 1950 at the foreign ministers' conference meeting at the Waldorf Astoria in New York, when Acheson summarily informed Schuman that the United States had decided to arm four German divisions. Efforts to provide reassurance that the United States was also prepared both to commit its own troops to Europe and to set up an integrated command structure in NATO did little to pacify the French.[48] Was this, Schuman wanted to know, where the courageous French initiative bearing his name was to lead, to a new *Wehrmacht* stationed on the Rhine?

In desperation, Monnet made two critical decisions. To defuse the rearmament issue he confected the so-called Pleven Plan, a proposal for a European Defense Community (EDC) composed of nationally-integrated fighting units, in October 1950. The EDC (which the United States soon strongly backed) would be one of Monnet's main preoccupations until August 1954 when the French Assembly, by refusing to ratify the EDC treaty, killed the idea of a European armed force.[49] His second decision was to turn the screws on the Ruhr: a new hard line was soon evident at the Paris conference and the decartelization program, which had been pursued intermittently since 1945, returned with a vengeance. The fate of the coal-steel pool would depend upon its outcome.[50]

Decartelization dominated the Petersberg, where the Allied High Commission maintained its headquarters. The official mood of Euro-affability prevailing at the Schuman Plan conference in Paris had no counterpart there. Negotiations were tough, anything but friendly, delayed the conclusion of the treaty for three months, and would have undone it all together were it not for a last-minute intervention by McCloy. Even after agreement had been reached the issue remained a sore point; the attempt to implement would cause more than two years of further conflict. Still, German agreement to decartelize saved the Schuman Plan; without it the French would have bolted, Monnet would have been repudiated, and Europe's great effort to integrate have ended in abject failure.

Decartelization involved three primary issues: the size of steel producing companies; the extent of their control over the mines; and the degree to which coal marketing could be centralized. The survival of the traditional vertically-integrated Ruhr trust was what was at stake in the taxing technical negotiations surrounding these matters, yet to trace in detail their complicated history, or even hope to capture the tense atmosphere in which they were conducted, is impossible in such a short article about so vast a subject. One can only hope to show how they generally unfolded.[51]

The struggle over decartelization began with a mutual stiffening of positions. On 28 September 1950 Monnet drafted a memorandum asserting the High Authority's right to approve or reject all further producer agreements and fusions. The same week witnesed the publication of the first three Regulations implementing Law 27, the general decartelization statute which, although on the books since May 1950, had until then not been enforced. Adenauer considered the decrees sufficiently draconian to threaten German withdrawal from the Schuman Plan, but was not taken seriously. Nor did the resignation a few days later of a prominent industrialist from an important German liaison committee elicit much of a French reaction. The 1 October 1950 speech of Robert Lehr, the newly-appointed Interior Minister, was what convinced the French that the Germans meant business. The ex-Lord Mayor of Düsseldorf, and a man known to have close ties to Ruhr industry, Lehr warned the French that in his view the occupation was over. The Ruhr would no longer accept controls and had to be allowed to expand, even if this meant curtailing future French investments.[52]

None of the several decartelization plans drafted by the

Germans in October came even remotely close to satisfying French demands. The 28 September memorandum, they declared, was the essential precondition of the coal-steel community. No decartelization, no Schuman Plan – it was that simple.[53] Yet the Germans, by this time supported by the other national delegations, refused to bend. The German Minister of Economics Erhard, a free-marketeer and outspoken opponent of *dirigismus*, recommended walking out of the negotiations on 12 December 1950, and ten days later the avuncular Adenauer intimated a German readiness to consider socializing heavy industry in order to pre-empt decartelization.[54]

Monnet had already moved forward the heavy artillery. On 18 December the French and the United States reached a *soi-disant* fundamental agreement on decartelization that reflected views long shared by Monnet and his American friends. 'McCloy and Bowie', he wrote to Schuman, 'are going to take the initiative in discussions with the Germans. It is therefore important that our representatives receive formal instructions to confirm the line of action I am going to lay down for them.'[55]

Neither anti-cartel fanatics, as the Germans believed, nor swooning idolators before the Schuman Plan idea, the Americans were troubled by the rapidity of German restoration, and continued to believe that the 9 May 1950 initiative was the best, and perhaps the only, opportunity to integrate the Federal Republic into Europe. They could see no conflict between doing Monnet's bidding and working in the national interest of the United States.

The Germans were still far from being ready to give in. Negotiations between Bowie and Erhard resumed in January, and appeared to be making some headway on the fifteenth when Hallstein stipulated that the Federal Republic would only sign the coal-steel treaty if allowed to protest decartelization and deconcentration provisions.[56] Monnet thereupon told Bowie over the telephone that 'If [the Germans] do not want to agree to a settlement that is reasonable ... and they are unwilling to accept, [one] that fits in with the Schuman Plan, then I think it [best] to know that and just blow off the whole thing'.[57] Monnet was still not ready to throw in the towel, however.

Instead he worked out a special coal deal with the Ruhr syndicate in order to undercut opposition from French steel producers, and then delivered an ultimatum to Hallstein, representing the Federal Republic, not only to accept the French position in its entirety but win endorsement of it both in the Ruhr and from the other delegations at the conference![58] This was beyond the German's power. The patience of the Ruhr producers with Adenauer's placatory approach was at an end, and the rest of the Six had come to reject both the particulars of Monnet's decartelization policy and his more general conception of the coal-steel community.[59] The negotiations were out of control. Only McCloy could conclude them.

Like Americans generally, McCloy blamed the Germans for the threatened breakdown. After accepting the German position on three minor reorganization issues on 12 February 1951, he wrote Adenauer that 'any effort to press for additional concessions will not only fail . . . but jeopardize the proposed compromises'.[60] The letter going unanswered until 3 March and the response even then being unsatisfactory, the High Commissioner thereupon summoned the Chancellor for a dressing-down, in which he blamed the Germans for delaying the conclusion of the treaty for two months. The next day the US and France imposed a decartelization plan by fiat to the accompaniment of a chorus of protest from the Ruhr. The Treaty of Paris was now ready for initialing, and the conference concluded on 18 April 1951 to the strains of the Belgian delegation singing in unison a hymn to Europe of their own composition.[61]

The treaty was not to take effect, however, until the decartelization process had been completed, and the 'monolithic structure' from which the Ruhr reputedly derived 'artificial advantages' been broken up. The coal cartel, the *Deutsche Kohleverkauf* (DKV), was to be taken apart by 1 October 1952 and during the period of transition remained subject to Allied authority. A total of twenty-seven separate steel companies was to be created, none of them any larger than any other such firm in the community or with capacity greater than 2.2 million annual tons. Only eleven steel companies would be allowed to retain mines, but only if they provided no more than 75 per cent of a mill's consumption requirements. According to one French calculation, this would reduce steel industry control from 56 per cent before the war to 15 per cent. Though the Ruhr producers repudiated this settlement, Adenauer refused to support them. He thought of the Treaty of Paris as a way station on the road towards sovereign status, a slightly leaky but still welcome shelter in which to rest and regain energy before moving on. It confirmed his confidence in the wisdom of gradualism.[62]

The 'Treaty of Instituting the European Coal and Steel Agreement', as the document initialed in Paris was officially called, consisted of an even 100 articles and a lengthy appendix describing transitional arrangements. The outlines of Monnet's original design were easily detectable in the document; the High Authority remained the exclusive source of executive power and an antitrust philosophy shaped its economic provisions. Many of the contradictions of the draft remained, however. The treaty's omissions were also significant. Regional groups were not mentioned and the relationship between producer associations and the High Authority therefore left open to dispute. Nor did the Treaty describe the internal organization of the executive branch. It thus reflected rather than resolved conflicts that had arisen during the negotiations, provided sketchy guidelines for dealing with some issues and failed to address others altogether. Though intended to serve as a constitution, the Treaty of Paris proved to be little more than a ceasefire agreement. The initialing that took place on 18 April 1951 provided only an interlude to the continuing struggle over control of the coal-steel pool.[63]

Its terms would become increasingly unfavorable to Monnet. During the interim period between the conclusion of the treaty and the inauguration of the community on 10 August 1952 several important trends strengthened the position of the German producers. Except for decartelization, remaining controls in the Ruhr were either abolished or fell in desuetude as a result of the mood engendered by the Korean War. The German economy also took on the distinguishing corporate features that many commentators consider responsible for its exceptional dynamism. In April 1951 Adenauer forced German coal and steel employers to accept that blessing in disguise, co-determination, as a reward to the unions for endorsing of the Schuman Plan.[64] Twelve months later the so-called investment aid law for the Ruhr was adopted. It was a levy the business community placed on itself in order to finance the renovation of heavy industry, a private equivalent to the French Plan. The extraordinary self-help measure completed the formation of the thing sometimes derided as the *Verbaendediktatur*, the dictatorship of industrial associations, that provided organization to the economy.[65] Finally, the old international cartels begin to revive in response to the common threat of Monnet's reforms. In November 1950 a standing committee to promote Franco-German producer cooperation was set up; in December cartel discussions began between many branches of industry, and in January 1951 the 'National Associations of the Schuman Plan Nations' was created to do battle against *dirigisme*.[66]

In June 1951, finally, the so-called Interim Committee convened for the first time. Composed of former representatives to the Paris conference but lacking an official mandate, the committee would meet intermittently over the next year in order to organize the High Authority's bureaucracy. The object of these get-togethers was to prevent Monnet from circumventing routine procedures and operating, as with the French Plan, through a small group of talented and intensely loyal 'commandos'.[67]

The struggle for control of the administration was unresolved when the European Coal and Steel Community first opened its offices in Luxembourg. In preparation for the event the head of the Federal Republic's Schuman Plan desk, Dr Ulrich Sahm, had drafted 'wonderful papers, full of grandiose organizational plans, personnel guidelines, compensation scales and so on' for the use of the designated Vice-President of the High Authority, the German Franz Etzel. Refusing to have anything to do with such 'German perfectionism', Monnet 'swept the whole thing off the desk, saying that he was going to begin with a small team and work from there'. He wanted, it seemed, 'to keep his hands on everything'. Sahm and Etzel discovered upon arrival at the opening ceremonies that 'there were French names tacked to every door. The entire thing was in French hands ... they had planned [it] down to the last secretary and concierge'.

Etzel immediately told every German in sight to attach a calling card to the nearest door 'no matter whether he planned to work [in Luxembourg] or not'. It was thus, Sahm deposed, that he found himself in the service of the High Authority.[68]

THE EUROPEAN COAL AND STEEL COMMUNITY

Little remained of Monnet's institution when he decided to step down as President of the High Authority in November 1954. The HA was beset by paralysis, heavy industry regulated the common markets, and decartelization had been replaced by reconcentration. The European Coal and Steel Community actually delivered on only one of its promises, the most important one: it advanced the integration process.

'Europe' did not disappear after the failure of the EDC but was rather 'relaunched' less than a year later at a meeting of the Six that took place in Messina.[69] The new round of diplomacy that began there led to the formation in 1958 of the European Economic Community (EEC). The term 're-launching' is a misnomer: this was the first such event that Europeans conducted by themselves. By 1955 the Six no longer needed the United States to act as silent partner, underwrite their venture, cohabit with them, provide nagging reminders of their need to cooperate, or in any other way coerce or entreat mutually beneficial cooperation. American absence indicated strongly that integration of some sort had occurred since the announcement of the Schuman Plan five years earlier.

It is hard to find direct evidence of it. The operations of the High Authority were gridlocked; the ECSC failed either to reform business practices or establish a new relationship between public and state power; and the economic impact of the community was slight.[70] Yet integration was no phantom; the term merely requires a qualifying adjective to take on historical meaning – it was the *Westintegration* sought by Adenauer. By 1955 the occupation was over, the Federal Republic was committed to rearming, and its industry had become a powerful engine of European growth. No one could seriously doubt that the West Germans would eventually dominate Europe economically. The acceptance of this reality by France, and the rest of the Six, is proof of rapprochement. The coal-steel pool did not deserve sole, or even primary, credit for it; other contemporary trends were equally important. Yet the ECSC was more than merely a diplomatic breakthrough; it led to the second stage of European integration.

On 10 August 1952 the nine members constituting the college directing the High Authority met for the first time. Broadly representative of the national and political composition of the community, these men had been chosen in part because they shared Monnet's European convictions and could be expected to cooperate with him. They had no idea of what to expect or do once in office. Advance arrangements were chaotic, the administrative machinery of the community was not in place and President of the High Authority Jean Monnet had not revealed his agenda.[71] To prevail he had to gain control of the administrative apparatus of the community. The effort would consume the first six months of its existence.

Procedures were one source of conflict. Monnet overlooked the treaty stipulation requiring the High Authority to act by majority vote, preferring to arrive at consensus if need be through exhaustion. Collective responsibility did not, however, imply collective action. By October 1952 dissatisfaction with Monnet's allegedly highhanded methods was so intense that he threatened to resign the presidency. Rebuking the members of the HA with a sharp reminder that they constituted a deliberative body rather than a 'college for action', he insisted that the President needed to intervene decisively and threatened to carve up the central administration into separate bailiwicks, each under an individual member, unless allowed to exercise it. The crisis passed without being resolved.[72]

The structures and functions of the administrative organs of the High Authority were another source of disagreement. To maintain tight control, Monnet kept hirings at a bare minimum and refused to give employees civil service status, preferring to put everyone on a contractual basis. He was also responsible for adopting a highly confusing organiza-

tional plan for the High Authority whose main purpose
seems to have been to immobilize the bureaucrats and leave
as much latitude as possible to his own people. There were
several key figures among them, such as Pierre Uri, who
headed the vaguely-named Main Branch for Economics.
Monnet's leading braintruster and a man both admired and
much-feared for his quick wits and sharp mind, Uri had
general responsibility for harmonizing policy between Luxembourg and the member-nations. Richard Hamburger was
also important. A German Jew who had hidden for four
years from the Nazis in a Dutch attic, Hamburger headed the
Control Section responsible for cartel and concentration
policy. HA Secretary Max Kohnstamm, the journalists Francois Duchene and later Richard Mayne (both Englishmen)
were other high-echelon Monnet-men. Apart from this hard-
core followership Monnet could count on sympathetic support from nearly all labor representatives as well as a great
many of the appointees from government. He never really
controlled the High Authority's *apparat*, however, quite
logically preferring to operate outside its framework.[73]
    Most leading positions in Luxembourg were occupied by
traditional businessmen and government officials. The German mining engineer Hermann Dehnen and director Tony
Rollmann of the ARBED steel enterprise in Luxembourg
co-directed the Main Branch for Production. The manager
of the German steel producers' association, WVESI, directed
its counterpart for investments. The chief statistician of the
Ruhr coal cartel, Rudolf Regul, played a strong second fiddle
to Uri at the Main Branch for Economics. Two of the HA's
three legal counsels were from the Federal Republic as was
the director of the important statistical section, the economist
Rolf Wagenfuer. As of January 1953 the Germans held
sixty-three leading positions, the French forty-one, the Belgians seventeen, the Italians nineteen, the Dutch thirteen
and the Luxembourgers (among whom office staff were
recruited) sixty-four. The Ruhr steel producers found the
distribution of offices wholly satisfactory.[74]
    Monnet's biggest problem in running the community was
the Consultative Committee (CC), the structure and authority of which were not clearly specified in the treaty. Monnet
tolerated this statutory body as a concession to big business,

but had no intention of allowing it to make or implement policy, or in fact do more than was implied in its official title. Though the President of the HA never admitted to trying to eliminate the CC, his actions speak more eloquently than his words. He refused to convene the CC in 1952 and before doing so tried to sap its potential strength by creating so-called External Committees to pre-empt it. It became obvious when the CC first met on 15 January 1953 that it would become a producers' club. Except for a small minority of labor representatives, delegates were chosen by national producer associations. Monnet therefore warned when first addressing the body that it would have to supply tangible proof of its goodwill before being allowed to exercise any authority: the opening of the common markets was to be the test.[75]

CONCLUSION

The creation of a single, community-wide area in which coal and steel products could be sold competitively was a laudable but unrealistic goal, because the coal and steel industries *and* Western Europe had been regulated for decades. Each nation had its own distinct system of controls and real costs were unknown. The ECSC furthermore lacked the power to correct the main causes of market distortion – currency parities, price controls, subsidies and tax, credit, and freight policies. To establish a single economic environment for business in Western Europe would require decades of work; even a single step in the right direction constituted an important achievement.

Notwithstanding official claims, Monnet knew that it was impossible to create genuinely common markets for coal and steel. The best he could realistically expect was for producers to publish, then lower, prices. This inevitably required their associations to meet nationally and internationally. In so doing they simplified pricing schemes, coordinated schedules between districts, and improved joint marketing methods.[76] Preparation for the common markets therefore accelerated the process of international cartel re-formation that had begun with the Schuman Plan. It did not, however, substantially change sales methods. The governments of the member-nations continued to set coal prices and the steel industry to determine prices, standards, and sales areas for its products.[77] Worst yet for Monnet, the ECSC was power-less to stop the rise in steel prices that began after the opening of the common market on 31 May 1953 and, though occasionally interrupted, would persist until his eventual retirement from the High Authority in June 1955.

The list of High Authority setbacks is long and depressing. Though the community received a huge American loan, Monnet did not succeed, as in France, in using investment funds to regulate industrial development. The expensive and time-consuming campaigns mounted to break up the German and French coal cartels were futile. The ECSC also tried and failed to prevent the operations of a new international steel export cartel. It made no serious attempt, however, to limit or otherwise influence industrial concentration. The ambitious labor policy outlined in the treaty remained confined to paper. Nor were the internal problems of the community ever settled. The CC became openly contemptuous of Monnet's leadership. The official explanation given for his resignation as President of the High Authority in November 1954 was disillusionment at the failure of the EDC; but he could only have been disappointed at the turn of events in Luxembourg. As an organization the ECSC had reached a dead end.[78]

One must not, however, overlook certain accomplishments. The ECSC set up effective machinery to regulate the European trade in scrap metal; dealt with the problems of labor re-training and re-adaption before they had become a priority of any national government; pioneered the harmonization of international freight rates; and engaged in the first really serious study of the comparative economics of taxation systems. Each of these achievements contributed to the development of more embracing forms of integration than the sectorial approach embodied in the Schuman Plan Treaty.[79]

The ECSC was significant for more than merely technical reasons: it substituted for a peace treaty with Germany. Though changing no borders, creating no military alliances, and being limited in scope economically, the coal-steel pool provided the political underpinnings for a new international settlement, premised upon the recognition that unlimited exercise of national sovereignty had become a prohibitively costly historical luxury. Monnet had grasped this elementary and powerful truth in World War I; another and even more devastating such catastrophe befell Europe before the Germans recognized it.

The solidity of the postwar settlement was due primarily to the conviction of the formerly revisionist nation that another European war had become unthinkable. The statement is easy to make but difficult to explain historically. One can speak of national shame, the traumas of war, defeat and occupation, transfers of power from one class to another, political division, a new sense of democratic responsibility, and geopolitical shifts from the center to the European periphery. And one can add to this already long list of factors and considerations the impact on attitudes of nuclear weaponry, consumer capitalism, and convenience technologies and *still* not come to the heart of the mystery as to why the *furore teutonicus* ended.

The story would not be complete without the coal-steel pool, however. The Schuman Plan broke the impasse in Allied policy towards Germany and cut a passage for the nation's re-entry into Europe. The ECSC itself was in many respects a disappointment. Monnet wanted to reform big business but instead restored it, and the High Authority was never able either to govern supranationally or create genuinely common markets. The statesmen at Messina adopted a different approach to advancing integration than that embodied in the heavy industry community.

To dwell on these points, however, would obscure the real significance of Jean Monnet's work. Monnet had a vision of the future, a plan of action, and the power to move events – all of which his critics lacked. No better alternative to his New Deal-inspired integration model existed at the time. Nor can one easily imagine a more boldly conceived and executed diplomatic initiative than the one taken on 9 May 1950. Without the extraordinary strength of Monnet's ties to Washington, finally, it would never have been possible to square the circle – to promise the Germans equality while guaranteeing the French security. As for the coal-steel pool, it was imperfect but by no means a failure. Like the Articles of Confederation, the ECSC would be a forerunner to a stronger and more permanent union. By creating it Jean Monnet enabled Europeans to resume control of their own destiny.

NOTES

1. The Truman Library Institute's Senior Scholar Award provided the author with the release time from teaching used to write this essay.
2. The subjects of this essay are treated in greater detail in Chapters Five and Six of John Gillingham, *Coal, Steel, and the Rebirth of Europe 1945–1955: The Germans and French from Ruhr Conflict to Economic Community* (Cambridge University Press, forthcoming).
3. See Jean Monnet, *Memoirs*, trans. Richard Mayne (New York, 1978), Chapter Three, '1919–1918: Working Together', 23f.
4. Ibid., Chapter Four, 'From Cognac to Poland, from California to China', 99f.
5. Interview with Robert Nathan, 15 August 1990.
6. Gillingham, op. cit., Chapter Two: 'The Greater and Lesser Wars'.
7. John Gillingham, 'From Morgenthau Plan to Schuman Plan: American and the Organization of Europe' in Jeffry Diefendorf and Hermann Rupieper (eds), *American Policy Towards Germany, 1949–1955* (Cambridge UP, forthcoming); Frances M. B. Lynch, 'Resolving the Paradox of the Monnet Plan: National and International Planning in French Reconstruction', *The Economic History Review* (second series) 1984/II.
8. George Ball, *The Past Has Another Pattern* (New York, 1982) 77f.
9. See John Gillingham, 'Die franzoesische Ruhrpolitik und die Urspruenge des Schuman Plans', *Vierteljahrshefte fuer Zeitgeschichte* 3/1986, 381–495.
10. John Gimbel, *The Origins of the Marshall Plan* (Stanford, 1968); compare with Gillingham, 'Die franzoesische Ruhrpolitik . . .', op. cit.
11. Archives Nationales de France (AN) (Allemagne 15 prov.) 'LeMinistère des affaires étrangères a M. le Général de l'Armeé Koenig, January 1948' and 'Instruction addressées a M. Schneiter', 7 January 1948.
12. See Erwin Hexner, *The International Steel Cartel* (Chapel Hill, North Carolina, 1943); also John Gillingham, 'Coal and Steel Diplomacy in Interwar Europe' in Clemens A. Wurm (ed.) *Internationale Kartelle und Aussenpolitik [International Cartels and Foreign Policy]* (Stuttgart, 1989) as well as John Gillingham, 'Zur Vorgeschichte der Montanunion. Westeuropas Kohle-und Stahlindustrie in Depression und Krieg', *Vierteljahrshefte fuer Zeitgeschichte* 3/1986, 381–405.
13. See Gillingham, *Coal, Steel and the Birth of Europe*, op. cit., 'The Dismantlement of Ruhr Steel' in Chapter Four, 'Neither Restoration

nor Reform: The Dark Ages of German Heavy Industry'.
14. Bundesarchiv, Koblenz (BA) Nachlass Lehr 18, 'Vorschlag zu einer Neuordnung der Vereinigte Stahlwerke AG unter Heranziehund auslaendischen Kapitals und mit einer Beteiligung der oeffentlichen Hand', (n.d.); also Sohl to Lehr, 6 October 1949.
15. See Gillingham, *Coal, Steel and the Rebirth of Europe*, op. cit., 'The Beginnings of a New Internationalism' in Chapter Four, 'Neither Restoration nor Reform . . .'.
16. See discussion in Alan S. Milward, *The Reconstruction of Western Europe 1945–1951* (London, 1984) 141f.
17. F. Roy Willis, *France, Germany and the New Europe, 1945–63* (Stanford, 1965) 70f.
18. Raymond Poidevin, *Robert Schuman: Homme d'Etat 1886–1963* (Paris, 1986) 219f.
19. Ball, op. cit., 78.
20. Ibid., also Gillingham, *Coal, Steel and the Rebirth of Europe*, Section III, 'The not so Special Relationship' in Chapter Three, 'From Morgenthau Plan to Schuman Plan: The Allies and the Ruhr'.
21. Among previous proponents of a coal-steel pool were John J. McCloy, William Diebold, Paul Porter, Walt V. Rostow, John Foster Dulles, Konrad Mommsen, Wilhelm Salewski, Hermann Puender, André Philip, Paul Reynaud, Georges Bidault, Jacques Gescuer and E. F. Schumancher.
22. Nathan, above, pp. 67–85; also Gillingham, *Coal, Steel and the Rebirth of Europe*, 'The Greater War is Launched' in Chapter Two, 'The Greater and Lesser Wars'.
23. Interview with Robert Bowie, Robert Nathan and Robert Schaetzel, 15 August 1990.
24. Alan S. Milward, 'Was the Marshall Plan Necessary?', *Diplomatic History* 13/2 September 1989, 234; also Ball, op. cit., 89f.
25. Richard F. Kuisel, *Capitalism and the State in Modern France: Renovation and Economic Management in the Twentieth Century* (Cambridge/New York, 1981) 201f; Michel Margairaz 'Autour des Accords Blum-Byrnes: Jean Monnet entre le consensus national et le consensus atlantique', *Histoire, économie, société* I/2 1982, 440–70.
26. Monnet, op. cit., 288f.
27. Ibid.
28. Foreign Relations of the United States (FRUS) 1950/III 850:33/5–2050, 'The United States Special Representative in Europe [Harriman] to the Secretary of State', 20 May 1950.
29. Dean Acheson, *Present at the Creation* (New York, 1969) 498f.
30. Monnet, op. cit., 464.
31. See US National Archives and Records Administration (NARA) RG84 (500: Coal and Steel Pool) Working Group on the Schuman Plan Proposal, 'Increasing Problems in European Coal and Steel Industries', 22 September 1950; minutes of 18 October 1950 meeting re Lehr Proposal, 'Railway Tariff for Coal and Iron Ore', 20 October 1950; 'Memorandum on the Institutions and the Permanent Economic and Social Dispositions of the Schuman Plan', 11

160 *Jean Monnet: The Path to European Unity*

October 1950; 'Restrictions to Trade in Coal and Steel among Schuman Plan Countries', 10 July 1950; 'Emerging Problems in Connection with the Schuman Plan', 14 July 1950.

32. Fondation Jean Monnet pour l'Europe, Lausanne (FJM), 'dossier George Ball'; see also Irwin M. Wall, above, p. 105.

33. FJM AMG 2/3/2 bis 'Note de P. Reuter, "Problèmes posés par l'Institution d'une Haute Autorité international en regard du statut actuel de la Ruhr," ' 5 May 1950; AMG 2/3/3/ 'Note (Reuter) sur la proposition francaise dans ses rapports avec le statut de l'Allemagne et celui de la Ruhr,' (n.d.); AMG 2/4/4a 'Note Concernant la Haute Autorité'. Domaine, Objet (n.d.); AMG 18/8/62 'Note Anti-cartel', 9 May 1950.

34. FJM AMG 3/3/9 'Document de Travail', 27 June 1950.

35. Ibid.

36. See Gillingham, *Coal, Steel and the Rebirth of Europe*, 'From Summit to Swamp' in Chapter Five, 'The End of the War Against Germany: The Coal and Steel Pool as Treaty Settlement'.

37. See Wall, above, p. 93.

38. AMG 18/2/1 'Note de la Chambre Syndicale de la Sidérurgie francaise exprimant ses premiers reactions face au Plan Schuman', 12 July 1950; USNA RG 84 (500: Coal and Steel Pool) Paris Embassy to Secretary of State, 17 July 1950; RG 84 (500: Coal and Steel Pool): Tomlinson to Ambassador, 'Views of Chambre Syndicale de la Sidérurgie on Schuman Proposal', 12 July 1950.

39. Bundesarchiv (BA) 102/5134 'Montanunionplan', 5 June 1950.

40. FJM AMG 2/3/11 'Entrevue der 23 mai 1950 entre M. Jean Monnet et le Chanceliere Adenauer'; AMG 2/3/4 Hans Schaeffer to Monnet, 5 June 1950; AMG 2/3/19 'Plan Schuman. Entretien avec le Chancelier', 16 June 1950; AMG 2/3/20 'Plan Schuman. Entretien avec le Chancelier' by Leroy Beaulieu, 16 June 1950.

41. See Walter Hallstein (ed.), *Probleme des Schuman-Plans. Eine Diskussion zwischen Walter Hallstein, Andreas Predoehl und Fritz Baade* (Kiel, 1951).

42. See Richard Griffiths, 'The Schuman Plan Negotiations: The Economic Clauses' in Klaus Schwabe (ed.), *Die Anfaenge des Schuman Plans 1950; 1951/ The Beginnings of the Schuman Plan* (Baden-Baden, Milano, Paris, Bruxelles, 1988) 35–73.

43. FJM AMG 3/3/9 *Document de travail*, op. cit.

44. See Alan S. Milward, 'The Belgian Coal and Steel Industries' in Schwabe, op. cit., 437–55.

45. See Ruggero Ranieri, 'The Italian Steel Industry and the Schuman Plan Negotiations' in Schwabe, op. cit., pp. 345–57.

46. BA B146/263 'Grundsaetzliches zum Schuman Plan (August 1950)' and 'Unterlagen zum Schuman Plan', 8 August 1950.

47. BA B102/5132 'Sekretariat fuer Fragen des Schuman-Plans 449/50, 8 August 1950.

48. See John Gillingham, 'Solving the Ruhr Problem: German Heavy Industry and the Schuman Plan' in Schwabe op. cit., 422f; also Thomas Schwartz, 'From Occupation to Alliance: John J. McCloy and the Allied High Commission in the Federal Republic of Ger-

many' (unpublished doctoral dissertation, Harvard University, 1985) 361f.

49. See Monnet, op. cit., 345–82 and 394–432, passim.
50. See Gillingham, 'Solving the Ruhr Problem', op. cit.
51. See Gillingham, *Coal, Steel and the Rebirth of Europe*, Chapter Five, Section III 'The Bashing of the Ruhr'.
52. FJM AMG 20/7/5, 4 October 1950, telegram of Francois-Poncet; AMG 18/0/6 'L'Importance de l'industrie de l'acier pour l'union économique européene', 14 October 1950; Archives Nationales de France (AN) 81 AJ 138, 'Fiche (Leroy Beaulieu) pour M. le Ambassadeur', (n.d.), 81 AJ 138 'Entretien (Leroy Beaulieu) avec Dr. Lehr, auhourd'hui Ministère de l'Interieur et un des Dirigeants des Vereinigte Stahlwerke', 13 October 1950.
53. FJM AMG 8/1/5, 'Observations sur le memorandum du 28 Septembere relatif aux institutions et positions économiques et sociales permanent du Plan Schuman', 4 October 1950.
54. BA B146/265 Erhard to Adenauer ('Stellungnahme zum Schumanplan'), 11 December 1950; B 146/265, 'Stellungnahme des Bundesministers fuer Wirtschaft zum Abschluss des Schuman-Plans', 12 December 1950; JM AMG 10/3/7 'Apercus sur le situation économique', 22 December 1950.
55. AN 81 AJ 137 Monnet to Schuman, 22 December 1950.
56. AN 81 AJ 137 'Extracts of a telephone conversation between Mr. Monnet and Mr. Bowie', 15 January 1951.
57. Ibid.
58. FJM AMB 20/5/13 Monnet to Hallstein, 10 January 1951; USNA RG 84 (500: Coal and Steel Pool) US Embassy, Paris, to Secretary of State, 8 January 1951; JM AMG 11/1/9, Monnet to Hallstein, 29 January 1951.
59. Kloeckner Archiv (KA), Guenter Henle Papers, 'Umgestaltung des deutschen Kohlenbergbaus und der deutschen Eisen und Stahlindustrie', 1.10.50–31.12.50, Henle to Pferdmenges, 21 February 1951; USNA RG 84 (500: Coal and Steel Pool) US Embassy to Secretary of State, 1121. 21 February 1951.
60. NARA RG 466 D(51) 19 D/B McCloy to Adenauer, 12 February 1951.
61. NARA RG 466 D(51) 353 US Embassy, Paris, to Department, 20 March 1951.
62. FJM AMG 13/27/10, 'Memorandum sur la Déconcentration de la Ruhr et la Conclusion des Negotiations sur le Plan Schuman', 8 March 1951.
63. FJM AMG 16/1/1 'Traité instituant la Communauté Européene du Charbon et de l'Acier'.
64. See Horst Thum, *Mitbestimmung in der Montanindustrie. Der Mythos vom Sieg der Gewerkschaften* (Muenchen, 1982).
65. See Heiner R. Adamsen, *Investitionshilfe fuer die Ruhr. Wiederaufbau, Verbaende und Sozialmarktwirtschaft 1948–1952* (Wuppertal, 1981).
66. FJM AMG 12/3/3, 'Les Fédérations industrielles de l'Europe de l'Quest et le Plan Schuman', 8 February 1951; JM AMG 11/2/5, BA

146/265 'Observations de fédérations industrielles nationales des pays intéressés par le Plan Schuman sur les clauses économiques de Projet de Traité en préparation', 17 January 1951; KA/Henle Papers EGKS. Schuman Plan. WVESI 1.151–31, 12.31, 'Die Industrieverbaende Westeuropas zum Schuman Plan' (n.d.).

67. See BA 102/12608, 'Vermerk ueber eine interministerielle Besprechung zur Frage der Organisation der Hoehen Behoerde', 26 September 1951; KA/Henle Papers EGKS. Schuman Plan. Wirtschaftsvereinigungen, 1.152–30.9.52. 'Besprechung zwischen Bundeswirtschaftsministerium, Auswaertigem Amt, Kohle und Eisen am 5.6.1952'; BA 102/8603a 'Besprechung in Den Haag am 26. und 27.2.52', BA 162/8603a 'Monnet Praesident der Hoehen Behoerde?' from *Le Monde*, 17 June 1952; B102/8603a 'Schuman Plan. Sitzung der Sachverstaendigungen', 23, 24, 25 June 1952.

68. FJM, 'Interview mit Dr. Ulrich Sahm', 27 February 1984.

69. See Hann-Juergen Kuesters, *Die Gruendung der Europaeischen Gemeinschaft* (Baden-Baden, 1982).

70. See above all William Diebold, *The Schuman Plan: A Study in Economic Cooperation, 1950–1959* (New York, 1959); Ernst B. Haas, *The Uniting of Europe: Political, Social and Economic Forces, 1950–1957* (Stanford, 1958; 2nd. ed., 1976), and Louis Lister, *Europe's Coal and Steel Community: An Experiment in Economic Union* (New York, 1960).

71. Sahm interview, op. cit.

72. FJM AMH 7/1/12 'Compte-rendu de la quinzième séance de la Haute Autorité', 2 October 1952.

73. AN 81 AJ 160, 'Note E. Hirsch. Réflexions sur l'organisation de la Haute Autorité', (n.d.).

74. Wirtschaftesvereinigung der Eisen-und Stahlindustrien (WVESI), 'Vermerk ueber die Vorstandssitzung am 13.1.1953'.

75. 'Einsetzung des Beratenden Ausschusses', *Bulletin des Presse-und Informationsamtes der Bundesregierung*, Bonn, 27 January 1953.

76. See Diebold, op. cit., passim; Gillingham, *Coal, Steel and the Birth of Europe*, 'Action and Inaction at the ECSC' in Chapter Six, 'The Success of a Failure: The European Coal and Steel Community in Action, 1952–1955'.

77. Ibid., 'The Common Markets Open' in Chapter Six; Werner Abelshauser, *Der Rurkohlenbergbau seit 1945, Wiederaufbau, Krise, Anpassung* (Muenchen, 1984).

78. Monnet, op. cit., 397f.

79. See discussion in Diebold, op. cit., Chapter Twenty-Two 'Partial Integration and its Consequences'.

6 What Type of Europe?

Robert Marjolin

This material was excerpted from Robert Marjolin, *Memoirs 1911–1986: Architect of European Unity* (London, 1989) with the permission of George Weidenfeld and Nicholson, publishers of the English edition.

PART I: CHARLES DE GAULLE

It would be true to say that, in the matter of Europe the post-war period and more specifically the fifties and sixties, was dominated by two great currents of thinking, one embodied by Jean Monnet, the other by General de Gaulle. The former and his followers thought that one day, in the not too distant future, national sovereignties would merge into a European sovereignty and that for headway to be made in that direction, national sovereignties had to be progressively dismantled.

The 'Europeans', as they were usually called, fell into several categories with different leanings: they ranged from the federalists, for whom none of the big problems facing France and Europe could be solved unless federal European institutions were rapidly set up, to the pragmatists, for whom the movement towards the ultimate goal was all that counted and who were ready to support any initiative, even of minor importance, as long as it tended in the desired direction. Jean Monnet himself was in this last category.

As for the position of General de Gaulle and the Gaullists, as set out in the former's *Memoirs of Hope* and in Maurice Couve de Murville's book *Une politique étrangère 1958–69*, it can be summed up thus: today and for all time, the fundamental political reality is and will be the nation-state; the latter may, by treaty concluded with other nation-states, relinquish certain tokens of its sovereignty, but these can only be individual and specific relinquishments, carefully defined and explicitly agreed to.

It was on the institutional issues – role and powers of the Strasbourg Assembly and of the Commission, possibility of majority voting in the Council of Ministers – that the 'Europeans' and the Gaullists were to clash most sharply. But

163

the actual existence of the Common Market would never be brought into question. I personally was to find constant support in Paris for the completion of Europe's construction as defined in the Treaty of Rome.

One may understandably be tempted to ask the following question: if General de Gaulle had come to power two years earlier, in 1956, when the Rome Treaty negotiations were only beginning, would they have led to the outcome we know or would they have taken a different course? This is one of those hypothetical questions to which there can be no precise answer. Assuming the best, which is to say that France would have agreed with her five partners to create the European Economic Community, it is almost certain, in the light of the years which followed, that the treaty would have been different in a number of important respects. The principle of unanimity would have been asserted without any limitation of duration. The Commission's role would have been reduced; it would probably have become merely a secretariat of the Council of Ministers. It is unlikely that France would have been content with the few articles in the treaty that laid the foundations of a common agricultural policy; she would have wanted that policy spelled out in the treaty, at least as far as its essential rules were concerned. Would the other five countries have agreed to France's demands on these different points? No one can tell.

When he became head of the government in 1958, de Gaulle accepted the Treaty of Rome as signed a year earlier. He accepted its economic philosophy, which corresponded to his own. In his *Memoirs of Hope* he makes himself clear:

Expansion, productivity, competition, concentration — such, clearly, were the rules which French economy, traditionally cautious, conservative, protected and scattered, must henceforth adopt.[1]

And further on, speaking of the Common Market itself:

I was concerned with international competition, for this was the lever which could activate our business world, compel it to increase productivity, encourage it to merge, persuade it to do battle abroad; hence my determination to [practice] the Common Market, which as yet existed only on paper, to [work towards] the abolition of tariffs between the Six, to liberalize appreciably our overseas trade.[2]

This resolve to put the Common Market into practice was one of the reasons that led de Gaulle to take the difficult monetary and financial decisions of 1958[3]; these put the French economy back on an even keel and enabled France on 1 January 1959 to make the same tariff cuts and the same advance towards alignment with the common external tariff as her EEC partners. 1958 was also notable for the adoption of France's new constitution, which put an end to the governmental instability from which the country had suffered so much under the Third and Fourth Republics. The end of the Algerian war in 1962 completed the decolonization process, and enabled the French government to devote itself entirely to the task of strengthening France's economic position in a Europe where the Common Market was being built stone by stone.

Over the ten years that followed de Gaulle's coming to power, France, often with the support of the Commission, played a decisive role in Brussels, where Maurice Couve de Murville, the Minister for Foreign Affairs, and Oliver Wormser, his principal collaborator, represented her in a continuous period of service unprecedented for length.... [I]t was thanks to them and a few others that France, working closely with the Commission, succeeded in pulling the common agricultural policy out of the rut of generalities in which it was liable to stick and made it a practical reality.

De Gaulle and the United States

Having paid my tribute, a deserved one, to the nascent Fifth Republic, I feel easier about expressing the reservations I have concerning some aspects of Gaullist policy. I wish to speak in particular of certain instances of extreme language, as in the condemnation of the Fourth Republic, which was presented as being utterly without merit. To read General de Gaulle, one would think that the years from 1946 to 1958 were a period of total anarchy in France, during which the United States all but dictated French foreign policy. It is true that French diplomatic action at that time was usually in line with American views. But it is not equally true that those American views were, essentially at least, in line with French interests? Why stand apart and oppose when there is fundamental agreement on the goals to be achieved? I would not deny that the USA, given its economic and military power, had great weight in the decisions taken at that time, but I find it very difficult to accept the theory that, on important issues, US policy ran counter to the interests of France and of Europe.

I shall say nothing about the definition of Europe as extending 'from the Atlantic to the Urals'. I have never understood it. On the other hand, I cannot conceal the fact that I feel distinctly uncomfortable with the idea of 'the two blocs' from which Europe had to demarcate itself, this particular expression being employed, more often than not, without any indication of the essential difference that exists between the two. I am the first to want 'Western', i.e. non-Communist, Europe to find an identity that will distinguish it from the USA. Moreover, America was never opposed to the union of Europe, whatever form it might take; at different times she even vigorously promoted or encouraged it. What I cannot accept is the apparent equation of Soviet Russia, the most absolute totalitarian regime that the world has ever known, and America, which has a democratic regime comparable to ours. In our dealings with America we, France, are not in the same position as countries like Poland, Czechoslovakia and Hungary are *vis-à-vis* Soviet Russia. We can say 'no' to the Americans, as de Gaulle did in 1966 when he pulled France's armed forces out of NATO, without our being threatened with invasion or even economic reprisals. For France's EEC partners, the movement towards European unification and the maintenance of a close and friendly alliance with the United States were not only compatible, but complementary. I think they were the ones who were right. The extremes of Gaullist language at times deeply disturbed France's relations with the other five countries. These extremes were all the more pointless in that France's foreign policy under de Gaulle was not essentially different from those of her European partners. At certain times even, such as in the Berlin and Cuban crises, de Gaulle showed himself to be the staunchest and most resolute ally of the United States.

Arguably, therefore, it was inordinate language more than acts or failures to act that brought France's membership of the Atlantic Alliance into question. The pity of it is that, since thought is expressed in language, the Americans and France's European partners themselves had cause to think, on certain occasions, that France's intentions were different from what they really were. The words through which the deed is expressed are often as important as the deed itself.

De Gaulle and Jean Monnet

There can be no question here of writing a Plutarchan account of two parallel lives: those of de Gaulle and Jean Monnet are comparable only in a few respects.

At once a thinker, a propagator of ideas and a statesman whose coming to power had a profound effect on France, de Gaulle realized at a very early point in the thirties what the nature of the coming war would be; if that war began with a disaster for France, it was because the prophet of mobile warfare with emphasis on large motorized and armored units had not been heeded. During the war he embodied resistance to the enemy; when the Liberation came he maintained peace at home. In 1958 he gave France the best constitution she has ever had. Finally, he completed the decolonization process by giving Algeria its independence, thus leaving France entirely free to concentrate on European matters.

Jean Monnet's sum of accomplishments was more modest, or different, if one prefers. The only political post he held in France was that of Commissioner General of the French Plan, to which de Gaulle had appointed him. Earlier, in Washington, he had played a big part in the Anglo-American war effort. At the beginning of the fifties he devised and created the European Coal and Steel Community, which represented an important stage in the construction of Europe.

The lives of the two men were thus very different. And yet, if one were to ask in France or abroad, especially abroad, which Frenchmen made the deepest imprint on the past half-century, almost certainly the two names that would be mentioned first would be those of General de Gaulle and Jean Monnet. Each was, in his own way, an illustrious Frenchman of whom France can be proud.

There is certainly nothing arbitrary or fallacious in drawing this analogy between the two men, even though the contrasts between their respective lives and philosophies are very marked. De Gaulle, apart from a sojourn in Lebanon and, of course, the London years, spent virtually the whole of his life in France in that most national of French institutions, the army. Jean Monnet, on the other hand, despite his peasant origins, to which he often referred, was a cosmopolitan who lived a large part of his life abroad, notably in America and China. Their passions were different. De Gaulle's sole aim, during and after the war, was to restore France to her rightful place in Europe and in the world. 'De Gaulle,' wrote Maurice Couve de Murville, 'was most certainly a man of unyielding passion, and his passion was France.'[4] Jean Monnet, too, was passionately devoted to his country; he undoubtedly saw no contradiction between the relinquishments of sovereignty that he was proposing and the greatness of France. For him, that greatness lay by way of a united Europe, which would include Britain, and close ties with the United States, whose hegemony he did not perceive as a threat.

It was probably on this last issue that the differences between the two minds were most marked. Jean Monnet felt deep affinities with the United States, where he had lived for a long time. He was at home there. He had many friends there. The idea that America could threaten France's independence seemed absurd to him. De Gaulle, on the other hand, had an invincible distrust of the giant across the Atlantic. There is a rational explanation for the way he felt: one result of the war had been to relegate France, like Britain and Germany, to the status of a second-class power carrying relatively little weight in world affairs, whereas the influence of the United States had grown prodigiously and asserted itself in all parts of the globe, with the exception of the Communist countries. How could one not conceive that one day the United States might misuse that influence? In

Europe, Britain was seen by many as an American outpost. Germany, feeling threatened by the Soviet Union, counted on the Americans to ensure her safety and was prone to follow them in all their economic and political moves. But de Gaulle's mistrust of, if not hostility towards, the United States had been aggravated by his treatment at the hands of Roosevelt during the war, who saw in him the leader of French faction instead of the man who embodied the Resistance. Not until the war was over did the American attitude change. I shall not discuss the question of how this misunderstanding arose; it is unlikely that all the blame lay on one side. The fact remains that US policy with regard to de Gaulle was singularly lacking in percipience for a number of years.

This contrast between de Gaulle's and Jean Monnet's feelings towards America was duplicated in their respective reactions to Britain's applications to join the Common Market, first in 1961 and then in 1967. Jean Monnet, immediately and with deep conviction, supported Britain's candidacy, once it seemed to him that the British had accepted the Treaty of Rome and the decisions that had been taken to implement it. De Gaulle opposed it with equal determination, not only because in his view the British presence would complicate or even prevent the treaty's execution in full, but because Britain's entry would in effect be America's entry. The Common Market, he thought, would become a worldwide free-trade area; that would be the end of Europe, which would cease to be European.

If one were to try to list all the divergences in the thinking and action of the two men, one would never finish. For example, de Gaulle sharply criticized the ECSC, of which Jean Monnet was the founding father, and vehemently opposed the European Defense Community, which Monnet tried so hard to promote. He was utterly against any form of 'supranationalism', the latter being in his view no less than tantamount to a plot to undo France, with Jean Monnet as one of the chief instigators, if not the chief.

At bottom, the nation-state for de Gaulle was something virtually immutable, fashioned by centuries of history. The idea that one day the European nation-states might be merged into a vast entity called 'Europe' or 'United States of

Europe' seemed to him the manifestation of a dangerous delirium that could only lead to the disappearance of France, without anything real, anything genuinely European, being able to take her place. His thinking, molded by a profound knowledge of history, centered on the balance of power between states, whereas Jean Monnet liked to ignore it, or to pretend to.

And yet, in spite of all these opposites, the two men were very close to each other in a number of fundamental respects. Both were modernists, they wanted a modern France in tune with the times. De Gaulle spoke of the need for the economy to grow, to expand investment, to increase productivity, to accept international competition, in terms that Jean Monnet would not have disowned. The two men came together after the war in the creation of France's Plan of Modernization and Equipment. De Gaulle accepted the Common Market without argument, when he could have brought the whole thing into question.

For de Gaulle, as for Jean Monnet, Europe, or perhaps it would be more accurate to say the cornerstone of Europe, was essentially Franco-German rapprochement. It was necessary to forget two centuries of intermittent war, to make sure not to compromise the future by trying to keep Germany in a state of subjection, to settle rapidly what might remain of the Franco-German dispute. Jean Monnet inaugurated this policy with the treaty establishing the ECSC; de Gaulle, when he returned to power, gave it added impetus by creating a relationship of close cooperation between himself and Adenauer. After the old Chancellor died in 1963, the special Franco-German relationship weakened somewhat but never disappeared completely.

Although firmly rejecting federalist ideas because he saw in them a threat to France's independence, de Gaulle constantly thought of a political Europe able to hold its own with the United States – a third force, so to speak. Hence the endeavor to establish political cooperation among the members of the Common Market in the early sixties. Jean Monnet, though following different paths and failing to share Gaullist ideas about the American peril, had goals that were not far removed from the General's. He too wanted a Europe that could treat on equal terms with the United

States; he had nothing to say against the efforts to establish political cooperation among the Six.

The dialogue, more often than not indirect, between de Gaulle and Jean Monnet, with its overt points of disagreement and its generally covert points of agreement, lasted for twenty years, from 1950 until the General's death. Throughout that time I saw Jean Monnet very frequently. As of 1958, de Gaulle received me regularly, perhaps once or twice a year. Above all, during the whole time that he was Foreign Minister, I had many long conversations with Maurice Couve de Murville. As a rule, I saw him every Saturday afternoon. I did not approve of General de Gaulle's extreme language, but in all the periods of tension that the Common Market experienced during the sixties, in all the crises that shook it, my stance was often close to his and to that which Couve de Murville expressed in Brussels. My relations with Jean Monnet were friendly and trusting, even if our views differed on some important issues such as Britain's entry into the Common Market at a time when the latter's construction was not complete. I also thought that the nation-state was not on the way out and that one could not expect the emergence of a European state in the foreseeable future. I often conversed on this subject with Monnet.

One man we both knew well, and who has remained one of my best friends, was a witness to many of these conversations. This was George Ball, for many years Under-Secretary of State in Washington – an extraordinarily clearsighted and courageous man who, though a member of the US government, strongly opposed the Vietnam venture. This is how he described the stances of Jean Monnet and myself:

> Monnet and Marjolin addressed [Europe's] problems from different angles of attack. Monnet invariably set goals that might be approached but never attained. Marjolin, whose task was to translate broad concepts into functioning institutions, was necessarily aware of the limits of the feasible and the need for compromise. I refrained from taking sides in the argument, since I was devoted to both men. But their disparate attitudes illuminated the basic question. Was Monnet really right in believing that a change in institutions would cause men and women to

conform their thoughts and actions to a new set of principles? Could allegiance to a united Europe some day play the same activating role that national sovereignty had played in the past? Or did it really matter whether he was right or not? Would not the insistent pressure for the unattainable goal at least lead toward greater solidarity and common policies and actions that could never be achieved by more modest objectives?

Marjolin did not believe that the concept of nationality could be displaced [by the concept of 'Europe'] within a single generation, or even several generations, merely by creating new institutions. Patriotism had seen the coalescing force animating Germany's neighbours to resist her ravaging armies in two world wars, and Britain, in Marjolin's view, was not ready for Europe. He did not think – as Monnet did – that deeply entrenched habits of thought could be quickly modified in the pressure chambers of new institutions.[5]

George Ball himself did not think that Europe could, in the foreseeable future, set itself up as a United States of Europe, but he did believe in the power of ambitious ideas, in their ability to change reality, at least to some extent.

The Inner Logic of Integration

The difference in standpoints which George Ball noticed between Jean Monnet and me was even more pronounced, as far as I am concerned, when it came to certain theories representing the views of a number of fervent 'Europeans', who were quite a strong force during the fifties and early sixties.

For them, federal Europe was within reach, if the political will were there. Practically speaking, once the first step had been taken in this direction, events would necessarily follow on from one another and inevitably lead to the desired result. This is the gist of the so-called theory of *engrenage* [chain reaction] or the 'spill-over effect'. It is set out in the fullest detail in what may be regarded as the political testament of Walter Hallstein, who, as a close collaborator of

Konrad Adenauer, then as President of the EEC Commission from 1958 to 1967, played a large part in the construction of the Common Market.[6]

The forces which the Europeans had let loose in deciding to create a common market, so Hallstein's thinking went, must inevitably take Europe to economic union, then to political union. If one started out with a customs union and a common agricultural policy, one would inevitably be drawn much further. Neither of them would be able to function, or at any rate to function satisfactorily, unless currency parities remained invariable, in short unless a European currency were created; which, in turn, would entail a merging of the economic policies of member states into a single economic policy; and this would necessitate the merging of national sovereignties into a European sovereignty.

One arrived at the same conclusion if one considered the European Community's relations with the rest of the world. Once the Common Market had been set up, there could no longer be national trade policies *vis-à-vis* third countries – only a common commercial policy, for which, moreover, the Rome Treaty would explicitly provide. But trade policy was an essential part of foreign policy, itself closely bound up with defense policy [. . .] Thus, a process that began modestly with the establishment of a customs union and a common agricultural or commercial policy would reach its logical outcome: a European federation, or as others would name it, the United States of Europe. This is what Walter Hallstein called the 'material' or 'inner' logic of integration.

My own reaction to these 'federalist' ideas was one of extreme skepticism. I did not believe in the *engrenage* or 'spill-over theory'.

To begin with, I did not think it true that the customs union or the common agricultural policy would be unable to survive unless Europe formed itself into an economic union, in the strongest sense of the term. Nearly thirty years after the signing of the Rome Treaty and some eighteen years after the completion of the customs union, Europe has still not become an economic union. National economic policies differ greatly; European currency parities change frequently against one another, despite the introduction of the European Monetary System; unity of agricultural prices has been shattered by the refusal of national governments to adjust domestic farm prices to the movement of exchange rates. I am not trying to say that the customs union and the common agricultural policy have been untroubled by these developments, but essentially the Common Market has survived. Above all, it would be a fundamental error to think that a government having to contend with acute domestic problems, often threatening its very existence, could be constrained to take crucial decisions involving relinquishments of sovereignty, simply because an 'inner logic', the reality of which is moreover debatable, left it no other alternative.

The Federalism Question

However, with these reservations, I was not then, nor am I now, in profound disagreement with the 'federalists'. I would be one myself if events were to take a turn that allowed me to think that the goal of a European federation could be achieved in the foreseeable future. At present I can do no more than ask myself sometimes whether the European peoples, or at any rate some of them, have a genuine aspiration, however confused, towards European unity? Is there such a thing as European sensibility, intrinsically distinct from, say, the American sensibility? Are we French, for example, further removed in our feelings and reactions from the people of North America than we are from the Germans or the British? Was Walter Hallstein right in stating that Europeans are intuitively aware that, beyond their native countries, there is a greater homeland, Europe? No one would deny the cultural unity of the Continent; but are not the United States and other countries with inhabitants of European stock a part of the cultural unity? I leave it to each reader to answer these questions, for the matter is eminently subjective. Not that the reply would necessarily resolve the issue. It is possible that there is no specifically European sensibility and that, nevertheless, European union is vital for reasons of international policy, in order to enable Europe to go on playing a world role and to preserve her freedom.

The institutional quarrel has always seemed rather pointless to me. Between maintenance of national sovereignties *in toto* and dismantlement of the latter, there is a middle way.

For me, this middle way represented the reality, the hypothetical extremes – full maintenance of sovereignties or their dismantlement – being mental constructs. The middle way was a treaty whereby the signatory states would pledge themselves to one another indefinitely and undertake to carry out certain acts by specified dates, such as the progressive abolition of customs duties and import quotas, the gradual derestriction of movements of labor and capital, the organization of agricultural markets, and so on. After a transition period, which might vary according to the circumstances, the result would be a Europe which, if perhaps not wholly unified economically, would nevertheless present a degree of unity unachieved hitherto.

Of course, a treaty is just a piece of paper. One or more signatory states can tear it up, admittedly, but that is equally true of any organizational formula: any legal construct is perishable. It is not by creating a pseudo-executive, to which sovereign powers would be given but which would have no means of enforcing them, that the problem will be resolved. The only answer is the existence of a will to live together, the realization by nation-states that, whatever the disadvantages of the Community, they are better off in it than out of it.

The fact that I felt so uncomfortable with extreme European views also explains why I never spoke of the 'United States of Europe', an expression used by many excellent minds fascinated by the power that unification had given the British colonies of North America in the late eighteenth century and thenceforward. This analogy between the two continents always seemed to be eminently superficial. What could there possibly be in common between the British establishments of the Atlantic coast in 1780 or thereabouts, which were less than a century and a half old, which shared the same language, the same law and, essentially, the same institutions, which had never fought one another, and the old states of Europe – France, Britain, Germany, Italy – some of which, admittedly, had unified only in the nineteenth century, but which all had national traditions going back to the Middle Ages? Because the term 'United States of Europe' creates illusions in minds that are ignorant of history, I have always refused to use it.

PART II: THE EUROPEAN COAL AND STEEL COMMUNITY

A European customs union could have emerged directly from the effort to reconstruct Europe after the war and paved the way for future expansion. It did not. The Marshall Plan made it possible to create the Common Market but did not actually engender it. The direct ancestor of the Common Market was the European Coal and Steel Community, which brought together a group of countries (the Six) that had decided to go further in the construction of Europe than Britain and a few small countries, notably the Scandinavian countries, were prepared to at the time. The ECSC was devised in 1950 and brought into being in 1952. It stemmed both from the aspiration to a closer unity of Europe than that embodied in the OEEC and from the need to define a new French policy *vis-à-vis* Germany. Its two protagonists were Robert Schuman, then France's Minister of Foreign Affairs, and Jean Monnet.

I shall speak only briefly of the ECSC as I had no hand in its creation, being engaged at OEEC in less ambitious tasks, namely the forming of a European market through abolition of import quotas and multilateralization of payments. If I mention it here, it is because it constitutes an essential stage in the formation of the Europe we know today.

Robert Schuman and Jean Monnet had similar ideas of Europe, but their immediate concerns were different. True, Monnet was convinced that France's policy in regard to Germany was on the wrong track and that it was vital to come up with an idea that would initiate the reconciliation of the two countries and enable them to work in partnership. He was certain that, in order to avoid future wars, Germany had to be recognized as having equality of rights. On this issue he was far in advance of French public opinion of the day. 'Peace can be founded only on equality of rights', he told Robert Schuman. 'We failed in 1919 because we introduced discrimination and a sense of superiority. Now we are beginning to make the same mistakes again.'[7]

But the idea uppermost in Jean Monnet's mind at that time was a different one. He wanted to create a Europe endowed with efficient institutions resembling, even very remotely, the

United States constitution, a Europe which could take its decisions by majority vote and which, in consequence, would go well beyond the Europe as represented by the OEEC where all decisions had to be unanimous. He made no attempt to hide his contempt for what he called 'intergovernmental cooperation'. True, he admits in his *Memoirs* that the latter, as embodied in the OEEC, if one accepted it for what it was, with its limitations, was a factor of progress for a European economy that was too compartmented. The abolition of quotas and the establishment of payments agreements would facilitate and stimulate trade; better knowledge of the other's resources and goals would enable each to direct his own efforts to better purpose. But that was where the effectiveness of this type of organization ended. To ask more of a system that entailed no delegation of sovereignty would have been unrealistic, and very soon, he said, the OEEC had become purely technical machinery. It had outlived the Marshall Plan because it had been able to serve as a source of useful information.[8] In a letter to the then Foreign Minister Georges Bidault, which must date from 1948, Jean Monnet wrote that the idea of sixteen sovereign nations cooperating actively was an illusion. 'I believe that only the establishment of a *federation* of the West, including Britain, will enable us to solve our problems quickly enough, and finally prevent war.'[9] And in a letter to Robert Schuman he wrote:

> Everything I have seen and reflected on here leads me to a conclusion which is now my profound conviction: that to tackle the present situation, to face the dangers that threaten us, and to match the American effort, the countries of Western Europe must turn their national efforts into a truly European effort. This will be possible only through a *federation* of the West.[10]

At the same time Jean Monnet, dominated as he was by one idea, was aware that it was unrealistic to think of a federation in the near future. He had become persuaded of this in 1949, when he proposed to the French and British a Franco-British union, a merging of the French and British economies, and a hark-back to Churchill's proposal of 1940. This would have been the first step towards a European federation. But the British would hear no talk of federation nor of delegation of sovereignty; it is not even certain that they understood what the latter expression meant. Edwin Plowden, a senior Whitehall official, was later to say to Jean Monnet: 'We'd won the war [we had worldwide responsibilities] and we weren't ready to form special links with the continent.'[11]

Jean Monnet found that his attempt to create a federal nucleus around which Europe might be formed had failed to interest the one great power in the Old World then in a position to take on a political responsibility of that magnitude. Even in France, national sentiment was still too strong for the idea of a federation to have any chance of winning acceptance. It was necessary to come up with a scheme of smaller compass, one that would go some way towards the final goal without offending public opinion, which was as yet unreceptive.

It was then that he devised the plan that was to lead to the creation of the European Coal and Steel Community (ECSC). Its whole underlying philosophy was summed up in a few lines: 'A start would have to be made by doing something more practical and more ambitious. National sovereignty would have to be tackled more boldly and on a narrower front.'[12] The word 'federation' was mentioned in the Schuman declaration that gave birth to the ECSC, not as something accessible in the short term but as the outcome of a long process of which the ECSC would be the starting point. The resulting new institutions defined what, for want of a better term, might be called 'supranational Europe'. The latter would be the result of more and more extensive delegations of national sovereignty to supranational bodies. These delegations of sovereignty would, according to the thinking of those who were promoting them, lead in the first instance to sectoral communities of clearly delimited scope, and later to a federation of Western Europe. The pooling of certain powers, hitherto national, would set off a process that would end in the emergence of a European state. Lastly, France's chief partner in this undertaking would not now be Britain, but Germany.

The project thus conceived would probably not have come off had it not matched the immediate concerns of Robert

Schuman, then Foreign Affairs Minister. He could not but be aware that French policy towards Germany was deadlocked. Since 1945 successive French governments had tried in vain to prevent the reconstruction of Germany as a great industrial power, essentially by restricting German steel output and thus releasing large quantities of coking coal that could be exported, notably to France. These efforts had encountered not only German resistance, as after World War I, but also, and infinitely more seriously, the American will to rebuild the industrial power and, soon thereafter, the military power of Germany, in order to make her a bulwark against Soviet political and military expansion. France could only fight rearguard actions, from which she regularly emerged beaten.

When Jean Monnet came to Robert Schuman early in 1950 with his project for the ECSC, the latter quickly recognized that here was a way out of the difficulty and a means of shifting the stance of French policy towards Germany, without appearing to capitulate to American demands. His *directeur de cabinet*, Bernard Clappier, later Governor of the Bank of France, played a major role as an intelligent and convinced intermediary between the two men.

The Germans for their part, in the person of the then Chancellor Konrad Adenauer, immediately perceived the prospects that the ECSC project held for their country. The controls that applied to their coal and steel production were discriminatory, and Bonn wanted them out of the way as soon as possible. On the other hand, the Germans accepted at once the idea of an authority that would oversee not only Germany's production, but also that of France, Belgium, Luxembourg, the Netherlands and Italy. The hope was even entertained for a while that Britain would join the Community. What the Germans wanted to avoid at any price, and they were ready to make heavy concessions to this end, was the differential treatment they had been receiving. Their objective was to regain sovereign power status as rapidly as possible. In accepting the principles of the Schuman Plan (as the ECSC project was christened), Adenauer publicly stated his satisfaction: 'The proposal that France has just made to us is a generous move. It is a decisive step forward in Franco-German relations. It is not a matter of vague generalizations, but of concrete suggestions based on equal rights.' With this habitual realism, the chancellor also recognized an immediate advantage: 'Since the production of the Saar will be pooled, one cause of tension between France and Germany will be removed'.[13]

Finally, the Americans threw their weight behind the enterprise, which fitted in perfectly with their plans for Germany. Like Jean Monnet, they also saw in it the embryo of the European unity for which they had now been hoping for several years. Disappointed by the attitude of the British in the OEEC, they turned to the ECSC; the vigorous support they gave it helped to convince the Germans.

On 9 May 1950 Robert Schuman made his formal declaration initiating the project. In 1952 the deal was settled and the ECSC became a reality; the six member countries (France, Germany, Benelux and Italy) formed a common market for coal and steel within which those products would move freely. Institutional machinery, comprising notably a High Authority, a Council of Ministers, a Court of Justice and a Parliamentary Assembly, was set up to keep markets orderly and ensure that they functioned smoothly. This was an institutional system similar to the one that would be adopted a few years later when the European Economic Community was established, but with essential differences which I shall come back to later.

The ECSC is estimable on two counts. First, it represented a step forward, a new start on the road to a united Europe. Second, it represented a revolution in Franco-German relations. Nearly a century of wars, of attempts at domination, of an antagonism that had come absurdly to be called hereditary, had given way to a will to cooperate on completely equal terms. It would take a few more years for mentalities to change and adjust to the new situation, but the movement was under way and there would be no stopping it until the goal had been achieved.

Even without the ECSC, Germany would have regained her place in Europe. The Americans, who were working actively for her reconstruction as a great industrial power, would eventually have carried the day. But this reconstruction would have been effected against France; a great deal of bitterness would have persisted for a long time in the two countries. If only in this respect, the ECSC was an inspired idea.

De Gaulle was unjust when, in his memoirs, he accused Jean Monnet and the French governments of the time of having undersold France's interests:

> Thus, the re-establishment of a central German adminis-tration in the three western zones had been accepted, in spite of the absence of genuine guarantees. Then, the European Coal and Steel Community had been inaugu-rated, under an agreement which, without offering us the means of restoring our devastated mines, exempted the Germans from having to provide us with fuel deliveries and gave the Italians the wherewithal to equip themselves with a large-scale iron and steel industry.[14]

The path that de Gaulle seems to be indicating as the one he would personally have followed would have been the surest way to preclude any Franco-German rapproachment; any form of European construction would have become impossible. But there was much that was intentionally polem-ical in what de Gaulle said. No one can tell how he would have behaved had he been in power at the time. When he did come back to power in 1958 his attitude would be quite different. He and Adenauer would join forces to make a Franco-German Europe. Even today, a certain complicity between France and Germany, a certain Franco-German political will, constitutes the hidden mainspring that enables the Franco-German mechanism to go on functioning.

But the contribution of Jean Monnet and Robert Schuman to Europe's construction does not end there. It was they who in 1950 brought the Six together under the leadership of France. The Luxembourg of the ECSC constituted a school in which the Six learned to work together. When the day of the Common Market dawned they were ready to continue their collaboration in a much wider area than that of coal and steel.

Admittedly, the ECSC did not fulfill all the hopes that its founders had placed in it, particularly with regard to its institutions. The 1951 Treaty of Paris had given the High Authority extensive powers in the coal and steel sectors; it had made the Authority a sovereign power whose decisions were, within certain limits, binding on national governments. By 1956, when plans for the EEC were taking shape, ideas had been scaled down concerning the prerogatives of the 'Commission' (the name was already less ambitious than that of High Authority). One of the reasons, in fact the most important one, was that the High Authority had found itself constrained, in the exercise of its powers, by the fact that any decision of consequence in regard to coal and steel inevitably had repercussions in other areas of the member countries' economies. As a result, close cooperation had become a practice between the High Authority and the Council of Ministers. Furthermore, the energy situation had changed radically during the fifties. With oil progressively replacing coal in many uses, the ECSC was no longer in the center of the European economic scene, contrary to what might have been expected a few years earlier. Finally, the failure, in 1954, of the efforts to set up a European Defense Community had rebounded on the ECSC, the two ventures being linked in the public's mind by the fact, in particular, that both sought to reintegrate Germany into the concert of nations while preventing her from recovering her might of prewar years. But on the whole, the verdict on the ECSC had to be a positive one. It opened the way to more ambitious ventures.

NOTES

1. Charles de Gaulle, *Memoirs of Hope* (New York, 1971) 134, first published in English-language translation London, 1971.
2. Ibid., 135.
3. These measures included a 17½ per cent devaluation of the French franc.
4. Maurice Couve de Murville, *Une politique ètrangére 1958–1969* (Paris, 1971) 10.
5. George W. Ball, *The Past Has Another Pattern* (New York, 1982) 81.
6. See Walter Hallstein, *Europe in the Making* (New York, 1972).
7. Jean Monnet, *Memoirs*, trans. Richard Mayne (New York, 1978).
8. Ibid., 273.
9. Ibid., 272.
10. Ibid., 272–3.

11. Ibid., 280.
12. Ibid., 274.
13. Ibid., 304.
14. Charles de Gaulle, *Memoirs of Hope*, op. cit., 10

7 Jean Monnet's Methods
François Duchene

European integration is young for myths, but it has the beginnings of a surprising one in the person of Jean Monnet. This seems odd because he was, to all appearances, a rather anonymous, technocratic figure. True, he was the source of the European Community, the first man to propose European union in a form governments had to take seriously. But this cannot by itself be the reason. For one thing, he shares the credit of innovation with Robert Schuman and others. Why then should Jean Monnet have become 'Mr. Europe'?

Personal qualities apart, there seem to have been two factors. The first is that no one else has been as uniquely identified with European unification. Europe may have been the apex of other men's careers, but it was not at all times their center. Political lives are inherently various. In contrast, after 1950, there was no dispersion of Monnet's activities. The identification of the man with the theme was clearcut and complete. It was also in most ways masterful. He was the one man who not only could, but habitually did, link up the whole European chain of being from the tiniest tactical maneuver to a political vision of the world. Monnet has thereby colored the European idea to an exceptional degree.

The second factor is that the daring old man on the flying trapeze performed much of the time without visible means of support. Monnet never held elected office and was never a minister in any regular government. No comparable European leader has depended so heavily on his own personal qualities and so little on institutional backing. In these circumstances, he was bound to trade on private networks of contacts. He worked mainly behind the scenes with small groups of key decision-makers. Inevitable, the bulk of this activity was, and remains, to some extent a mystery. The fact that Monnet seemed to be involved in a surprising number of major decisions, without the non-initiative being able to see why such a publicly anonymous man had influence, or indeed exactly what he did, contributed, and still contributes, to a vague sense of intangible power.

Monnet had a reputation in many quarters as a 'gray eminence'. It suggests a man in the shadow of someone else. The shadow, if there was one, was very much his own. Still, the label suggests someone endlessly tortuous, secret and calculating. Monnet could at times be conspiratorial. But in general his approach was almost incredibly natural and simple. Basically, he went straight to the place where what he wanted could be obtained, and walked in. He was only mysterious in that he succeeded, and assumed he would succeed, in doing what most people would not even think of attempting.

Monnet, it is worth noting, was an adult before 1914. Born in Cognac in 1888, although he could profess a well-nigh 'American optimism', and dress in well-worn Savile Row clothes, he nevertheless gave off an indefinable sense of the rural France of his youth. From time to time, those who met him – like René Foch – commented that he was 'almost Chinese', an inscrutable, shrewd old man:

> I had tried to be as clear as I could. He listened to me, he looked at me, and he said: 'What you have told me is so clear it cannot be correct'. That struck me as rather profound. . . . [Monnet] impressed me as very much a peasant. Unlike the people you meet in the French establishment, he was not adept with words, he did not use them well. He mistrusted words.
>
> What was peasant for me was his circumspect manner of inspecting a problem from every angle, his refusal to rush to conclusions. Like a peasant buying a cow.

Monnet was superstitious, if that is a rustic characteristic; and a walking barometer, to judge by the number of times he tapped his chest and complained the weather was close. Another aspect should perhaps be added. Sir Michael Palliser, who knew Monnet first when he was a private secretary to Harold Wilson at 10 Downing Street, says, 'I found him a very good listener, which is not true of all great men. But, I think, not a very patient man. Underneath that calm manner, there was a good deal of impatience.'

Friends, for Monnet, were made through work and for work. They might come from any background and any country, and he often worked informally at the lunchtable, though he ate little himself. But Monnet took no part in the cocktail round of politics and shunned conferences as a waste of time. He was provincial and international. He was neither Parisian nor a mandarin.

A passage in the *Memoirs* concerns the moment when proposals for the American program of araments for the Second World War, in which Monnet had played a prominent part, reached Roosevelt.

On the basis of what I had told him, Beaverbrook produced figures which to the American experts seemed fantastic: 45,000 tanks in 1942 instead of 25,000; 24,000 fighter aircraft instead of 5,000; three times the number of anti-tank guns, and so on. Only Roosevelt listened to those requests without demur. 'All that's out of the question', he was told. 'It's not a matter of what we *can* do but of what we *must* do', he replied. I recognized in his attitudes and decisions that same philosophy of action that I myself had acquired ... Events were to show that this philosophy, which concentrates on what is necessary, is more realistic than one which takes account only of what is possible.[1]

Necessity of this kind assumes exceptional confidence in one's own insight and a clear visualization of what does not yet exist, but might be made to.

Monnet wrote in his *Memoirs* that he was never short of ideas. His fertility of resource can be gauged by the many relevant, or semi-relevant, proposals launched in a long career. Monnet's 'power of the imagination', as Max Kohnstamm called it, was particularly noticeable when some shock bruised previous assumptions. The implications would immediately be blown up into dramatic and sometimes quite exaggerated proportions. But soon the critical process would begin, and the visions be steadily whittled down to what seemed a hard core of immediately relevant conclusions. George Ball, who was with Monnet when the news of the Korean war broke, has testified to his speed and accuracy of insight into the effects it would have on American policy and European integration.

Monnet rarely had difficulty in imagining the concrete and immediate step which, in complex and changing situations, might change the flow of action. He said himself, without undue modesty, 'in crises people do not know what to do. I do know what to do'. His usual attitude to crises was that they were opportunities. In many ways, he reminded one, in administrative and political terms, of the instant *coup d'oeil* which is said to be the hallmark of good commanders. The launching of the Schuman Plan offers astonishing analogies with *Blitzkrieg*. The secrecy of the preparations, the bold objectives, the precise first targets, the speed of operations and the sharp acceptance of the tactical choices demanded by the strategy, all smack of it. There is much in Monnet's doctrine and practice of an 'expanding offensive' where one goal opens up another in chain reaction, to the extent that the *coup d'oeil* broke through first to bold conclusions. These in turn became springboards for further ideas that other people would not be placed to conceive so soon.

The integration of the two qualities, imagination and realism, produced an existential style that was rather intellectual by the standards of most politicians, yet owed little to theory and books. The Monnet and Schuman Plans have a familiar ring – both notions were present; though not exactly common, among the minorities alive to problems at the time. But the fact that Monnet and not others achieved them was no accident. Their vitality – as with most creative achievement, of any kind – was in the detail.

The Monnet Plan was an object lesson in picking one's way round potentially lethal pitfalls. This can be seen in the political balances engineered with the powerful bureaucracy, all too ready to reject an intruder. His Commissariat General du Plan was a tiny body, with only a hundred people including the cleaners and chauffeurs. One reason for this was not to appear a competitor to the ministries. At the same time, Monnet threatened several times to resign in order to make sure he was responsible only to the Prime Minister.

The idea of planning in 1945 in France was centralist, partly inspired by the obvious Soviet model, and with the idea that a superministry could impose coordination on the traditional ones. This proved a complete misconception. Monnet substituted a form of corporative 'democratic' consultation which involved all the key actors in devising the investment targets and then working together to achieve them.

Similarly, the art of the Schuman Plan in making it difficult for 'liberals' or 'interventionists' to mount effective opposition campaigns can be drawn up as a long list of antitheses. It was 'interventionist' by the very fact of being a sectorial plan, a line of approach to which the Germans, the Dutch and most economists were to object five years later. On the other hand, a common market was, in European terms at least, 'liberal'. The crisis powers of the High Authority of the Coal and Steel Community to deal with 'lack of sales' and 'penury', and the rules it had to administer on prices, were all 'interventionist'. On the other hand, it was 'liberal' in that ownership (a highly symbolic issue) was not dealt with at all in the Schuman Plan and the anti-cartel provisions were, by European standards, very strict. Such pairs of paradoxes are a measure of the care taken to circumvent rehearsed responses and the lobbies based on them.

Monnet's fusion of idealism and the pragmatic approach produced his dynamic notion of how reform was to be accomplished. He believed, like W. H. Auden, that we are changed by what we do. If the problem is insoluble in today's terms, then the context must be changed. 'The German problem cannot be settled in the present conditions', Monnet wrote on 3 May 1950, 'the conditions must be transformed',[2] which was the aim of the Schuman Plan. To him, political propaganda in favor of generalized ideas (such as Europe) was useless. The conditions that make today what it is, also buttress the outlook of today. The art is to seize the opportunity offered by a crisis to break through the conditions that protect the *status quo* and introduce new elements that favor further change. The Schuman Plan was consciously launched with this in mind. 'Europe will not be conjured up at a stroke, nor by an overall design; it will be attained by concrete achievements generating an active community of interest.'

Monnet talked often about this dynamic outlook to change. He liked the metaphor, culled from his own frequent mountain walks to concentrate his thoughts, about the changing view as one climbed up the mountain path. The perspective changed minimally but inexorably with every step. It followed that it was a fallacy to extrapolate from the present.

Several things ensued. One was that the crucial step was always the first. Obsessive attention would be paid to every facet of it. On its success everything would depend. Another was that anything but the most general statement of final ends was studiously avoided. Political union was clearly in his mind well before 1950. Simply, a statement so committing about anything so distant was false to the political process. Third, of course, different moments might require apparently different attitudes. Monnet was never a systematic 'functionalist'. He was rather favorable to de Gaulle's proposals for a political union under the Fouchet plan. He thought it more important to inveigle de Gaulle into the system to conduct a static defense of the Community institutions. Fourth, the process of continuous creation would not necessarily lead where its own promoters imagined. The very existence of a uniting Europe might produce political options at the international level quite unforeseen at the beginning. Monnet's attitude was open-ended.

In many ways, Monnet's outlook is best understood in terms of James McGregor Burns' distinction between 'transactional' and 'transforming' leadership. Transactional leadership is the art of tying up compromises between political forces in the normal operation of a settled system. Transforming leadership requires an altogether rarer capacity to change the terms in which the political debate is carried on. Monnet's approach makes much more sense as transforming than transactional leadership. He was aware of that himself.

In the end, the test of political leadership is the capacity to bring ideas down to earth in action. Monnet's visible achievements would probably never have materialized had he not been an artist in moving bureaucracies and governments well before he stepped onto the political stage.

Monnet's mode of operation, the originality of which was a major part of his persona, is the aspect which, in those who worked with him, evokes instant recognition, often with a kind of laughing admiration. The basis of it was a completely matter-of-fact approach to power. He used and respected power, but defined it in low key as the capacity to act and (in his own eyes at least) use it 'for the individual'. He was unimpressed by the State, whose pretensions he deeply distrusted. He had a correspondingly sharp nose for real information and influence, irrespective of where they were located, high or low. All his operations have to be seen in terms of this pervasive and purposeful informality.

THE IDEA

It will not be surprising from what has already been said that there was a strong ruminative element in Monnet's process of conception. Though in general he hated being alone, a large part was played in the whole of his working life by long walks. Mountains especially appealed to him. He relaxed among them and found an inner balance there to confront the tensions of his calling. To prepare for great occasions, he went off on long expeditions in the Alps.

At the next level, though, Monnet was a man for whom discussion was vital. All his proposals were hammered out in intense debate with a small circle of argumentative advisers who were a kind of slowly changing office family. 'You put your head through the door, you were called in, and you were kept there for the rest of the day', as Max Kohnstamm said. Anyone with something to contribute might suddenly be added to the group for a while, irrespective of who they were or where they came from. Both the Schuman Plan and Euratom seem to have been worked out first with individuals with whom Monnet had in one case only casual prior acquaintance and in the other none at all.

A graphic description of the process has been given by Stanley Cleveland, one of several outstanding members of the American Marshall Aid Mission in France, led by David Bruce:

> The Monnet method was quite special. Monnet never wrote anything in his life, as far as I know; he developed the ideas and let other people write them up for him. But whenever Monnet attacked a new problem he would gather a bunch of people around him. Some of them would be his intimates – Hirsch, Uri – people who were close to him, Tommy [William Tomlinson], when he was alive, and others. Some would be people he hardly knew

but had somehow laid his hands on. They knew a lot about the particular subject. He would begin a sort of non-stop *Kaffeeklatsch.* It could go on sometimes for a period of one or two weeks – hours and hours a day. It generally started out with a rambling discussion of the subject in which relevant facts would be brought out. People would begin to argue (these were a very argumentative bunch). Gradually two or three approaches and positions would develop in the group. Monnet would remain silent, occasionally provoking reaction, but not saying much . . . Then gradually, as the conversation developed – and it often took several days or even a week before this happened – he began venturing a little statement of his own. Usually it was a very simple statement, just a few words, almost a slogan. It distilled, out of all this argument among highly verbal, brilliant people, a couple of kernels of an idea. These he would throw into the conversation. The people would react to him. Gradually, Monnet would begin to expose a little more in a few sentences, then in a couple of paragraphs. The process then was that people in the group who had been arguing against each other would all turn against him. They would argue with him, indicating all the things that were wrong about what he was saying. Monnet would listen, reformulate his ideas – taking into account what somebody had said, refusing to heed what somebody else had said. It was like taking a rough piece of stone and gradually chipping edges off until it became a sculpture.

At this point he would begin to come out with a formulated concept, an idea. It was usually action-oriented and contained all the necessary elements. Then he would go through what was, in some ways, the most excruciating part of the process. Yet it was the ultimate refinement. Monnet would go on saying the same thing, over and over again, in practically the same words, occasionally modifying a detail to take account of a legitimate criticism. People would still argue with him but gradually the arguments would die out because he would have taken into account all of the legitimate arguments that were made. In the end, there was . . . in Monnet's head, and ready to put on paper, a perfectly formulated idea. [Interview by Leonard Tennyson]

This account evokes memories in anyone who helped prepare the versions – often the ten, occasionally the thirty, versions – of a Monnet proposal, declaration, speech or memorandum. It is a rather heightened version of routine moments, but it corresponds to the bigger ones, and they shared the same basic character.

THE USES OF SIMPLICITY

One of the hopes of the process described by Cleveland was to distill ideas to an essence, as Richard Mayne has said, transparent as water with the force of gin. That was the precondition of the next stage, persuasion of the men of power. Robert Marjolin recalled in his memoirs that 'Monnet had a greater capacity to win people over and convince them that I have encountered in any other human being'. Reducing the idea to its simplest possible form was a structural feature of that capacity, fulfilling many functions.

The first was largely to convince Monnet himself so that he could be the more convincing to others. He frequently said that when people were not clear, they had failed to understand what they were saying.

Second, simplicity was essential to communication. It was not a matter of talking down to people, but of laying a clear path for understanding to advance. It was necessary to eliminate at source the ever-present scope for misunderstanding, which is a potential weapon in the hands of opponents. In this perspective, intellectual adornments that might complicate the desired impression must be avoided. Monnet's relations with the press, his main channel for broadcasting his views, would warrant a study in themselves. He was very successful, in ways that were not showy but potent in the long run. Leonard Tennyson put it like this:

> Monnet attracted the press. He attracted politicians, he attracted a lot of other people, because of his apparent – not apparent, obvious – disinterest in personal power [giving the impression] that he was concerned with an idea, that he was pursuing this, and was an accurate exponent of something exciting and interesting that was happening in

Europe. He was quite articulate. The press found in Monnet someone whom they felt they could trust and rely upon. It's that simple.

That Monnet cumulatively obtained the kind of press that politicians dream of was largely a tribute to the service he shrewdly provided. He liked publicity, especially being photographed. At the same time, *exegi monumentum* was his bet with fame, and he was content to tie his reputation to his works. The publicity was for them, not directly for him.

Third, thoroughly preparing a notion and paring it down to essentials was important in forestalling criticism that must arise when it was held up to public gaze. Once an idea had been streamlined, simple though it might seem, it had in fact been designed to resist friction. On the whole, the Monnet team were adept at confounding critics and responding quickly to unexpected lines of attack. The brilliant Pierre Uri would usually produce the last argument or note.

Fourth, well-selected simplicity was a way of imposing one's own categories on the collective debate. As early as the negotiations on the Schuman Plan and the first days of the Coal and Steel Community in Luxembourg, Monnet's terms tended to be taken up and become orthodoxies, for those in close contact with him. Phrases like 'non-discrimination', notions such as the importance of institutions, or that Britain will 'accept facts' became the categories in which many people thought and moved. This was undoubtedly one of the secrets of his long-term influence.

Fifth, and possible most important, simplicity was an instrument for building trust. It helped Monnet to address all partners and all audiences in the same, or virtually the same, language. This was specially important in a multi-national undertaking. Latent mistrust between nations and groups was always ready to rear its head. It was vital not to be observed speaking in different terms to different people.

PERSUASION AND POWER

The stage of finding the man in power who could implement his ideas was perhaps the most idiosyncratic of Monnet's whole approach. The pattern seems to have been established from the first attempt. In a way, the most astonishing thing he ever did was, at the age of twenty-six in 1914, to persuade a lawyer friend of his father, Fernand Benon, to give him an introduction to the then Prime Minister, René Viviani. In essence, he did exactly the same thing with de Gaulle on the Monnet Plan, with Bidault and Schuman on the Schuman Plan, with Spaak on the *relance de Messine* and even, it has been claimed, much later with President Giscard on the European Council. There were many smaller cases.

All this is inherently straightforward. Monnet worked always from the center of a small circle which was never large enough for him to lose personal contact with each of its members. In much the same way, when he reached out into the world beyond, he worked with only a few people at a time. Gradually, he built up networks of such individuals, powerful and not so powerful, on whom he could call as occasion demanded. The amazement lies only in the success of Monnet's uncanny ability to by-pass the obstructions which prevent most people from passing through the bureaucratic labyrinth.

The list of the prominent postwar politicians and officials, especially in the two decades after the war, with whom Monnet had close relations, virtually all formed through work, is almost endless. By the 1950s, these associations went back, in some cases, for thirty years. René Pleven, the French Prime Minister who launched the EDC, was Monnet's personal assistant in refloating the Polish zloty in 1927; and John Foster Dulles, Monnet's lawyer on the same occasion. Two other postwar French Prime Ministers, René Mayer, and Felix Gaillard, had at one time been Monnet's assistants. In the United States, the list of friends and associates was particularly long. They included Felix Frankfurter, Philip Graham, Oscar Cox, John McCloy, Harry Hopkins, the Dillons (father and son), George Ball, David Bruce, 'Tommy' Tomlinson, Donald Swatland and a host of others at different times on the highest steps of the establishment.

At the same time, the striking point about his dealing with the great was his wariness and caution. His technique of dealing with them was to offer a service; to avoid any appearance of competing with them; and as far as possible –

without making it obvious – to make them feel they needed
him more than he did them: in short, to disguise and
minimize in every way his basic dependency on their goodwill.

The essence of the service to be rendered was, of course, to
propose and carry out policies because, as an acerbic passage
in the *Memoirs* remarks, men in power are short of ideas, for
lack of time and information, and they would like to act
constructively, so long as they can take the credit. Accordingly, Monnet was careful not to compete for jobs, nor for glory,
at least openly and in the short run. That was one of
Monnet's great strengths. He never tried to take other
peoples' jobs, according to Baron Robert Rothschild.

INFLUENCE IN OBSCURE PLACES

It is of a piece with his caution that Monnet often conditioned the great by working through influential but not
necessarily prominent subordinates. As a man of power but
not of show, he had a nose for others in a similar situation,
high or low, and a sharp eye for their strengths and
weaknesses. He was unerring in locating unknowns behind
the bureaucratic screen, irrespective of their youth, status or
experience, who exercised influence over crucial holders of
power, provided a route to them, or simply conveyed important information. He had no snobbery. A useful contact
would be cultivated as carefully as a prime minister or
president. Although in his last three decades he could walk
through the door of virtually all the heads of Western
governments more or less when he wished, most of the time
he seemed to prefer to lay indirect siege to the men of power.
This was virtually the hallmark of Monnet practice.

Everyone who experienced these blandishments comments on them. At the simplest level, it was a matter of
picking up information. As Berndt von Staden, later the
German ambassador to the United States, has said:

Monnet was able to make a distinction between people of
influence, and people who were well-informed. If it came
to information, he did not hesitate a moment to call a very

junior man and to ask him questions. Then he was quite willing to spend two hours of his time and his time was precious, with somebody who had no political influence of his own, but who was able to give him the picture of the situation. [3]

If subordinates were useful to Monnet, he wooed them with the same assiduity and charm as their masters, and paid them the same basic respect. There is a long roll-call of workers in the vineyards of great men more or less enlisted on the side by Monnet. But if the great man acquiesced, his staff became almost as important as he was himself. Monnet was well aware of how dependent the great are on intense bureaucratic preparation. To influence that preparation was to shape, even to make, their decisions. Close liaison with subordinates also made it easier not to see the great man too often and so not only avoid overloading his goodwill, but also to arrange meetings as far as possible when he felt the *demandeur*, relieving Monnet of the role. And it ensured optimal timing for initiatives.

Of course, Monnet's networks were an 'elitist' phenomenon. It is hard to see how another would have worked. The populist tactic had been tried in the Council of Europe. The result had been virtually nil. Unfortunately, neither the motor nor the brake on European integration was public opinion. In the founder countries of the Communities, the popular attitude was then, and has always tended to be, more permissive than that of the governments. To pursue integration was not, therefore, to go behind the back of public opinion. On the other hand, integration rarely, if ever, was the top political priority at any given moment. As a result, working on governments from within, or through party leaders, was the only plausible strategy. But the establishments were also where most of the opposition concentrated. This tended to be located among the corporatist establishments, the machinery of state and its agencies, as well sometimes in the industrial lobbies. All this necessarily meant operating at the top of the pyramid. At that level, personal networks were one of the keys to effective action.

TACTICS AND PRINCIPLE

Once Monnet, often after much hesitation and discussion, had decided what his priorities were, his instinct was normally to strike while the iron was hot. Monnet's team prepared a forty-article treaty for the first meeting of the Paris conference on the Schuman Plan. Monnet's *Memoirs* say specifically that the intention was to deprive potential opposition of the time to mobilize. Again, on the very afternoon of the day the treaties of Rome were signed, Monnet saw the Clerk of the French Assembly to remove any technical obstacles to ratification.

Monnet was ready to work at most times of night or day to gain or keep the initiative.

I never sat down to a table to discuss anything without having a proposal. It did not matter to me that it should be the first or the only one. It was our side's contribution, and all the better if it was accepted by the other because it was the best, or for any other reason. I must say that our initiatives often won the day for lack of competition.[4]

Monnet paid the same obsessive attention to seeing that a note had reached its destination.

This was, of course, all part of Monnet's 'determination (*acharnement*) to achieve results', as Etienne Hirsch noted. Monnet's determination in adversity was legendary among his associates. The rejection of the EDC was a terrible blow to the European integrationists. Yet the EDC was barely thrown out but he was consulting even the most junior of his associates on plans to seize the initiative again. In one of Monnet's favorite stories, 'a Western visitor asked Ibn Saud the secret of his success. Ibn Saud replied, "God appeared to me in the desert when I was a young man and said something which has guided my actions throughout my life: He told me, 'For me, everything is a means – even the obstacles.'"'[5]

Monnet did not give way easily on what he thought crucial and when he was determined to have his way. There was, for instance, no compromise with Britain over the supranational principle which Monnet had decided was basic to the strategy of the Schuman Plan. He fought a number of battles with German industry, sometimes with and sometimes without

American help. On the other hand he was not a fanatic either. He was as much a man of discussion in negotiation and other dealing as he was within his own circle. He did not rush to premature conclusions or try to ride roughshod over opposition unless he felt it was disingenuous or irreducible. He was not apt to paint himself into a corner through vanity or pride.

There was one more important factor in Monnet's mode of operations; what might be called the imperative to pursue the tactics of principle. If one is trying to introduce a new political principle into contemporary practice, it has to be exemplified to spring into life. Being new, the principle is alien to the scene on which it breaks. It will be hard to implant against ingrained habits which have evolved for other reasons and from a different background.

The best example of apparently quixotic tactics is probably the surprise of the hardened negotiators of the Schuman Plan treaty when they found Monnet arguing with his own French team in front of everyone else about the shape of the new Community. Representatives of other countries, unused to this, suspected a trap. When they found it was not, and that Monnet was behaving in some sense as if he were already leader of a European Community and seeking the most reasonable way forward, they became involved with some enthusiasm in a joint and unfamiliar search for a common goal, as Max Kohnstamm has noted.

THE OUTSIDER

All these are aspects of the fact that if Monnet's extraordinary personal talent for detecting and manipulating the levers of influence in country after country made him, in one sense, a virtuoso inside the corridors of power, nevertheless, in another sense – in terms of bureaucratic hierarchies and government, that is, at the political levels to which his career finally rose – he was virtually the classic outsider. As Robert Bowie has said, 'He never really had a political base. He only had persuasiveness'.

This may somewhat overstate the case. Monnet could never have been effective if he had not been one of a kind of shadow party of internationalists on both sides of the Atlantic. From such a point of view, it is an error to speak of the integrative policies of the postwar period as if they were clearly those of states such as America, France or Germany. To a significant extent, they were due to small but temporarily dominant groups of people in key positions, with converging ideas, working together across frontiers, often against latent or active opposition at home.

On the other hand, the limits of Monnet's influence were evident even in a matter like the determination of the Belgians and Luxembourgers to share the spoils of housing the European Community institutions, a deal which destroyed Monnet's dream of a European federal district on the model of Washington. The scope and limits of Monnet's influence are a complex issue. In a brief compass, it can perhaps best be gauged through considering his alliance with the American policy-makers in Washington. A prior question must be who influenced whom in Monnet's relationship with Washington. Many Frenchmen, not only Gaullists, more or less assumed that Monnet was the agent of the Americans. It is true that American support for the revival of Germany forced the French to envisage both the Schuman Plan and the EDC. On the other hand, in Euratom the Americans made big concessions to European, indeed to French, ambitions, and European industrial interests could have gained as much as American from the cooperation agreement. Moreover, Monnet's hand was visible in a number of specifics of American policy. In Eisenhower's change of attitude to EDC in 1951; the backing for Euratom's system of nuclear controls; the US resignation to Euratom building a gaseous diffusion plant; the current of influence seemed to flow from Europe to America rather than the other way.

Because France was one of the crucial pillars of any European policy, Monnet reduced the risks of losing control, and his influence was at its height, when in effect he played a direct part in running French policy, essentially in the first half of the 1950s. Also, an individual working as he did, was likely to have maximum influence in relatively open, or decentralized political systems. This was clear not only in the French Fourth Republic, where rule by Assembly created potential for influence through personal networks (though even these had to be built up from a base like the Monnet Plan); but also from the USA in wartime, where Monnet's success as a foreigner is a sign not only of his talents but of the access to influence at that time in the American system. Monnet's influence could also be strong in the case of a closed system where, for whatever reason, the dominant leadership was ideologically close to what he was trying to do. Adenauer is the outstanding (but not constant) case.

However, an outsider like Monnet was ineradicably weak when his strategies came up against rooted domestic interests, as in the federal district matter, but also, and with the most far-reaching implications, when he was dealing with relatively closed hierarchical systems with uncommitted or hostile leadership. The example which leaps to mind is the elective monarchy of the French Fifth Republic under de Gaulle. But the other, which is at least as significant, because less exceptional than de Gaulle, was Britain. Despite a range of discreetly influential contacts, Monnet had little or no direct impact on British policy to Europe. Here again, this was partly because the British leadership, until around 1960, had no intention of being inveigled into Europe. On the other hand, that cannot explain Churchill's refusal to recognize Monnet as a legitimate French voice just before France fell in 1940. This was because Monnet was not invested with official status as the designated representative of the French government. Without that, Monnet was a nobody to Churchill. As far as Britain was concerned, Monnet usually had to work indirectly – with marked success – through the Community Six and Americans.

INSTITUTIONS AND VALUES

Monnet's career until World War II was largely technocratic. As Deputy Secretary-General of the League of Nations in 1919, at the age of thirty-one, he saw salvation very much in the terms of the kind of functional cooperation one might expect of an international civil servant. It was the failure of this approach which left a lasting political impress on Monnet's mind. He felt the tragic contrast between inspiring cooperation among allies in wartime, when things were desperate, and its rapid collapse as soon as peace returned, so that the catastrophic cycle started up again. By the time the Schuman plan appeared, it already had a substantial prehistory in Monnet's mind, and a context larger than the scheme itself. Cooperation, of an incremental kind, was blocked by deep-seated 'structural' obstacles to change. It followed that radical measures, deep enough to uproot them, must be undertaken.

In a folksy formulation to which Monnet was addicted, most negotiations set people on opposite sides of the table, confronting each other, with the problem never addressed. What needed to be done was to bring them all round to the same side of the table, with the problem by itself on the other side. The question was how relations could be reshaped to do this.

A common task is the starting-point, but not enough. If men are to trust one another enough to sit on the same side of the table, they must be confident of having equal rights by the rules of the collective, not just in form but in substance. 'Equality is absolutely necessary between people as between individuals', Monnet wrote. 'We lost the peace in 1919 because we built discrimination into it, and the will to dominate (*esprit de superiorite*).'

Monnet had long been a devotee of the *bilan*, or balance sheet (he often preferred the English expression). It comes up frequently in the *Memoirs* and was familiar to all of Monnet's associates. Even at this level, the 'bilan' was still an administrative yardstick of what needs to be done. But in 1950, the notion of the balance sheet was expanded into a political concept as the general view (*vue generale*). This logical extension was much more profound and, in effect, still underpins the whole rationale of the Community system. It is necessary to every stage of it: to the formulation of federal objectives, which are beyond the member states responsible solely to the domestic electorate of each; to the general trust in their equity of those policies because they belong to the Community as a whole, not to a dominant partner; and to the exercise of common responsibility for the differentiated effects on the members. It embodies all the powers given in the Communities to the 'executives', from the High Authority of the Coal and Steel Community to the

Commission operating on behalf of the three European Communities as they exist today.

In principle, all this is a form of federal doctrine, but Monnet's approach to institution-building was much more psychological and conceived from the ground up than inspired by constitutional blueprints. Indeed, because the Community has been economic and only very partially federal, whereas most of the classic federations began, however shakily, with the traditional fields of sovereignty, defense and foreign policy, there is very little analogy with precedent. It is astonishing how little the Community has owed to historic models.

Still, the pragmatic approach to the form taken by the Community, on the other hand, does not mean Monnet regarded institutions as in some sense contingent. For a man who was not normally high-flown, his pronouncements on institutions are notable for an almost lyric strain. He was particularly fond of an aphorism of the Swiss nineteenth-century thinker, Amiel:

> The experience of each person is a new beginning. Only institutions grow wiser; they store up the collective experience and, from this experience and wisdom, men subject to the same laws will gradually find, not that their natures change but that their behavior does.[5]

And again, 'Institutions govern relationships between people. They are the real pillars of civilization'.

THE FERMENT OF CHANGE

Monnet's views on institutions had deep roots, he meant them very seriously, and they are perhaps his most characteristic pronouncements. Yet the matter is more complex, even in his own practice, than his declared beliefs might make it appear.

At one level, not the most important, there can have been few professed admirers of institutions as suspicious as Monnet of the bureaucratic routines to which it is fairly predictable they will lead. The small size of the Commissariat-General du Plan he regarded as a diploma of quality. He tried to treat the sizable bureaucracy of the High Authority rather as he might a private office. Though he gave his staff the impression they were at the creative center of the world, he was administratively exhausting. He expected the whole cumbersome body to veer like a weathercock with every tactical, and in his eyes overriding, shift of priority. He believed creation demanded a certain disorder. Administration bored him.

More profoundly, there was a potential contradiction between the theory of institutions and the pragmatism of a dialectical strategy based on the transforming power of successive actions, each one conditioning the next, to produce 'continuing change'.

The first aspect of this strategy was the deliberate calculation that the Schuman Plan would create contradictions with national policies which could be resolved only by further steps down the European and presumably federal road. The danger that the nations might absorb the excrescence back into the pre-existing system was dismissed. In fact, there have been signs of both processes at different times in the history of the European Communities. But on the whole, the Monnet bet has proved correct. In the last resort, none of the opponents of the Communities has dared, or thought it wise, to dissolve the new system; and so at least to some extent they have been saddled with its logic. The supporters on the other hand have several times seized changes to expand its scope.

The second factor was the tactical leverage created by the mere fact that the European policy, without Britain, was based on an unfamiliar Franco-German tandem. This political innovation changed all international calculations. Once the European Economic Community was set up and it became evident that the new political entity had come to stay, and had general implications, the British could no longer remain on the sidelines.

In practice, this implied a great power directorate with a united Europe in effect joining the superpowers to run the world. (Japan was not then in European minds.) It appeared as early as 1959 in Monnet's proposals for a transformed OEEC with an executive committee composed of the United States, and the Commission speaking as a 'single voice' for the European Community. Potential for rivalry between America and Europe, if the latter really revived as a major power, was an obvious risk of such a 'partnership'. But on the whole the fear of competition between the two Western blocks was rejected, notably in Washington. This may have been because American power was so great that any real challenge seemed an intellectual abstraction. The expressed grounds, however, were different.

The first was that factors holding the Americans and Europeans together were far stronger than those pulling them apart. They were all democracies, so innately pacific, with a common stake in the prosperity and stability of the world. Their association was vital to a world compatible for both. Second, the pressures of 'interdependence' were such that the need of common control over blind process overrode traditional competition between states. There would be difficulties. They could be handled. Third, the Europeans would squander their collective resources for all practical purposes of international policy if they remained divided. Europe could only acquire dynamism and understanding of world problems if it attained the size and reach that unity would bring.

Whatever the practical force of these arguments, they are very different from the institutional ones Monnet used for European integration. It is not surprising that Monnet, as a practitioner, never addressed the contradictions involved in how Europe and America would finally relate to each other in terms of 'interdependence', common values or common institutions.

There are, indeed, two themes, not one, in Monnet's political philosophy: first, European unity; and second, through Europe, the search for improved international government. This was a natural extension of the theme of reconciliation in Europe, but it did not rest on the traditional response of many 'Europeans' who simply saw European unity as the creation of a 'nation writ large'. Monnet did not think in these terms. He wanted a political framework to manage common international problems, and to move beyond the fragmented purposes of a world seen by many nation states. This made it difficult for traditionalists, especially in France, to understand what he was about, or believe him if they did. Few contemporaries beyond a restricted circle of like-minded reformers ever fully grasped the paradox, in traditional, national terms, of Monnet's refusal to be a European nationalist, and yet his determination that a uniting Europe should achieve 'equality' with the United States. It is ironic that Gaullists saw Monnet as a pawn of the Americans (thus jettisoning Monnet's cherished goal of association in equality); while Kissinger, in the *Years of Upheaval* (ch. V) viewed him as a subtler kind of European Gaullist proposing to obtain from America by stealth what de Gaulle hoped to snatch by defiance (thus jettisoning the stress on interdependence and cooperation). What they wrote off as camouflage, because neither would, nor could, see it through the same spectacles, was in fact the clue to his strategy and values.

CONCLUSIONS

If the question is asked why others equally near the seats of power did not seize the initiative as often as Monnet, the answer is that, while being close to power, he detached himself from the distractions of day-to-day politics and set his own agenda. He had a chance to stand for election to the French Assembly in 1945. He turned it down. He was a poor speaker and would no doubt have made a colorless public figure. But he made a virtue of his limitations. He said that it was easier to propose policies to men in power than to try to keep power oneself. This was largely true in the French Fourth Republic, of which he made himself in effect the strategist. Throughout his life, Monnet isolated the task which at the moment seemed to him essential and in effect imposed his own priorities. He achieved this by a capacity to relate general goals to all the detail relevant to putting them into practice.

At one end, his vision of generalities was telescopic. He was too concentrated and focused to be what people usually think of as 'romantic', but he let himself go at least once to admit there had to be a utopian stand in all political innovation; his highest word of commendation for a statesman was to call him, as he called Roosevelt and Willy Brandt, 'generous'; and much of his appeal came from his controlled idealism. He had a breadth of vision which identified him with a cause. At

the other end of the scale, dealing with detail, Monnet went
to infinite pains to hone his plans in open-ended discussion
with able associates.

He expended much effort in retaining the initiative. He
lavished practical psychological insight on bolstering his
persuasions. He found a common language of carefully
selected simplicities for all audiences. His axioms sprang
directly from the matter in hand.

In short, Monnet's methods depended on a high and
well-balanced level of excellence right across the board, from
representation of the idea down to the slightest relevant
detail. This is much easier said than done in mobile situations
and therefore impossible to reduce to a formula.

There are nevertheless a certain number of characteristic
Monnet traits that can to some extent be held up to scrutiny.
One of them is the talent for building up and keeping
working alliances of influential people, high and low, in
different countries over long periods of time. Part of this was
obviously a tribute to his personal qualities. But the informality of it was also exceptional, and, probably, necessary.
Contacts were always person-to-person, never hierarchical
nor official. He raised the bypassing of formal channels to a
fine art. He was probably most at home working with
Americans, because their combination of meritocracy and
informality suited him. His fluency in English, not just as a
language but from his experience of the United States and
Britain, at a time when this was rare among Frenchmen, was
an added advantage.

A second striking trait of the Monnet working stance was
the importance he accorded to the 'general view'. This
stretched all the way from the 'balance sheets' of his technocratic days to the powers to propose policies 'in the general
interest' of the 'executives' of the European Community in
his political ones.

Third, Monnet rooted large political goals in concrete
proposals worked out not just in obedience to his own
priorities but also to those of the immediate political scent.
He did not believe that ideas standing outside urgent topical
preoccupations could capture attention. They needed to be
advanced at times when the contradictions of the *status quo*
forced political leaders to question their own assumptions.

To what extent are such practices and precepts transferable? Clearly personal alchemy played a role. In the unending competition for influence, Monnet's assets were exceptional. Individuals would not be exceptional if they were all exceptional in the same way. By definition, they tend to be idiosyncratic. They will be no more likely to obey his recipes in the future than he was to look for models in the past.

The postwar years were also exceptional. They gave more openings to a person of no institutional status than he could possibly hope to have in run-of-the-mill situations. Monnet's personal standing in the United States is a clear instance of this. He acquired backroom influence in Washington during the war even though he was a citizen of defeated France working for the British. Such a *tour de force* is almost inconceivable outside an emergency. As for France, Monnet would probably not, without two wars, have come from private business into the center of affairs. In France, as in most of Europe but more so, institutional resistance to someone outside channels is virtually insurmountable. He could never have acquired the central postwar position he did in the French establishment without the break-up of former cadres, the massive administrative renewal and the fluidity resulting from the muffled civil war of the occupation.

Lost wars are times of exhaustion and often of revolution. Most of postwar Europe was destroyed; institutions and networks of loyalty were deeply shaken. The shadow of Hitler was hardly lifted before that of Stalin fell. The new Germany was desperate for rehabilitation. France, after the shame of 1940 and the occupation, was equally in search of salvation. Europe looked for ever dwarfed by the superpowers. Unity seemed not so much bold as the one answer basic enough to meet new and extreme circumstances.

Monnet was, as he said himself, 'a man of beginnings'. It is one thing to set up a European Community or proclaim an Atlantic partnership, and quite another to make them work over a long period. The Community has progressed despite long dispiriting intervals. But two favorable factors in its case – the breadth and depth of economic commitment in the Common Market, and the sense of a single potential identity subsumed in the very word, 'Europe' – are probably not transposable, at least in the foreseeable future. As for partnership, Kennedy enunciated a theme, but its problems had yet to be lived with. Much of the coherence of the postwar period came in fact from the unique power of the United States. As recovery elsewhere has reduced this pre-eminence, decision-making has become hydra-headed. It has in fact become increasingly tangled in competing national priorities. The history of macro-economic diplomacy between the three dominant currencies is an object lesson in the obstacles to coherence. Significantly, the equivalents have been experienced even in the more highly-structured Community. The more one encroaches upon the vitals of sovereignty and society, the harder the going proves to be.

How the Monnet 'method' or methods, might apply to the future of global relations is, of course, in the eye of the beholder. Yet, on the record, a few points about the basic approach seem plausible. It is fairly safe to assume Monnet would be trying to promote the maximum practical union in the European Community, with a Franco-German agreement at the core of it. He would be preoccupied with 'Europe in the world', as he said of his difference with George Pompidou who was concerned with 'France in the Common Market'.

As regards the world, he would not be satisfied with the 'five-power balance' that seems attractive to some. To go beyond it, he would try to work from the ground up, that is, through concrete answers to one priority concern at a time, seeking to pave the way to subsequent ones. He would not try to persuade everyone to agree. He would seek limited agreements between limited numbers of core partners. He would see these as bases from which to extend later. He would try to give the resulting contacts the maximum content, institutional strength and power to develop.

He would certainly be very attentive to changes in the Soviet Union and Eastern Europe and to the opportunities they might offer. That was already his preoccupation for the Atlantic 'partnership' in 1962. In short, he would try to turn latent common interests between nations into active ones; and temporary convergencies of perception into permanent structures confident that these alone could provide a step-by-step approach to a safer, more effective and also juster international system, less dependent on naked power and more on commonly accepted law.

SOURCES

Quotations, unless referenced below, are from interviews available in the Fondation Jean Monnet pour l'Europe in Lausanne. Among these are the following, done by the author and cited here: George Ball, Robert Bowie, Paul Debuvrier, René Foch, Max Kohnstamm, Michael Palliser, Robert Rothchild, Berndt von Staden and Leonard Tennyson. Monnet's own statements are usually from his *Memoirs*, in the London and New York editions translated by Richard Mayne, or translated by the present author.

NOTES

1. Jean Monnet, *Memoirs* (New York, 1978), 173–4.
2. Ibid., 291.
3. Ibid., 323.
4. This story in similar words appears in Monnet's *Memoirs*, 399.
5. Monnet used this aphorism often, in varied forms. See *Memoirs*, 393.

8 Jean Monnet As He Was
Jacques Van Helmont

Translated by Margot Lyon

Stocky, of medium height, Jean Monnet was built to be a lumberjack or a boxer. In New York a taxi driver who said he was a Turk, took Monnet for a fellow Turk and what is more, a general.

His eyes were brilliant. Earnest but often mischievous. His expression was attentive, his gestures quiet.

He dressed simply. For years he wore suits and shoes made to measure in London, much the same in style, well looked-after until they gradually wore thin. His two or three hats and overcoats ended up showing signs of wear, but still served him.

While he was speaking his eyes never left the person he was talking to. He seldom raised his voice, which was low in pitch, limited in volume, but clear. It had a metallic vibration that one noticed. It could become insistent, almost irritating.

It was a voice made for confidential conversations, his favorite method of operating. With one or more people in an office, a hotel room, the corner of a meeting hall, or by telephone. His voice helped him, not to impose himself but to be listened to. It communicated something of his energy.

He took care of his voice. He was concerned about the impression it made. He asked people to tell him if he was in good voice, as clear as usual, the way one says to other people that they are looking in good shape. In summer he went off alone to have it attended to, at out-of-the-way spas that have not been fashionable for a century. American friends made gentle fun of these obligatory cures, calling them his fad, a superstition that was behind the times. He paid no heed to them. At eighty, he had vague wishes for lessons in diction. He dropped them after a few sessions.

He imposed a daily discipline on himself, to give himself as much energy and future time as possible. He watched his health continually, weighing up diagnoses and cross-checking them one against another. He dined out only a few times a year.

With some exceptions he liked to sleep and wake in his country home. Then he would take a walk across the fields before he was driven to his office reading the newspapers, sitting in front beside his chauffeur. When he got to the office, when he left, and often several times during the day, he felt the need to talk on the telephone to his wife or daughter.

The discussions he began toward the end of the morning continued during lunchtime. He mostly ate on the spot, in the office dining room. In the beginning he liked to be served a light meal, but as the years went by the meals, though not elaborate, conformed more to the habits of his guests. After a break or a short walk, he would work through again until the evening.

He put up with weekends and vacations, seeing them as interruptions that he did his best to delay, or at least to shorten, except when he went off to the mountains.

When he was alone his usual pastime was to go over his thoughts and his documents, endlessly. Until his last active years he was prepared to work late into the night if necessary, or to go off to take a plane or a train. Earlier, he had liked taking the ferryboats between Calais and Dover and even more crossing the Atlantic or the Pacific in great ocean liners. He remembered seeing a typhoon in the Sea of Japan.

He was an expert on journeys, and he liked them. Once he had arrived at the train station, he would go off himself to find a porter. At each stage of the trip he would count and recount his baggage. One bag, and one or two valises. He would not let them out of his sight and unless it was impossible he went along with the porter. He kept a flat document case in brown leather, with a zip fastener, under his arm. Inside was his passport, his tickets, part of his money and his most important papers. His baggage was worn but solid and in good condition. It served for a long time.

He was happy when he was on a journey, heading by plane or train toward some capital, in the hope of getting the cooperation he needed and of revealing hidden treasures. He easily got into conversation with people of all conditions, in any country. His conversations fed his reflections. Often he would try out the basic line of argument and the decisive formulas he was looking for.

He would come immediately to the point. He let important people know he had taken the trouble to come and see them, and let everybody know their thinking was valuable to him. He chose the words he wanted. He spoke precisely, yet at the same time in half statements, like drawings where everything is lightly sketched in except one figure, one movement, one detail.

On the telephone it could happen that he suddenly feared a misunderstanding. He wanted people to repeat what they had said to him. Throwing away all caution about who might be listening he would begin to talk openly, mentioning names and speaking unambiguously. His telephone would not have lasted long under a police regime.

Once his visitor had left he would consider what to retain of the conversation. Sometimes he would keep a few words, and sometimes a sentence or two, that he would write down on a pink notepad, in blue ink. The clear line of thought that he expressed well in conversation grew blurred when he wanted to note down an entire discussion. Instead of keeping to the other person's phrases he had a tendency to transcribe them into his own personal style, and in this way into his own mode of thinking.

His rule was to go by exactly what he had heard, including intonation and silences. But occasionally he would plunge into a fit of mistrust, and would have to fight it. Although he was obstinate he would come to terms with an objection if he recognized it was weighty. He was inclined to imagine that talk could resolve all conflicts. But he also acknowledged that a government might have to take drastic measures, and turn to force. Even so, all violence evoked profound repulsion in him.

Sometimes he condensed his thought with the rapidity and force of a maxim. But more often, after a few lines something blocked within himself and he would not be able to find any other good formulas. He would get round this obstacle by asking someone else to draw up a project, after the two had talked about it in depth. Through a series of discussions he gradually worked out the document he wanted, and shared in drafting it.

He attached great importance to clarity and conciseness. If a certain degree of emotion was expressed, it was held in check. He disliked a high-flown vocabulary and unusual words. He rejected them, without appeal. He excelled in evaluating the overall impression a text would produce, the way it was set out, the avenues it opened here and there, or closed for whoever was to receive it. He would try his text out on passing visitors.

Before the final version was reached the text had to go through multiple drafts. They had to be begun again, and rearranged. Through all this he wanted to verify that his conclusions were suitable and that the text would hold its recipient's attention, so reaching its target. Sometimes too he simply wanted not to be left alone. Toward the end he went beyond the good text. He would realize this and turn back. The best proposals he worked out in this way always included, according to the circumstances, a certain procedure, and a prescribed mechanism so that the public powers could get to work.

He hardly ever spoke of what he had already done, except in a few sporadic anecdotes. But his past, and the relationships he had had or was thought to have had, were always implicitly there and spoke in his favor. He carefully limited the engagements he took on, in the same way as, without being stingy, he was careful about his expenses. To persuade certain people, he appealed to their idealism. Others turned to him of their own accord, and told him in confidence of their anxieties. He would pacify and satisfy them by recruiting their expertise, their experience or their contacts.

He never took the initiative in paying for work contributed. When he was asked for money he paid, without thinking any the less of the asker.

He aroused long-lasting attachments, but he hardly ever showed his friendship, and even less his affection. He did not play on the feelings he inspired. He did not try to keep anyone who left him, even if he came to regret the departure. He himself was able to detach himself smoothly and never cluttered himself up with what he left behind, when he started out on a new activity. Experience had polished him like a pebble.

He was born and raised in France. He had had neither the help nor the limitations of a university or a *grande école*. He had more general knowledge than he showed. He kept quiet and listened when the talk turned to subjects he did not know about. He trained himself without great booklearning, watching persons and situations and reflecting on what he saw. Until the end of World War II he lived outside France, mainly in Great Britain, North America and the Far East. He had drawn lessons from the two wars and the disruption that followed them. During each of these tragedies he played an active role in the economic organization of the Allies' victory, and afterwards in the work of reconstruction.

He never limited himself to one occupation or one career. His activities were a series of widely differing chapters that might have been taken from several novels: brandy selling, pooling of the merchant fleets in World War I, the League of Nations, negotiating international loans, Wall Street, financing of Chinese railroads. Then, when half his life was over, the ordering of aircraft engines, the United States armament program, the food importation program for liberated France, the pooling of the Franco-German production of coal and steel, Euratom, and the Action Committee for the United States of Europe.

Contrary circumstances and the weight of years settled him down at last. If he had still been able to change he would not have stayed twenty years in his last field of activity. In his life and spirit, change was inscribed as the supreme law. He wanted change and accepted the disorder that followed, although he had no taste for disruption.

For him it was natural to keep a low profile, and not to waste time on personal rivalries. The role he looked for was to initiate changes that brought people together who had previously been divided or rivals. With this aim he made use of his outstanding ability to think up and carry out new combinations. His action was not guided by an intellectual system nor by references to history, which he knew little about. He took never-ending pains to adapt whatever he had undertaken to changed circumstances or people.

He took great trouble to find out who the leaders were in the countries he dealt with: the heads of government and of the political parties, of the labor unions; those who left and those who replaced them. They made what he called the 'magic circle', inside of which the essential options and decisions are made.

He was never one of these, in spite of his gifts as a trainer of men and a strategist. His most important actions were subject to the decision of the men in power. He carefully kept up the personal relations he had with them. Contact with them rejuvenated him and made his face shine with joy. Meeting and talking with presidents, chancellors, or prime ministers, watching them operate, gave him a kind of professional pleasure. He would speak to them very bluntly when he thought it necessary. He compared them one with another and one country with another, sometimes one period in time with another. He imagined himself in their place. Of the people around them, he cared more for reputable independent-minded newsmen than for government officials.

Ordinarily he kept his distance from current events. He watched circumstances evolve, calculated tendencies. He would beat about the bush until the obstacle took shape. Then he decided to act, and with a determination that made one forget his age he would launch into his campaign with total concentration. He himself would deliver his proposition to the man concerned or to his closest counsellor. He kept a watch on how the document or the project passed from one person to another. He kept ordinary risks in mind quite as much as exceptional hazards.

When the moment of decision came he forced himself not to intervene anymore. Until the affair was in the bag he would stay close to his telephone, pretending to be unconcerned.

He used circumstances and ideas that were not of his making. Through a general idea, or by imagining the worst, or through the influence of his personality, he did his utmost to get political leaders to link the circumstances that forced them to act with the project he put to them. The result he counted on was a precise procedure catalyzing this unstable mix of people in power (himself not being one of them), of circumstances and projects. Several times, he had succeeded in transforming these transitory moments into clearly outlined practical organizations. While he was still young he had concluded that unlimited ambition is impossible and fatal. He always acted on that basis. When he was over sixty he turned to the idea of uniting Europe. Developments were no longer limited in time. Moral justifications had become more and more important and had taken on their own reality. For many years for him – wary as he was of abstractions – and for some of his associates, the procedures of delegating sovereignty to European institutions and of organizing peace were by no means general notions or structures appearing out of the mist, broad general ideas floating on the future. He saw the future globally. He had become convinced that nations needed common institutions, and that such institutions, well thought out and backed up by improvements in material and social life, could guide collective behavior in good directions. But he did not become a creator of constitutions. He refused to sketch advance outlines of the final stages that would be reached later. These would result from what had been done in the interval. An *a priori* scheme would have been a hindrance. He refused to be the prisoner of a formula. During the years when parliaments had the last word in France and elsewhere, he brought the parties and the labor unions of the six member countries together, to make sure they would get the parliamentary majorities that were needed. When the balance of power altered he preferred direct and informal contacts between himself and government leaders, or their closest associates.

By temperament as well as experience he did not bow to the religion of sovereignty, in the sense of absolute power for the States. He favored a constitutional authority, moderately innovative, that acted in the interests of all. He was not spontaneously drawn toward the separation of powers. He was a man for discussion, but without any personal preference for a parliamentary role. He never aimed at a seat in the national assembly. He was suspicious of assemblies not led by a government.

He constantly incorporated a moral aim into the different actions he took up, although he showed no particular religious interests. The two wars and the crisis of the 1930s had not shaken his confidence in human reason or in its ability to find the good, recognize evil and, in spite of this, to achieve some progress through working together. His natural field of concern was the problem of handling the public affairs common to France and to other Western nations. He was enlivened and stimulated every time he found himself among the passers-by on the sidewalks of London, New York or Washington. He saw himself as a citizen of the Western world. After the trials of the first half of this century he could not conceive that Europe and the United States could develop divergent futures, nor France and Germany.

Some obstinately faithful friends notwithstanding, he took a severe view of Europe. Citizens of France, Britain and Germany, and even more their leaders were still, in his eyes, caught up in the shackles of the past.

His preference went to the United States. He saw it favorably because of what it had done for the cause of freedom, and because of memories of outstanding moments in his own life. It was in the United States that he found his closest friends and his most important relationships, among them, several presidents. When at last his hands were empty he had no further influence in America and stopped going there. Even then, what happened in the United States still touched him personally. He disliked and blamed the impulsive movements and the unilateral actions that reminded him of the 1920s. However he was still enchanted by the dynamism, the vast resources and the spirit of organization of the Americans. They inspired confidence in him to the end.

When he reached his last active years and had become frail, he talked of stopping work for a year or two and of going to Arizona where there is constant sun and the air is pure. Then, of coming back to Europe and finding things still in the same state. After so many journeys, he did not achieve this one. Neither did he get two wishes, that he would mention with a smile: to win the Nobel Peace Prize and to live to be a hundred.

We had got into the habit of always seeing him there, living through key periods of time and surviving them upright, like a Roman statue. He was not indestructible. Eventually, he was forced to end his active life. For him it was a wrench to distance himself from the magic circle. He withdrew by letter, with no goodbye visits or farewell meetings, with no pretenses and no successor. He did not achieve the transmutation of economic institutions into a political union. He was a man for beginnings. He did not enter the Promised Land.

Bibliography of Jean Monnet and His Times

BIBLIOGRAPHICAL NOTE

The basic record of Monnet's life and accomplishments remains, ten years after his death, his own *Memoirs* (Doubleday, 1978). Several works, undertaken at various points during his lifetime, attempt to gauge the whole man and his work; and since his death several authors have begun serious studies of his life.

Francois Fontaine, whose fine essay, written after Monnet's death in 1979, appears in this volume, also wrote in 1963 a short essay called simply *Jean Monnet*, in the Cahier Rouge series of the Foundation Jean Monnet Pour l'Europe and the Centre de Recherches Europeennes in Lausanne, Switzerland. This is still valuable although now out-of-print. The remarkable Cahier Rouge series, which now numbers over 150 works and is still growing, covers both Monnet and the European Community as well as other aspects of Europe. It is especially useful for the recollections of Monnet's contemporaries, including Jacques Van Helmont, whose very personal and moving tribute to Monnet also appears, with the Fontaine essay, for the first time in English in this volume.

Another major source of documentation about the European Community, of which Monnet has been called both the architect and the master builder, is its Publication Office in Luxembourg. A quarterly and an annual catalog, as well as specialized catalogs, list the hundreds of publications which document the day-to-day details of the work of the Commission, the Community's executive branch, and from which the careful reader can gain a good perspective of the accomplishments of the Community. Although relatively few of these documents concern Monnet and his era directly, the series 'European Perspectives' does attempt to give accounts of the history of major Community programs and periods. For example, Van Helmont expanded his essay on Monnet in this volume into *Options Europeennes 1945–1985*, which appeared in 1986 in this 'perspective' series. Unfortunately it is only available to date in French, but several other books in the series are in English, including Daniel Strasser's *The Finance of Europe* (1980); Jacques Van Ypersele's *The European Monetary System* and Tommaso Padoa-Schioppa's *Money, Economic Policy and Europe* (both 1985); and Hans Von Der Groeben's *The European Commun-*

ity: The Formative Years (1987). Following are some general works on the Monnet era with special emphasis on those which cover the main periods of his long and productive life.

The publisher of works marked * is the Fondation Jean Monnet pour l'Europe/Centre de recherches européennes, Ferme de Dorigny, Lausanne. The Fondation is the repository of Monnet's papers, while the Centre is the publisher of the Cahier Rouge Series concerning European integration and Monnet, only some of which are indicated here.

MEMOIRS

Acheson, Dean, *Present at the Creation* (New York, 1969).
Adenauer, Konrad, *Memoirs 1945–1953* (Chicago, 1965).
Ball, George, *The Discipline of Power: Essentials of a Modern World Structure* (Boston, 1968).
Ball, George, *The Past Has Another Pattern* (New York, 1982).
Berard, Armand, *Un Ambassadeur se souvient* (Paris, 1978).
Clappier, Bernard, 'Bernard Clappier Temoigne' in *L'Europe Une Longe Marche** (1985).
De Gaulle, Charles, *The War Memoirs* (New York, 1955).
De Gaulle, Charles, *Memoirs of Hope, Renewal and Endeavor* (New York, 1971).
Eden, Anthony, *Memoirs: Full Circle* (Boston, 1960).
Hirsch, Etienne, *Ainsi va la Vie** (1968).
Kennan, George F., *Memoirs 1925–1950* (Boston, 1967).
Kennan, George F., *Memoirs 1950–1963* (Boston, 1972).
Marjolin, Robert, *Memoirs, 1911–1986* (London, 1989).
Macmillan, Harold, *The Blast of War* (London, 1976).
Macmillan, Harold, *Tides of Fortune 1945–1955* (New York, 1969).
Macmillan, Harold, *Riding the Storm 1956–1959* (New York, 1971).
Monnet, Jean, *Memoirs* (New York, 1978).
Monnet, Jean, Diaries, unpublished, located at Fondation Jean Monnet pour l'Europe, Lausanne. The Fondation is the repository of Monnet's personal papers, which are being catalogued. The sections concerning Monnet's life as an investment banker (1933–1940) and his years in public life from 1945–1954 are completely classified and available on microfiche at the Fondation's offices in Ferme de Dorigny on the campus of Lausanne University. Work on the other sections of the Monnet papers is continuing.
Schuman, Robert, *Pour l'Europe* (Paris, 1963).
Spaak, Paul Henri, *The Continuing Battle: Memoirs of a European* (Boston, 1971).
Stimson, Henry L. and Bundy, McGeorge, *On Active Service in Peace and War* (New York, 1948).
Van Helmont, Jacques, *Options Europeennes 1945–85* (Brussels, 1986).

BIOGRAPHICAL WORKS

Beyer, Henry, *Robert Schuman, L'Europe Par La Reconciliation Franco-Allemande** (1986).
Brumberger, Merry and Serge, *Jean Monnet and the United States of Europe* (New York, 1968).
Kaspi, Andre, *La Mission de Jean Monnet a Alger* (Paris, 1971).
Kohnstamm, Max, *Jean Monnet: Le Pouvoir de l'Imagination** (1982).
Lacouture, Jean, *De Gaulle*, 3 vols (Paris, 1986).
Teissier Du Cros, Henri, *Louis Armand: Visionnaire de la Modernite* (Paris, 1987).

COMMENTARIES AND HISTORIES

Barnet, Richard, *The Alliance: American-Europe-Japan – Makers of the Postwar World* (New York, 1983).
Beloff, Max, *The United States and the Unity of Europe* (London, 1963).
Brugmans, Henri, *Le Message Europeen de Robert Schuman** (1965).
Brugmans, Henri, *L'idee europeenne 1918–1965* (Bruges, 1965).
Cappeletti, Secombe and Weiler (eds), *Integration Through Law, Europe and the American Federal Experience* (Berlin, 1986).
Cook, Don, *Floodtide in Europe* (New York, 1965).
Charlton, Michael, *The Price of Victory* (New York, 1985).
Diebold, William Jr., *The Schuman Plan: A Study in Economic Cooperation 1950–1959* (New York, 1959).
Diebold, William Jr., and Camps, Miriam, *The New Multilateralism: Can the World Trading System be Saved?* (New York, 1986).
European Community Liaison Committee of Historians (ECLCH), Raymond Poidevin (ed.), *Origins of the European Integration*: Papers presented at a colloquium November 28–30, 1984 in Strasbourg (Brussels, 1986).
ECLCH, Klaus Schwabe (ed.), *The Beginnings of the Schuman Plan*: Papers presented at a colloquium (Baden-Baden, 1988).
ECLCH, Enrico Serra (ed.), *The Relaunching of Europe and the Treaties of Rome*: Papers presented at a colloquium March 25–28, 1987 in Rome (Brussels, 1989).
Flanner, Janet, *Paris Journal. 1944–1965* (Cambridge, Mass., 1977).
Grosser, Alfred, *The Western Alliance* (New York, 1980).
Haas, Ernst B., *The Uniting of Europe* (Stanford, 1968).
Hackett, Clifford, *Cautious Revolution: The European Community Arrives* (Westport, Conn., 1990)
Hogan, Michael F., *The Marshall Plan: America, Britain and the Reconstruction of Western Europe, 1947–1952* (New York, 1987).
Kohnstamm, Max and Hager, Wolfgang, *A Nation Writ Large?* (London, 1973).
Kuisel, Richard F., *Capitalism and the State in Modern France*, (esp. chapter on the Monnet Plan) (Cambridge, 1981).

Lipgens, Walter, *A History of European Integration*, vol. 1, 1945–7 (London, 1982).

Mayne, Richard, *The Community of Europe* (London, 1962).

Mayne, Richard, *The Recovery of Europe* (London, 1970).

Mayne, Richard, *Postwar, the Dawn of Today's Europe* (London, 1983).

McCloy, John J., *Amerique-Europe. Relations de Partenaires Necessaires a la Paix** (1982)

Mioche, Phillipe, *Le Plan Monnet* (Paris, 1987).

Milward, Alan S., *The Reconstruction of Western Europe, 1945–1951* (London, 1984).

Monnet, Jean, *Amerique-Europe. Relations de Partenaires Necessaires a la Paix** (1963).

Monnet, Jean, *La Communaute Europeenne et l'Unite de l'Occident** (1961).

Monnet, Jean, *Le Chancelier Adenauer et la Construction de l'Europe** (1966).

Monnet, Jean, *Les Etats-Unis d'Europe ont Commencé* (Paris, 1955).

Monnet, Jean, *L'Europe et l'Organisation de la Paix** (1964).

Monnet, Jean, *L'Europe Unie: de l'Utopie a la Realite** (1972).

Newhouse, John, *De Gaulle and the Anglo Saxons* (New York, 1980).

Pleven, Rene, *L'Union Européenne** (1984).

Pollard, Robert, *Economic Security and the Origins of the Cold War, 1945–1950* (New York, 1985).

Pollard, Sidney, *European Economic Integration 1815–1970* (London, 1974).

Reuter, Paul, *La Naissance de l'Europe Communautaire** (1980).

Rieben, Henri, *Des Guerres Europeennes a l'Union de l'Europe** (1987).

Schaetzel, J. Robert, *The Unhinged Alliance, America and the European Community* (New York, 1975).

Schonfield, Andrew, *International Economic Relations of the Western World 1959–1971*, 2 vols (Oxford, 1976).

Von der Groeben, Hans, *The European Community: The Formative Years* (Luxembourg, 1987).

Zurcher, Arnold, *The Struggle to Unite Europe* (New York, 1958).

DOCUMENTS

Comite D'Action Pour Les Etats Unis D'Europe, *Declaration et Communiques** (1965).

Jean Monnet-Robert Schuman, Correspondence 1947–1953* (1986).

ARTICLES

Brooks, John, 'The Common Market', *New Yorker*, September 22 and 29, 1962.

Davenport, John, 'Jean Monnet of Cognac', *Fortune*, August 1944.

Index